D1563395

THEY SATISFY

They Satisfy

THE CIGARETTE IN AMERICAN LIFE

Robert Sobel

ANCHOR BOOKS
Anchor Press/Doubleday   *1978*
Garden City, New York

ISBN: 0-385-12956-4
Library of Congress Catalog Card Number 77-27681

To Owen and Margie

Contents

Preface

Smoking is one of the human race's more curious and paradoxical habits. We spend far more money placing pollutants into our lungs by means of cigarettes than in cleansing the air of noxious gases. Almost all habitual smokers appear to be sorry they ever took to tobacco, and warn their offspring not to follow their examples. This message has been taken up and augmented by public service advertisements and slogans with some degree of effectiveness. At the same time it is literally impossible to read a newspaper or magazine, or drive along a road, without coming into contact with dozens of messages spelling out the enjoyment a cigarette can bring. Smoking still is accepted as an accompaniment to civilized discourse; we have become accustomed to taking a "smoking break."

Motion pictures and television dramas tell us that smoking can be a prelude to sex and a means of relaxing afterward; however, some doctors claim that heavy smoking can damage sexual performance. Smoking is supposed to kill the taste buds, but there are those who seem incapable of enjoying a meal without punctuating it with one or more cigarettes. The habit makes no sense at all to confirmed nonsmokers; those with the habit claim themselves unable to begin the day without the help of a cigarette.

There is no satisfactory way of explaining why people smoke. Some psychologists speak and write of oral fixations that require sublimation, but this tells us little of how they were satisfied prior to the advent of tobacco. Certainly the initial act of smoking is not pleasant—often it prompts a gagging reflex. One has to put some effort into becoming habituated to cigarettes and even more, later on, when trying to quit the practice.

With all of this, the cigarette doubtless will remain an important accouterment to our civilization. We may be able to adjust to a deepening shortage of petroleum and higher prices for coffee, but a complete and sudden cutoff of cigarettes would create an intolerable situation for many people throughout the world. In most ways it would be a more drastic change than that brought by alcohol prohibition in America during the 1920s. Then speakeasies appeared and people could imbibe bootleg booze in their homes. In contrast, the cigarette is an out-of-doors as well as indoors habit, one engaged in on impulse, and not after some planning. How these ways of smoking could be controlled, much less ended, cannot easily be imagined. For whatever good or evil it may bring, we are wedded as a civilization to those paper tubes containing small amounts of granulated weed.

✿   ✿   ✿

Twenty or so years ago, during the height of the Cold War, authors dealing with the subject of communism found themselves labeled either as "witch-hunters" or "pinkos," and sometimes both, though from different quarters. There seemed no way out of the quandary. It was an emotional subject, and such emotions evoked invectives.

A similar situation exists today insofar as smoking is concerned, though of course the arena is much smaller and the stakes not so large. In the process of learning more about the cigarette, I have come into contact with dozens of corporation executives and advertising men, doctors and researchers. Although most did not ask the question outright or in blunt terms, it overhung all discussions. "Was I writing a pro- or anticigarette book?" Or to put it another way, "Do you believe cigarette smoking causes cancer?"

The answers are simple enough. This is an effort at history, not propaganda, and should be read and judged in this light. There are scores of diatribes on the subject; most of those appearing in recent years have been written in emotional terms by medical men or health crusaders, whose goal is not understanding, but conversion. We have several histories of cigarettes and tobacco; all but a few have been sponsored or subsidized by the tobacco companies. This book emanates from neither camp. Such organizations as the American Cancer Society and the Tobacco Institute have provided statistical information and answers to specific questions, no more than that.

As for the second question, I am not a doctor, or even a scientist, but in the process of conducting research have had to learn the vocabularies of these professions. Fortunately I have had the help of colleagues at Hofstra University who are both. While sparing me their personal views on the subject (almost all were strongly opposed to the habit), they translated scholarly papers into conventional prose and provided me with a crash course on etiology and the current status of research in the field. It was during this part of the investigation I found many honest and unbiased (meaning unsubsidized) scientists who believed heavy smoking causes lung cancer and related ailments—and almost as many others who are equally proficient and fair-minded who took an opposing point of view, or were simply uncertain regarding the question.

Does smoking *cause* lung cancer? Anticigarette forces observe that 5 per cent of heavy smokers die of lung cancer, implying a link, since the percentage for nonsmokers is much smaller. Their critics respond by noting that this means 95 per cent of these two-pack-a-day individuals do *not* die of the disease. Why is this the case? There are no clear answers to these questions.

On January 11, 1978, Secretary of Health, Education and Welfare Joseph Califano announced a new government war against cigarette smoking, one that would cost several millions of dollars. Actor Tony Randall, a vocal opponent of smoking, had been invited to Washington for the occasion but couldn't make it, since he was to appear on the Johnny Carson show in Los Angeles that evening. It was an interesting program, for just as Randall strongly dislikes cigarettes, so Carson not only lampoons the reformers, but is known to be a chain smoker, and their discussions of the subject often are amusing and diverting. That evening, in the course of their expected dialogue on cigarettes, Randall noted that Califano spoke on the fourteenth anniversary of the Surgeon General's Report, a major document in the struggle, a paper which put forth the concept of a link between smoking and cancer. To this Carson replied, "Yes, and I'm still here."

So were millions of other smokers, who either didn't believe the Report or couldn't quit if they wanted to. Randall was quick to note that Carson was correct, and probably would go coughing to his grave. He conceded there are some people who don't seem to be affected in a serious fashion by smoking—for some reason—and their longevity and health convinced others that there is no danger in smoking. This is another problem that hasn't been answered by either side in the controversy.

In the course of this research I have been asked whether I smoke. The answer should be irrelevant, but sadly this is not the case. So I confess to having smoked a pipe while in college and for many years thereafter. As a freshman I had been informed by a girl I much admired that a pipe clenched between my teeth would make me appear mature and worldly-wise. Additionally, Ronald Colman was portraying a college professor in a now-forgotten television series, "The Halls of Ivy." Colman was one of my boyhood idols. He smoked a pipe in the role. So would I.

Had I met a different girl and preferred Humphrey Bogart, doubtless I would have taken to cigarettes. As it is, they never appealed to me.

I don't smoke today. Perhaps there is no causal link between tobacco and cancer. Then again, one might exist. It doesn't make sense to take chances while awaiting the verdict. Besides, I have forgotten everything about that girl except the business regarding the pipe, and long ago decided I'd never resemble Ronald Colman, no matter what I did.

ROBERT SOBEL
New College of Hofstra

I

Origins

Traditionalists and some of the old-fashioned types puffed on pipes, while "real men" and hayseeds in both city and countryside chewed from the plug. Urban dandies and those who affected the style of European aristocrats utilized dry snuff. Affluent businessmen waved their long Havanas like scepters, while poor workingmen masticated penny stogies. Few American women smoked, or at least admitted to using tobacco. To be seen with a cigar or any other form of the weed marked a woman as being eccentric, rustic, fast and loose, or "advanced." Few sought those labels a century and a quarter ago.

The tobacco industry of this period supported a large array of fabricators. There were importers of Mediterranean briars and meerschaums, and the small shops that turned the raw materials into pipes. Country boys made their own corncobs, but those who relocated to the cities purchased them for a few cents apiece. Though not for long. Corncobs were the mark of the unsophisticated rube, the hick, and even then Americans wanted to avoid that stigma.

Fine artisans still fashioned elegant snuffboxes, but the business was declining along with the use of that product. The plug market was expanding, however, and spittoon sales were booming. The decline of the snuffbox and the rise of the spittoon, one of those footnotes in social history, were seen as more indications of the growing barbarism of American life by several observers. But not all chewers used spittoons—or were able to when working or walking through the city's streets. As a result, wooden sidewalks were stained with tobacco juice, and gobs of expectorated plug were so common as not to cause comment or even command notice.

The cigar was deemed the cleanest form of the leaf, since its only residue was ash, and the butt could be disposed of in a more sanitary fashion than chew or pipe dottle. Elegant cigar smokers had humidors, silver cutters, and pocket cases fashioned of leather or some precious metal. Many cigar users employed amber holders, while others favored ivory. The ability to judge, enjoy, and collect cigars was considered as much a social grace as the knowledge of fine wines and their proper maintenance, service, and rating.

American men liked their tobacco. The first homemade pipe, that initial chew, the cheap cigar lit behind the barn—all were important rites of passage. Some parents might warn that smoking stunted the growth and fouled the breath, but few outside of dedicated antismoking circles made any significant effort to prevent their boys from taking up the habit. The only question was: What form of tobacco would be used? President Grant smoked cigars, as did Robert E. Lee, then in retirement. Tycoons and actors used them as well, and so it appeared did most American males. There were forty million Americans in 1870, slightly less than half of whom were men. That year the nation's cigar factories produced, and importers brought into the country, more than 1.2 billion cigars. Thus, the average American male from infants on up smoked sixty cigars that year. To this was added the over 100 million pounds of smoking, snuffing, and chewing tobacco—five pounds per male.

Usage was on the increase. According to official government

figures derived from production and tax statistics, Americans consumed 2.5 billion cigars and another 150 million pounds of pipe tobacco, snuff, and plug in 1880. But in the South and many parts of the North, the products were made and sold by individuals who avoided gatherers of taxes and statistics. Perhaps another quarter of a billion cigars and an additional 50 million pounds of other smokes and chews should be added to these numbers.

The biggest tobacco news of the decade was the emergence of the cigarette as something more than a novelty but less than a socially acceptable habit in most parts of the nation. There is no way of knowing how many of them had been consumed prior to the Civil War, since the government did not keep such statistics at that time. But in 1880 half a billion were sold, and this figure is for the manufactured varieties alone—roll-your-owns added another billion or so to the total.

The cigarette had a constituency of sorts. As far as we can tell it was small and marginal in the 1880s, comprised of dandies in eastern cities, immigrants, and poor people seeking cheap smokes. Cigarettes were used by young children and old hoboes. Should a middle-aged, middle-class man light up a cigarette in New York or Boston, he would attract glances and would run the risk of being considered effeminate or un-American. No "real man" considered their use on a regular basis, even though it was common knowledge that cigarettes were the vogue in "smart society" in London and Paris. Of course, all of this would change drastically within three decades, the result of smart advertising, new methods of distribution and production, several key inventions, and a change in the tempo of American life.

How did it happen?

When Columbus landed on San Salvador in 1492 the natives offered him food and drink, artifacts, and a few handfuls of dried leaves. The Spaniard consumed the first, kept the second to show to Queen Isabella and her court, and discarded the leaves, thinking them worthless. A few days later the explorer was offered additional leaves, and this time shown how they could be smoked in long pipes. As most everyone knows, Columbus took tobacco leaves back to Europe, where in time the habit caught on and became the basis for a major colonial export industry.

The Indians also used cigars—rolls of tobacco leaves held together by sputum. If the point were to be stretched, it might be said the same Indians invented the cigarette. Invariably, scraps and bits of tobacco were left over after cigars were rolled. Also, there were the stems of the leaf and inferior leaves not worthy of the pipes. These would be crushed together—later on the term would be "granulated"—wrapped in straw, reeds, or cornhusks, and then smoked by lower-class people, members of the lesser breeds, and inferior individuals—which translated into children, the poor, and women. So this kind of small cigar—cigarette—remained in the Americas for the next two centuries, and in some remote areas, even longer.

Europeans "invented" the cigarette independently of the Indians, but with the same idea in mind: to develop a cheap smoke. Beggars in cities and towns would scavenge through garbage seeking food and discards that might be used or sold. In the sixteenth century they came upon cigar butts, snuff dust, and pipe dottle. These were isolated with care, then combined and crushed—to produce a blended mix?—and wrapped in scrap paper, to create a cigarette, which was smoked by the group, usually huddled in a circle. Since Spain was the largest user of tobacco in this period, and Seville the city which used more of the product than any other, the Sevillian name for the smoke—*papalete*—took hold throughout most of Europe. The "paper cigar" was considered cheap, the dregs of tobacco smoked by the dregs of society.

This was the situation when the French Revolution erupted, altering not only the politics and economics of European society, but its habits as well. In France those who survived the initial collapse of the monarchy eschewed aristocratic ways and affected those of the workers and peasants. Gone were the wigs, bustles, sweetmeats, and embroidered clothes of the aristocratic age—along with snuff, fancy pipes, and long cigars. Those wanting to indicate sympathy with the Revolution took to short peasant pipes, made of clay or fruitwood. Cigarettes were not *de rigueur*, but their use did imply membership in the lower classes which some expected to inherit the nation.

Cigarette smoking enjoyed a vogue in revolutionary cadres, though the use of the small smokes was by no means universal.

Outside of what later would be known as Bohemian circles they were scarcely to be seen. The British, who as a nation opposed the Revolution, considered their use a sign of lack of respect for the Crown and stable society in general. Confrontations between cigar-smoking middle-class individuals and shabby cigarette users were mentioned in the London press at the turn of the century. And as might have been expected, the eventual defeat of the French resulted in the decline of cigarette use, except among artists, writers, and others who remained true to the revolutionary cause—and in Latin America and Spain, where the custom continued long after the Bonapartists had been crushed elsewhere.

Visitors to Central America in the middle of the nineteenth century noted that while men smoked cigars, women used papalete, and in public. There even were differentiations to indicate marital status, with the wives using *puros*—all tobacco—and unmarried women the *blancos,* which were granulated tobacco wrapped in paper or straw. At a time when European women scarcely would dare smoke in private—when George Sand caused a commotion by puffing on cigars in restaurants—the daughters of Latin American grandees lit up after dinner. "Every gentleman carries in his pocket a silver case, with a long string of cotton, steel, and flint, and one of the offices of gallantry is to strike a light; by doing it well, he may kindle a flame in a lady's heart." So wrote an English traveler in the 1850s. Nor were papalete confined to women. A Spanish proverb of the time went, "A paper cigarette, a glass of fresh water, and the kiss of a pretty girl, will sustain a man for a day without eating." The popularity and knowledge of cigarettes, and their identification with Spain, may further be seen in Prosper Mérimée's novel, upon which was based Georges Bizet's opera, *Carmen.* The heroine, of course, worked in a cigarette factory in Seville around 1820. Carmen was at the same time vulgar and exotic, and the cigarettes she helped turn out were for those like her. On the one hand they were used by individuals who could not afford cigars or chew, while on the other, upper-class women in urban areas took them up, perhaps more for shock value than anything else. By the early 1850s they were seen in New York. "Some of the *ladies* of this refined and fashion-form-ing metropolis are aping the silly ways of some pseudo-accomplished foreigners in smoking tobacco through a weaker and more *feminine* article, which was most delicately denominated cigarette," wrote a critic of the practice in 1854, insinuating that no self-respecting man would touch the white tubes. Even then, however, cigarettes were smoked by artists and even businessmen in Paris. At first most were manufactured in small shops, perhaps by cigar makers seeking a market for their leavings. The Parisians made a distinction between a poverty-stricken painter or writer and a teamster in the same economic circumstances; the former might be admired, even courted, while the latter was beyond cultural redemption. Both might roll their own cigarettes from dry snuff, since they were unable to afford cigars. Middle-class men might reject the habits of the manual workers, but they would imitate those of the artists, and so they did. Cigarette smoking became the vogue in Paris in the 1840s, so much so that in 1843 the French tobacco monopoly, seeking new profits, began manufacturing them and advertising cigarettes for sale by brand names.

A similar situation developed in Moscow and St. Petersburg. For years the Russian nobility had slavishly copied everything French, thinking that to speak, act, and behave Parisian was to be civilized and sophisticated. But as is customary in such things, the French imports were filtered through the Russian cultural screen. The Czar's officers would not import French cigarettes, but rather developed their own varieties. This meant the use of several Turkish and south Russian dark tobaccos, especially the small Dubek and Yacca leaves, grown in the Xanthi district, which were both mild and sweet-smoking. These aromatic tobaccos and others from the southern Mediterranean and Black Sea areas were difficult to grow and thus quite costly. Some small cigars were rolled from the leaf, which was not large enough for the bigger cigars. But the Turks and others in the area preferred to use pipes or to create their own cigarettes, the latter deemed the most economic method of taking a smoke.

The Russians combined the French and Turkish customs to produce their own cigarettes. Like the Turks, the Russians used unsized paper to wrap the smokes, to which they added cardboard mouthpieces. French cigarettes were round and Turkish ones oval; the Russian varieties were round and packed in hard-paper containers. By 1852–53 they were the vogue at court. But nowhere else. Russian peasants smoked pipes and would not dare be seen with cigarettes in public. Russian noblemen, usually officers in elite regiments, smoked cigarettes in court, where they were viewed as affectations, a counterpart to the Prussian saber scar. In other words, they were part of a uniform or life style, and not primarily a habit to be enjoyed. The ruling family did not smoke cigarettes at this time, however—at least, not in public.

So the new smoke had a disparate constituency—aristocrats in Russia, poor people in London and Paris, and Bohemians in most European political and cultural centers.

These cigarette cultures combined during the Crimean War, that Russo-Turkish conflict that involved Britain and France in 1854. For close to two years the Western Europeans fought beside the Turks on that Black Sea peninsula. Or to be more precise, the soldiers were stationed there, died of dysentery and other diseases, and on occasion engaged in battles and minor skirmishes.

Londoners and Parisians fraternized with their counterparts from Constantinople, and lacking amenities from home, adopted some of those of their ally. There was considerable intermingling between the rival armies, especially among officers, and so the West Europeans met with and even became friendly with Russian aristocrats and borrowed some of their customs as well. Finally, as with all wars, this one saw the diminution of rank distinctions; privates in the field shared rations—and tobacco—with officers, and vice versa.

So tobacco migrated across national boundaries and between the classes. British and French soldiers, unable to obtain their customary brands and forms, bought and took what they could from the Turks and Russians. In this fashion they came into contact with the dark-leaf cigarettes with their long cardboard holders. These carefully rolled smokes clearly were meant for gentlemen, and not peasants and proletarians. They were wrapped with special papers, often yellow, and not scraps and leavings from newspapers or old books; and they gave off exotic aromas, which filled the tents and lingered for a while after the last shred of tobacco had turned to ash. This last point was important, for cigarettes wasted less tobacco than did cigars, and even that weed was often of an inferior variety to that of the conventional smoke. Also, the cigarette butts could be recycled more easily than cigar stubs, an important consideration in wartime and other periods of scarcity. Thus, they added a bit of elegance at a lower price and mystery to life, welcome at a time when soldiers were trying to escape the dreariness and monotony of their lots.

Just as the Crusaders acquired from the Orient a taste for spices, so the West European soldiers tried to purchase Turkish and Russian cigarettes when they returned home. Veteran officers would smoke them after dinners at their clubs, while swapping stories about the war. In the late 1850s these cigarettes were as much a symbol of overseas duty as medals and service stripes. Sensing the creation of a fad and hoping to cash in on it, several tobacco merchants and cigar manufacturers tried to interest the general public in cigarettes. Robert Gloag, a tobacconist who had fought in the Crimea, imported a small quantity of Latakia, granulated the small leaves, and turned them into Turkish cigarettes with the brand names of Xanthe and Kohinoor, hoping in this way to evoke the oriental atmosphere and create an army of buyers. Philip Morris, a leading English tobacconist, followed suit, and after the veterans had indicated interest in his brands tried to sell them throughout Britain, on the continent, and in the United States. Several Parisian firms did the same, and for a while cigarettes were the rage of the social set, as rising young politicians, including Louis Napoleon Bonaparte, smoked them in public. But the fad died quickly, so that by the early 1860s cigarette smoking was only slightly more popular than it had been prior to the war. Gloag abandoned production and concentrated on marketing cigars. Philip Morris expanded his Bond Street shop and turned his energies to the export trade for a variety of products. Louis Napoleon stopped using cigarettes, smoking instead the long, thin Havanas and Brazilians.

The "Crimea fad," as one newspaper called it, made only a small mark upon European social life, but the cigarette no longer was the exclusive smoke of the poor or the occasional one for the artists. Cigarettes were inexpensive, convenient, and capable of delivering more actual smoke per ounce than the pipe or the cigar. They were the sensible way to use costly leaf, and they were handy in stress situations, when smokers wanted only a few drags before discarding them. Thus, they would be a perfect substitute for cigars in time of war—when soldiers smoked out of doors, and their rest periods might be interrupted by renewed fighting. During times of relative peace and calm, however, most smoking took place indoors and often was accompanied by ritual—brandy and good talk. Cigars were not inhaled, but rather puffed, so the smoker and his friends could savor the aroma. Fine cigar smoke was for men what perfumes were for women—a smell that was both attractive and disguised other body odors. Just as a woman's perfume was supposed to excite men, so the cigar and its smoke offered sexual connotations, both for the eye and nose. The same could not be said for cigarettes. The West European "paper cigars" had an indifferent aroma, were not savored, and were not yet part of any social ritual. Too, there was some question as to whether it was an indoor or out-of-door product. Farmers might chew upon unlit stogies or masticate plug while in the fields, but their pipes were for after hours, at home. The city dwellers of the 1850s rarely smoked while out of doors; why do so when the cigar could not be savored? Engravings of the Wall Street scene of this period show individuals smoking on the street, but usually they had just emerged from their offices and were on the way to some other indoor spot. Generally speaking, chewing and working went together; smoking was identified with, and meant for, repose.

In America, as already has been indicated, the cigarette was used by sophisticated upper-class women in large eastern cities. They purchased Turkish and Russian brands in somewhat the same spirit as middle-aged Americans today might make a deal for a few joints of marijuana—the buying produced a sense of guilt and excitement, and the actual smoking, the thrill of tasting forbidden fruit. These women smoked in the privacy of their parlors or bedrooms and often in secrecy. Some would smoke in attics so the draperies would not catch and retain the aromas of the exotic tobaccos. These smells were considered effete by most American men, who were accustomed to Havana cigars and Vir-

ginia leaves. Those who saw Europeans smoking cigarettes must
have thought them either aristocrats or homosexuals, the former
disliked, the latter despised. In the early 1860s, there appeared
to be no way that middle-class American men—the prime market for smokes—would take to cigarettes.

However, war and advertising have always been the two most
important methods of spreading cigarette use. Just as middle-
class Western Europeans came to smoke them as a result of the
Crimean War, Union soldiers learned to use cigarettes while
campaigning in the South, or after coming into contact with
Confederate troops. During lulls in the fighting the soldiers of
opposing armies would mingle and trade for necessities and lux-
uries. The Confederates usually needed food, and the Union
troops, many of whom came from eastern cities, were interested
in tobacco. So northern biscuit and beef went for pouches of Virginia and Carolina tobacco. The enlisted men chewed it, but
some made cigarettes from the granulated leaf. It was not considered fashionable to do so. The American leaf lacked the fragrance of the Russian and Turkish tobaccos, and such hand-
mades were not for officers. Ulysses S. Grant and William T.
Sherman rode off to battle with unlit stogies clenched between
their teeth. Only after the battle would these be lit, as though in
celebration.

This was the practice of gentlemen, and those aspiring to such
status; Grant, Lee, and other generals on both sides would never
have been caught smoking a cigarette, and neither would their
underlings and imitators. But the common soldiers, lacking
money for cigars or the time to smoke them, made do with hand-
rolled cigarettes. By about 1863 such cigarettes were seen in the
major northern cities as well, brought there by soldiers on leave.
Thus, the war reinforced the habit and added to the constituency
of the cigarette. In places like Philadelphia, New York, and Boston, they were used by poor scavengers, society women, and
young men, each for reasons different from the others, and each
with a different kind of smoke—the lower class had hand-rolled
"recycled" cigarettes, the women preferred perfumed, exotic
brands, while the soldiers and middle-class young men rolled
their cigarettes from plug tobacco or pipe mixtures.

Soldiers and others who used American tobaccos in their cigarettes had learned to inhale the smoke. This was not a novel idea; the Indians had inhaled on occasion, and there were some pipe and cigar smokers who seemed to enjoy drawing the smoke into their lungs and leaving it there for a while. Still, most smokers prized tobacco for the aroma, and so inhalation usually took place through the nose. In contrast, the cigarette smokers of the 1860s inhaled by means of mouth and throat. For them the smell of the smoke was unimportant. There was something in the tobacco that produced a pleasing effect on the senses, or so it was said, and enjoyment not only was enhanced by this kind of inhalation, but was made possible. Thus, the smokers of this time were looking for a "kick" and not mere fragrance.

It was nicotine, an oily, colorless, highly volatile substance that set tobacco apart from other plants. A few drops of pure nicotine upon the tongue could kill; inhalation of tobacco smoke produced a narcotic effect, the extent of which depended upon both subject and the nature of the tobacco. The rich, heavy Havana leaf contained relatively little nicotine, usually less than 1.5 per cent, while the lighter Virginia tobaccos could have as much as 9 to 10 per cent in the harsher leaves. Cigarette smoke seemed lighter than that of cigars, yet it had more kick, something the Union soldiers came to appreciate.

At the time, most soldiers of the invading armies cared little for the reasons; they simply enjoyed their smokes. Farmers in the Virginia and Carolina tobacco fields may not have understood the chemistry of their leaves, but they did know how to produce the kind of tobacco prized by chewers. Only a generation prior to the war they had evolved a new kind of tobacco and method of curing it that was becoming known throughout the South. This Bright tobacco was one of the major keys to the acceptance of the cigarette. The industry might have developed without it, but cigarettes would never have become popular so rapidly were it not for this leaf.

Its appearance was a fluke. During the colonial period and the early national era, the best and most popular American tobaccos were grown in the Tidewater area of Virginia, where rich soils and beneficial climate combined to produce a strong, pungent, dark leaf. Tobacco grown in other parts of the nation was considered inferior to Virginia. One of these was Bright, a yellow leaf grown in the poor soils of the Piedmont in Virginia and North Carolina.

Like other tobaccos, Bright was cured over burning logs, in a fashion originated by the Indians of the region. In 1839 a slave who had been supervising the curing of Bright on the Slade farm in North Carolina fell asleep on the job and awoke just in time to see the last embers becoming dull. He heaped charcoal upon the fire and managed to revive it, not knowing that this sudden heat would alter the curing process. What emerged was a deep yellow tobacco, unlike any ever seen before—in 1860 the Census Bureau would call it "one of the most abnormal developments in agriculture that the world has ever known." This tobacco had an unusually mild, sweet, and pleasant taste and was quickly adapted for use as the wrapper for many plug brands.

The Union soldiers came across this plug through trade, purchase, or confiscation. Some of it was chewed, but increasingly they used it to roll cigarettes. In this way, the Bright tobacco cigarette appeared in the North in 1863 or 1864. At the same time the Turkish blends were enjoying a spurt of popularity, partly due to the increase in tobacco use during wars, and partly to the fact that European manufacturers had lowered their prices (usually by using cheaper tobaccos) in an attempt to broaden their markets.

It was then that antitobacco forces initiated a new campaign against the weed. Opponents of smoking and chewing had been present in national life since the colonial period and had gained many followers during that great reform era that preceded the Civil War. But the antitobacco crusade was far less important than the one against slavery, or that opposing alcohol. In that period the crusade against smoking attracted little attention; even its leaders cheerfully conceded that an end to slavery was of primary importance.

Ordinarily the opponents of tobacco might have been ignored, but Congress had to raise funds with which to carry on the conflict, and some legislators thought they had come upon a means of obtaining revenues while pleasing some vocal constituents. Since the Turkish and Russian cigarettes were popular only in large cities along the Atlantic, congressmen from interior areas, especially the Midwest, sponsored bills to place tariffs upon smokes, and they were approved by the House and sent on to the Senate for consideration. At this point the antismoking forces demanded taxes on domestic as well as imported smokes, and they won their point. Under the terms of the Internal Revenue Law of 1864, which passed by large margins in both houses and was signed into law by President Lincoln, a tax was to be placed upon all manufactured cigarettes. Initially it would be a dollar per thousand units, but in subsequent years it was raised to two dollars and then to three. By 1867 the levy was five dollars per thousand.

At that time there were no important American cigarette manufacturers, and so the tax largely affected the imports. In 1864 duties were paid upon 19.7 million cigarettes, almost all of which had arrived from Europe and presumably were purchased in the eastern seaboard cities. The Midwesterners pressed for higher taxes, and the government was pleased to have additional revenues. Sales of imported cigarettes increased, however, despite their higher costs. For a while, some small shops in New York, Philadelphia, Boston, Albany, and Rochester turned out the Turkish smokes for what seemed to be a growing group of customers.

This market declined after the war. The easing of social pressures, the return to a slower pace of life, the desire for status rather than satisfaction—plus the taxes—combined to force imported cigarettes back into relative obscurity, while cigar sales soared once again. The reformers rejoiced, while at the same time they mounted a new campaign against cigars that was poorly received by a nation weary of crusades of any kind. And the government searched for new sources of revenues.

Northern and midwestern veterans of southern campaigns continued to use domestic cigarettes, however, and just as the Crimean officers had demanded Turkish and Russian smokes, so the Northerners wanted cigarettes of Bright tobacco. The importation of Bright in bulk form increased in the late 1860s. While cigarettes were taxed, tobacco in this form was not. So the merchants would granulate the leaf, pack small portions in cotton bags, and sell the "makings" for a fraction of the cost of the finished imported brands. Some purchasers chewed Bright, but increasingly they used it for cigarettes.

Thus there were two different kinds of markets for cigarettes in the cities. First, there were those smokers who wanted imported brands. As indicated, such individuals usually lived in eastern cities and considered themselves sophisticated lovers of esoterica. The second category, growing rapidly, was for domestic Bright cigarettes. These smokers lived in all parts of the country, were lower and middle class, and seemed to prefer cigarettes primarily for the cheap price and the enjoyment of inhaling.

Could these two markets be united? Some small tobacco dealers, most of them foreign born, thought they could and made an effort in that direction. At first they imported Turkish leaf in bulk form, to avoid paying tariffs, and from it fashioned American-style cigarettes—without cardboard holders or filters. These were far less expensive than the imported European brands, and although they captured a segment of the market for the higher priced smokes, they made little impression elsewhere. One foreign house, Bedrossian Brothers, experimented with a blend of Latakia and Bright in their cigarettes, but with minor commercial success. Others followed, and all failed.

Import houses headed by native-born Americans watched the experiment with interest. The idea was sound, they concluded, but the marketing misplaced. The Bedrossians and their group had tried to sell their blended cigarettes as though they were Turkish or Russian. Some of their names indicated this drift—Turkish Elegantes, Moscows, St. Petersburg, and Sultana. These did not appeal to the Union Army veterans, most of whom distrusted the names and would not purchase the smokes. What was needed was a native approach to cigarettes, even though the items themselves contained foreign tobaccos.

F. S. Kinney was the first tobacconist to understand this and act upon his beliefs. In 1868 he hired some foreign-born cigarette rollers—taking some from the Bedrossians—and opened a small shop in lower Manhattan. Little is known of most early Kinney brands, though like several other newcomers he did use more Bright leaf than could be found in Bedrossian's smokes. Also, Kinney packaged his cigarettes in paper packs to save money and lower the prices. The Turkish smokes, packed in their cardboard containers, remained the more elegant cigarette. And the two kinds of cigarettes were different. One Kinney brand,

Halves, probably contained equal amounts of Bright and Latakia, hence the name. This native American touch was also found in Full Dress and Straight Cut. Finally, Kinney experimented with a cigarette that was almost wholly Bright, which he called Caporal. It was a success, though some buyers indicated a desire for more flavor. Kinney added sugar and licorice to the tobacco to produce Sportsman's Caporal and finally found the right mix in Sweet Caporal, which quickly became the city's leading cigarette and made Kinney the premier firm in the developing industry.

By no means was Sweet Caporal thought of as a national brand, but it was the first to achieve more than a local reputation and soon became the most imitated cigarette in the land. By 1870 they could be found in Boston and Philadelphia, brought there not by Kinney, but by visitors who had heard of them and wanted to try the new "taste sensation." Kinney finally awoke to the fact that he had a gold mine and took on jobbers to sell Sweet Caps along the eastern seaboard. The demand was so great that he had to erect a manufacturing facility in Richmond, close by the tobacco auctions. The price of Bright soared, creating a small pocket of prosperity in the occupied South, but eventually lead to overproduction and distress. The foreign brands were swept from the field, except those for the few urbanites who wanted an exotic smoke and disdained the popular variety.

New companies were formed to take advantage of the demand. Goodwin & Company of New York turned out Old Judge and Welcome, neither of which was very popular. William S. Kimball of Rochester had been convinced the Turkish brands and names could be sold to Americans, and he tried first with Three Kings, Turkish Orientals, and Vanity Fair. All had small sales and were hardly profitable. So Kimball reformulated the blend of one of his brands to include larger amounts of Bright, transforming Cloth of Gold into Old Gold, and this new cigarette achieved a measure of success.

Lewis Ginter, a Northerner who resettled in Richmond prior to the war, enlisted in the Confederate Army and rose to the rank of major. Afterward he returned to Manhattan seeking a new career and soon displaced Kinney as the nation's leading cigarette manufacturer. Joining with John Allen, a New Yorker, he formed Allen & Ginter which he hoped would become a major tobacconist. Ginter quickly recognized the potential of the cigarette and apparently felt the key to success rested in the purchase and processing of southern and imported leaf. He returned to Richmond in 1875 and after establishing good relations with the farmers there and setting up a distribution system, began turning out cigarettes blended from dark Havana and Virginia leaves. None sold very well, and so Ginter experimented with Carolina Bright. Some of his newly formulated brands were successful, especially Richmond Gems, Richmond Straight Cut No. 1, and Our Little Beauties, though none was able to challenge Sweet Caps for leadership. Ginter even managed to convince John Wanamaker—an opponent of the cigarette—to permit him to have a display at the Philadelphia Centennial Exposition and so was able to introduce his smokes to visitors from all parts of the nation. By the early 1880s Allen & Ginter was opening factories in Britain and luring experienced cigarette rollers to America.

Cigarette use increased after Bright made its appearance and Kinney developed Sweet Caporal. In 1869, the first year for the Kinney brand, only 1.7 million cigarettes were produced and taxed in the United States. The following year, when Kinney began selling them outside of New York, and new companies appeared to exploit the market, 13.8 million were consumed. By the time Allen & Ginter started selling its brands in late 1875, 42 million were being sold. This figure almost doubled the next year, and in 1877, 150 million cigarettes were smoked in the United States.

The market appeared saturated and due for a shakeout. This had taken place in other American industries, and there was no reason to believe it would be otherwise with cigarettes. In 1877 there were 121 different brands registered with the government tax authorities, and doubtless several score local smokes were overlooked in the tally—which also did not include the roll-your-owns. For the first time the cigar manufacturers and distributors were taking note of the cigarette, and its popularity had them worried, at least a trifle. As they saw it, the cigarette boom was the result of the depression which had begun in 1873 and lin-

gered for most of the rest of the decade. According to the conventional wisdom, individuals who previously had confined their
smoking to cigars had turned to cigarettes temporarily in order
to save money. The cheap cigar went for two cents, though some
might be had for a penny. Cigarettes were five cents for a pack
of ten, and roll-your-owns came to half that price. Given this
difference, and the lure of Bright, the cigarette did well. Thus,
cigar sales which peaked at 1.835 billion in 1874 fell to 1.776 billion in 1876 before leveling off. In good times, said the cigar
men confidently, the cigarette would be discarded.

The publicity for *Carmen,* which opened at the Opéra Co-
mique in Paris in 1874, seemed to buttress this opinion; once
again the cigarette was associated with unsavory lower-class
individuals in the minds of those people of taste. The cigarette
was alien, said the cigar manufacturers. Their variety of smoke,
on the other hand, was advertised as being purely American, this
being the best approach for the consumers of the 1870s.

Their analysis was only partially valid, and perhaps not even
that. Tobacco consumption would tend to rise during most subsequent depressions, or if the sales dipped temporarily when hard
times began, they would advance again—and often sharply—
once the manufacturers put out cheaper brands. Price had something to do with it; certainly quite a few American men were attracted to cigarettes because they couldn't afford cigars, and
probably a large number of them remained converts when good
times returned. On the other hand, sales of dry snuff and
granulated pipe tobacco, used for roll-your-owns, did not advance markedly in this period. From 118 million pounds in 1873,
the sales rose to 124 million in 1874 and remained stable for the
next two years. There was a decline to 123 million pounds in
1877 before sales advanced once again, reaching 146 million
pounds by the end of the decade, at which time there was a brief
period when snuff was in vogue and roll-your-owns became a fad
in the countryside.

One can easily understand why cigarettes were popular during
the depression of the early 1870s; price is always a consideration
at such time. But sales continued upward even after the worst of
the hard times had ended. Clearly the cigarette had caught on
by then, and use would spread steadily for the rest of the cen-

tury. There were many reasons for this growing market, as will be seen, and these included demography, organization, invention, and marketing. In all of these areas the cigarette had advantages over other forms of tobacco. It was a young person's smoke, and this segment of the population was increasing more rapidly than any other. The cigarette companies would be better organized than those in the cigar field and by men who were willing to experiment, since they had no clear tradition upon which to rely, and which might hold them back. In time cigarettes would be mass produced, a technique the cigar makers could not develop. Finally, the cigarette manufacturers demonstrated skills at marketing that not only were superior to those of the cigar producers, but that provided models for individuals who turned out a wide variety of consumer products for the mass market.

The cigar was by no means a declining luxury or necessity, but after the 1870s it was clear the cigarette would never again return to its old status of the smoke for poor urban wretches, idle wealthy women, and the effete. Around 1880 it became the kind of smoke the middle-class male might not have preferred, but one that he would accept.

II

The Duke of Durham

Any fair-minded person who understood the cigarette business as it existed in the early 1880s would have had to conclude that Lewis Ginter was the most important and innovative personality in the industry. Early in the game he had seized leadership from F. S. Kinney and the rest and, through the development of a workable distribution system, had been able to sell his brands all along the eastern seaboard. For his time Ginter was considered a bold publicist, and he knew his tobaccos.

This last factor was of no little importance. Ginter was the only one of the early tycoons who had any long association with the growing and marketing of the leaf. He studied agricultural policy, fraternized with farmers, visited the auctions, and in general appreciated tobacco as a creation of nature. Kinney, Goodwin, Kimball, and the other northern manufacturers were just that—they knew little of farming and preferred life in the factory and shop. While they may have been skillful at blending,

these men tended to think of the leaf as something that came out
of a package, was processed, and then placed into another package for sale. Ginter could be amazed at the accident that
resulted in the creation of Bright; the others were merely thank-
ful the new curing method had developed. Ginter was not the
first to use Bright in cigarettes, but more than any other manufacturer he did it in a way that pleased smokers. More important, perhaps, as far as the development of the cigarette was concerned, he pioneered with the use of another kind of leaf, White
Burley.

As with Bright, the White Burley strain resulted from an accident—what writers of the time called a "sport" of nature—on a
farm run by George Webb near Higginsport, Ohio, in 1864.
Webb planned for a record harvest that year, as demand for the
three types of Burley (Red, Little, and Twist Bud) had risen
sharply during the war, while the traditional southern sources
were lost for the duration. Burley was a particularly desirable
variety, being hardy, large-leafed, and dark, the kind preferred
by users of plug. Needing additional seed, Webb crossed the
Ohio River into Kentucky to obtain a supply, which he planted
in the conventional manner. The seedlings came up as usual except those in one bed, where the Kentucky seed had been
placed. There the leaves appeared light, a creamy yellow. Ordinarily Webb might have abandoned that patch, for along with
others who saw the seedlings he assumed them to be diseased.
But tobacco was in short supply and the price was rising, so he
decided to wait and watch.

The leaf grew irregularly, first slower than normal and faster
toward the end, so it ripened two weeks before the rest of the
crop. Webb cured some of the yellow leaf and found that it had
a strong, bitter taste, in part due to a higher than normal nicotine content. Most of the crop was destroyed, but on a hunch,
Webb saved some seed to plant the following year, so that in the
autumn of 1866 he was able to send two hogsheads of this White
Burley to Cincinnati for auction.

There the Burley was studied and analyzed and, much to
Webb's surprise, fetched a premium price. The tobacco men had
discovered that while the new strain lacked a pleasant taste of its
own, it had an unusual ability to absorb liquid additives. Most

tobaccos could hold around 4 per cent of such sweeteners and flavorers as glycerine, rum, licorice, sugar, and tonka bean; White Burley could take up to 25 per cent. Furthermore, the leaf took on new tastes with each blend of additive. White Burley could be used as a filler for plug that could transmit whatever tastes the manufacturer hoped to create, and even its color changed with additives. In this fashion, it acted like a wild card in a poker game—White Burley could become almost anything that was desired.

For several years this new strain was used exclusively in plug tobaccos, and its culture spread throughout southern Ohio and into Kentucky, just as Bright was conquering North Carolina and parts of Virginia. Almost immediately some cigarette manufacturers experimented with White Burley, but none had much success, in part because at the time they lacked an understanding of how it could be utilized. Ginter was aware of the potential for such an absorbent tobacco—with the proper additives it could be made to taste like the most expensive Turkish leaves, and at a fraction of the price. White Burley offered the means by which the two markets for cigarettes, that for expensive imports and the other for less costly domestic ones, could be united, or at least brought more closely together. Other manufacturers already used additives to enhance tastes, but none had attempted to create a flavor, or imitate one. Ginter became the pathbreaker in this field, and it was his major contribution to the industry.

Ginter experimented with Burley and Bright mixtures, and in the end created several new brands, among them Bonaparte, Matchless, and Old Rip, all of which had substantial amounts of White Burley treated with flavoring elements. These quickly captured the public fancy, and imitations followed. White Burley had emerged as a major component for smokes turned out by hand in small shops along the eastern seaboard and interior New York and sold in urban areas, usually ten for fifteen or twenty cents. These cigarettes of White Burley, Bright, and other domestic tobaccos were distinctively American, quite different in taste, aroma, and appearance from the Turkish, Russian, and other European varieties that were more familiar and continued to have loyal followers.

Much of this had been made possible by Lewis Ginter, the

first important figure produced by the cigarette industry. Yet Ginter, who in the mid-1880s was close to the end of his career, is a forgotten man today, at least as far as the general public is concerned. He left no visible monument bearing his name and did not create a major fortune or found a dynasty; even his company would soon be swallowed by a more vigorous enterprise.

This was not the result of flaws in his abilities or a lack of vision, but rather of his age. Lewis Ginter had begun his career in the 1840s and by the time the cigarette had become established was too old to capitalize upon it and create a business empire. He had done more than anyone else to create the product, a distinctively American cigarette sold at a low price and wrapped in a soft pack. But much remained to be done, especially in the areas of mechanized manufacturing, advertising, and business organization. Ginter contributed nothing of importance in these vital areas. Another man would do so, thus capitalizing on Ginter's creations. In the mid-1880s, when he replaced Ginter as industry leader, Buck Duke was not quite thirty years old.

Duke was a man of superlative organizational skills, a master manager, one of those individuals who had the knack for making money with every throw of the dice—which, on occasion, he had carefully loaded. After organizing his tobacco empire and then seeing it dismembered by the government, Duke lost interest in the industry and retired for a while. Then he re-entered the field to create one of the largest electric utilities in the nation and help found what was arguably the finest university in his part of the country.

With all of this, however, Duke had little vision or imagination. Certainly he was not on the scale of a Carnegie or a Rockefeller, though his control of tobacco was more complete than theirs in steel and petroleum. What he did possess was an unusual ability for selecting the right people for difficult jobs, and for negotiating clever deals. Upon his death, one of Duke's former associates, Clinton Toms of Liggett & Myers, was asked to evaluate his contribution. At no point did Toms use words like "brilliant," "innovative," or "creative." Instead, he spoke of "his power of concentration—his ability to put into any one task his whole power, and then to turn around and do the same thing with another entirely different problem." It was the kind of obituary that might have pleased the man who once said "superior brains are not necessary" in order to get ahead in the world. "Any young man can succeed if he is willing to apply himself."

So he did, and of course Duke was a roaring success by most standards. The irony of it all was that he was credited with accomplishments he never intended. Throughout his career in tobacco, Duke remained convinced that the key to power rested in domination of the cigar business. He appreciated the profits cigarettes returned and thought they would do well overseas, especially in the Orient, where the poverty-stricken masses could afford little else in the way of a "soft drug," but in his heart Duke believed Americans would always prefer cigars and plug. In dealing with the domestic market he excelled in detail work and the creation of the business structure, but he spent too little time considering whether he was headed in the right direction. This often occurs in the careers of individuals who possess brains and energy but are short on imagination. Such was the situation with Buck Duke.

He was born in Durham County, North Carolina, in 1865, and named James Buchanan Duke in honor of the President elected that year. His father, Washington Duke, was an independent dirt farmer, engaged in what today would be called subsistence agriculture. Like many others in the region, he raised a little tobacco on the side for sale at market, using the proceeds to purchase necessities. Washington Duke opposed slavery, not so much because the institution was inherently evil, but rather as a bulwark of the plantation class he hated. So he rejected secession, and served in the Confederate Army as a guard only after being drafted in 1863. After a brief stay in a Union prison, Washington Duke walked home to Durham.

The area had been overrun by Sherman's soldiers, who were stationed not far from the Duke farm. When news of the armistice reached North Carolina, men on both sides threw down their arms, fraternized, and by way of celebration broke into tobacco warehouses and corn whiskey distilleries and looted them with fine abandon. The Union soldiers, partial to the Bright leaf grown and cured in Carolina, packed some in their knapsacks to enjoy on the way home. Behind them they left the wreckage of most farms in the area, including that of Washington Duke. Naturally, the Carolinians were bitter about the destruction. They could not have known that they had unwittingly provided "free samples" to the northern soldiers. In time they would want more, and then they would pay for what they received.

As Washington Duke told it, his farm had been stripped of everything of value by marauding soldiers. All that remained were barren fields, the wreckage of the barn, an old wagon, and in a corner of the barn, overlooked by the soldiers, a small quantity of Bright tobacco. Together with his sons, Duke granulated the leaves, packed them in muslin bags with the label Pro Bono Publico—For the Public Good—and then sold them in order to get food and other goods.

Somehow the Dukes managed to survive that winter, and the following spring they planted the fields with tobacco. That year they sold fifteen thousand pounds of Pro Bono Publico, and were on their way to a more comfortable life than they ever could have imagined prior to the war. The North Carolina farmers benefited from the demand for Bright that appeared in the North. Within two years, Duke was able to leave off farming to concentrate upon the production of granulated Bright. He was one of several to do so in the Durham area, and Pro Bono Publico was by no means the best-known or most-favored Bright chew.

Bull Durham was another Durham brand, with a formula pretty much the same as all the others. One could hardly tell it apart from Duke's chew or such brands as Lone Jack, World's Choice, and Brown's Mule, all of which were based on the Bright leaf. Like them it was a local product in 1868, when its owner, John Ruffin Green, sold a half interest in his factory to a firm headed by William T. Blackwell. A merchandiser and distributor, Blackwell knew little about production, which he left to others. Instead, he concentrated on publicizing the brand, and eventually spent $100,000 a year to do so. He obtained testimonials from prominent people and broadcast them throughout the Northeast by means of newspaper ads, all of which served to fix the name Bull Durham in the public eye. It worked. Bull Durham became the nation's leading brand by the late 1870s. More important perhaps, Blackwell had demonstrated that it was possible to take an unknown, relatively undifferentiated

product and through clever advertising and efficient distribution
make it a huge success. At a time when there was no national
cigar brand, Bull Durham was chewed from the Mississippi to
the Atlantic.

Pro Bono Publico was only one of the mob that trailed far
behind in sales. The difference was not so much in the taste—
which could have been duplicated—but in the sales effort
mounted by Blackwell. Washington Duke understood this, but
lacked the energy and interest to do anything about it. James
Duke had both. After working on the farm and then in the factory where he clashed with his oldest brother Brodie, James had
gone to business school in Poughkeepsie, New York, to learn
bookkeeping—and there he also came into contact with Yankee
ways, which he liked. Late in 1874, shortly after his eighteenth
birthday, James asked his father for a thousand dollars, to start
his own business. Wash countered with an offer to take James
and his other brothers into the tobacco firm. They accepted and
thus formed W. Duke Sons & Company.

Brodie left the company soon after to enter real estate specula-
tion and dabble in funeral supplies. Then Wash sold an interest
in the tobacco business to outside investors and gradually withdrew from active management. Meanwhile James—whom everyone called Buck—traveled throughout the country, trying to sell
Pro Bono Publico and other Duke brands. Wherever he went he
found Bull Durham the leading seller, and nothing he did in the
way of lowering prices or developing new brands could alter the
situation. Furthermore, he didn't like selling or life on the road.
He yearned to return to the pleasures of Manhattan. "My company is up against a stone wall," he wrote. "It can't compete with
Bull Durham. Something has to be done and that quick. I am
going into the cigarette business."

Duke returned to Durham in 1881 to lead the conversion to
cigarettes. He did not relish the change, for like most middle-
class Southerners he considered them effeminate and alien
smokes. Men inhaled them openly in New York and Boston, but
those in Richmond and Savannah puffed cigars and used plug.
Duke himself preferred plug, though he did enjoy fine cigars in
the evening. Cigarettes were not smoked in Durham, Winston, or
other tobacco towns in the South. In 1881, they were still the

habit of the recent enemy. Having spent most of the past five years traveling through the North, Buck felt he knew these people and was even able to think and talk like them when the occasion demanded it. He also had studied cigarettes with care and appreciated the problems and bottlenecks as well as the potential.

As Duke saw it, there were four basic aspects to the cigarette business: the growing, purchasing, and blending of the tobaccos; the manufacture and packaging of the cigarettes; the distribution of the smokes to favored locations; and advertising. There were no important secrets in tobacco cultivation and curing, and the leaf was sold at auctions where all could bid. Although processors guarded the exact formulas of additives used to produce plug and granulated brands, all the constituents were known. In a matter of hours a skilled tobacco man could approximate the taste of any on the market. The same held true for cigarettes. Duke could imitate any one he liked, merely by purchasing a pack, turning it over to one of his foremen, and waiting a day or so for the results.

This is what he did initially, though later on some Duke brands might be said to have been new. Yet for all of his work in the industry, Buck Duke never created an important product or brand. He had little feel for the leaf; he was not that kind of innovator. Duke simply wanted to fashion a major industrial empire. The accidents of birth and history placed him in tobacco. Had he been a Northerner or a Midwesterner he might have drifted into railroads, oil, or steel, and perhaps made his mark there. Tobacco and cigarettes were means to an end for him. Even at the peak of Duke's career, industry insiders did not look upon him as one of their own.

Worse, many viewed him as a turncoat. Wash Duke had opposed slavery and after the war joined the Republican Party. Buck followed his example. The Dukes were deemed "nigger lovers," and though the family did little to aid blacks, they never bothered to answer the charges and refused to participate in antiblack organizations such as the Ku Klux Klan. Buck always felt more comfortable in Manhattan than in Durham or any other southern city. To those who remained at the old factory, who never went north and so rarely saw the top management, Buck Duke was a traitor.

Duke's talents and disregard for tradition showed in his production methods. He had entered the cigarette industry at a time when a generation of research attempting to create a cigarette-manufacturing machine was about to bear fruit, but in 1881 all cigarettes were produced by hand, and all the experienced rollers were foreign born. In small shops near Astor Place in Manhattan, groups of East European Jews would bend over their benches, ten hours a day, with the best and fastest of them turning out around three thousand cigarettes a shift. Most had learned their craft in Russia. Some went directly to New York when they heard of employment opportunities there, while others had come from London, attracted by higher wages and the shortage of cigarette rollers after the Civil War. These men, and not the tobacco farmers, were the key ingredient in the manufacturing process. At the time, the labor cost of producing cigarettes was close to a dollar per thousand, and of this amount, almost ninety cents went for the rolling, the men receiving seventy cents of it in wages.

These people lived in ghettos on Manhattan's East Side, rarely venturing into the Gentile world except to work. They were aware of their premium wages and of managements' desire to cut them, so the rollers organized a union in self-defense. Late in 1880, Goodwin & Company, which finally had come up with a popular brand in Canvas Back, tried to force the rollers to accept lower wages. Led by Moses Gladstein, a nineteen-year-old firebrand who had arrived in America the previous year, the men went on strike.

Duke knew of this situation when deciding to switch over to cigarettes. He had already hired J. M. Seigel, a well-known London Jewish cigarette maker, who was on his way to America and leadership of the Durham work force. Now Duke rushed to New York and approached Gladstein with an offer—the old wages for all workers who relocated to Durham, with Duke paying fare and expenses for the men and their families.

It sounded good. The Jewish immigrants lived in hovels in lower Manhattan often worse than the huts and farmhouses they had known in Eastern Europe. Anti-Semitism was well-established and rising in New York, and Gladstein and others probably knew that hatred for Jews was relatively quiescent in the South. The costs of living were lower in the Carolinas than in the city, and the workers learned they could hope to own their own homes—and even some land—if they made the move.

This was the picture Buck Duke painted. With no reason to remain in New York and in the knowledge they would move as a community, and not be alone, Gladstein and around 125 other rollers accepted the deal, and were in their new homes—really a new Jewish ghetto—on the outskirts of Durham by the autumn of 1881.

No sooner had they adjusted to this rural setting and the factory than Duke learned of a successful cigarette-manufacturing machine. This was no great surprise, since several inventors had been working on cigar and cigarette devices for over a decade, ever since Allen & Ginter had offered $75,000 for such a machine. Albert Hooks, a New Yorker, came up with one in 1872, but the cigarettes it turned out—when the contraption worked, which was seldom—were loosely packed and irregularly shaped. Two years later the Abadie Company of Paris received a patent for its machine, which also failed in test runs. William and Charles Emery presented their machine in 1876. In three stages it segregated a small amount of granulated tobacco and shaped it into a tube, then delivered it to a roll of paper where it was placed in position for the final step, which was the cutting and sealing. The Emery machine had limited success, and a model was purchased by Goodwin, who used it as a threat against the hand rollers. It was this machine that helped precipitate the 1880 strike that led to Duke's raid for workers.

In 1881, as Goodwin worked to perfect the Emery machine, James Bonsack of Virginia, a twenty-one-year-old mechanic, announced the perfection of his own device, which like the Emery utilized a three-stage process. Bonsack tried to interest Allen & Ginter, Kinney, and other cigarette manufacturers in his process, but all turned him down, as they pinned their hopes on the Emery and perhaps were fearful that Bonsack had impinged upon the patents of others. Also, some cigarette men weren't sure the public would accept the machine-made smokes, which they believed were bound to be of lower quality than the hand-rolled ones.

Duke took a different view. As he saw it, the others thought of cigarettes as small cigars and were trying to create them as though the cigar-making process had to be imitated. He considered cigarettes a cheap smoke, which would capture cigar smokers on the basis of price and advertising, but could also go further, convincing nonsmokers to light up as well. While most manufacturers thought in terms of a fixed, limited market for their wares, Duke believed that every American male was a potential cigarette smoker. This was an important distinction. Of all the major manufacturers of the period, only Duke believed cigarettes represented a wholly new product, and not simply a paper cigar. Still, so long as hand rollers were employed, the price would remain high, so much so that cigarettes would have to compete with small cigars for the customer's nickel and dime. A successful machine would enable him to lower unit costs and drop prices, expand advertising and volume, and drive competitors from the field, all the while increasing net profits.

Whether due to an inability to work out a deal with Emery or because he believed the Bonsack a superior machine that would withstand patent challenges, Duke decided to back the Virginian. The inventor and his engineer, William O'Brien, got rid of most of the bugs in the complicated device by 1884, by which time it could produce over two hundred cigarettes a minute, and do so with relatively little down time. Now Duke moved in and tied Bonsack to a series of unbreakable, airtight contracts. He would pay the inventor a royalty of thirty cents per thousand cigarettes produced (thirty-three cents if a Bonsack printing device was used to emboss each smoke) and guarantee to remit to the inventor at least $200 per month for each machine. Bonsack was to be free to lease his machines to other manufacturers on these terms, but a secret codicil in the contract provided for rebates, so that Duke's net royalty payments would fall to twenty-four cents per thousand. A subsequent clause guaranteed that Duke's payments would be at least 25 per cent lower than those paid by the others.

The reasoning was clear. Duke expected the Bonsacks to drive the Emery machines and others from the market, and that all manufacturers would have to purchase them or leave the business. Under the terms of his contract, he could undersell his competitors and turn a larger profit at the same time. In a matter of a few years he would crush the others, leaving him in command of the field. Prices would decline, consumers would be lured to cigarettes, and Duke would prosper. Everything was falling into place. Even the tax situation was brightening. Federal levies had reached $5.00 per thousand in 1867, but were down to $1.75 in 1875. Eight years later, as Bonsack perfected his machine and Duke moved to conquer the market, the government lowered the rate to $.50.

The newly relocated rollers appreciated the implications of mechanization and must have realized the precariousness of their position. A strike might have succeeded in New York, a polyglot city where separate communities coexisted and political and economic power was diffused among several groups. But Durham was a tobacco town, dominated by the Dukes and others like them. The workers could not expect success from a challenge to authority there. Nor could they afford to leave their jobs, for they lacked funds for another move. So they worked and waited.

The Bonsacks were performing well by late 1883, and Duke decided to act. He cut wages to $2.90 a week, forcing the workers to strike. Then he locked them out of the factory and brought in local men for those jobs the machines couldn't handle. Some of the rollers shrugged it off and struggled to return to Manhattan. Others remained in Durham and tried to find work in other areas. Perhaps due to a twinge of conscience, Buck Duke gave Moses Gladstein a thousand dollars, which he used to open a small clothing store.

The age of the hand roller was coming to an end, at least insofar as American-style cigarettes were concerned. The question remained whether the Bonsacks, Emerys, or some other machine would take the bulk of the business, but no industry figure of importance expected to continue doing business in the old way. A single Bonsack, working for fifty-five hours a week (the norm for rollers in this period), could turn out as many cigarettes as all the hand workers in America combined. Mechanization was inevitable; one of the residues and casualties of the change was the small East European Jewish community in Durham.

No sooner had things settled down at the old factory than Duke visited Manhattan, seeking a site for a new installation. He would expand operations in Durham and, in fact, began work on a larger factory there in 1884. But at the same time he knew that a move to New York would be necessary to place him in the midst of what then was the biggest market for cigarettes of all kinds. In time, as his new brands gained acceptance in different parts of the country, Duke would establish regional centers for sales and distribution. But New York was the corporate and financial hub of America in the 1880s, and Duke yearned to be at the nation's true locus. For personal reasons too, he wanted to make the move. He had come to enjoy the pace and excitement of the great city far more than he did the placid, provincial society to be found in Durham.

Duke arrived in New York just in time to witness the financial panic of 1884, a collapse which for the most part was confined to Wall Street, but which shook public confidence in other parts of the nation. As had been the case in previous periods of economic upheaval, cigar consumption declined while that of the cheaper cigarette rose. Taken together with the perfection of the Bonsacks and the cut in federal excise taxes, the panic appeared a good omen for the cigarette industry in general and Buck Duke in particular. After locating a small factory building for a low rental on Rivington Street—ironically, close to where the hand rollers lived—Duke surveyed the cigarette scene in the city.

Burley and Bright cigarettes were still deemed fads in the early and mid-1880s, enjoyed by Civil War veterans and some middle-class males. Fashionable society leaders smoked cigars, and when they wanted a change of pace might try a Latakia-based cigarette, usually Russian or Turkish. These were hand-rolled and would remain so even after the Bonsacks were perfected. Machines could not form the rough-cut foreign tobaccos as well as they did the granulated American leaf. In addition, the hand-rolling added another touch of authenticity to the romance of the "Oriental smokes."

Some manufacturers were experimenting with blends of Bright and the dark Turkish and Russian tobaccos, though with little success. Most tried to have representation in both markets, for at the time it appeared certain there would remain two distinctive kinds of cigarette smokers. The urban class would continue to use premium foreign and domestic cigarettes containing dark leaf. Not many of these would be sold, but the profit margins could be quite high. Meanwhile cigar smokers might switch to the cheap domestic brands, for which there could be a large market but low profit margins.

Throughout his career Duke would be convinced there was no future in the premium-priced market. In the 1880s he felt the foreign cigarettes were little more than a fad. These sold for twenty-five cents for a package of ten and were not out of place in drawing rooms and fine salons. The American brands, which he had decided to back, were sold on a price basis, and the lower the price, the more popular they became. In the mid-1880s, the lowest-priced manufactured brands went for ten for a dime. These might never achieve an audience among people of quality, thought Duke, but he could make up in volume what he lost in status and profit margins.

Duke recognized that Americans were upwardly mobile. Didn't his own career illustrate the point? And it would be the same with smokes. Men might start with American cigarettes, but if they did well, they would graduate to foreign smokes and cigars. Thus the cheap cigarette had a limited future, unable to cut deeply into the public that chewed and incapable of rising above its station. Yet the fates had placed Duke in this market. He appeared destined for the role of the initiator of the young into smoking, and he would keep them so long as they were unsuccessful in life or business. Depressions and war would help Duke insofar as sales were concerned. Prosperity for others might see lower profits for his company, or at least so it seemed at the time. Duke would try to make cigarettes the universal smoke for the proletariat and parts of the middle class. Considering the times, this vision was not at all limited; rather, it was ambitious and even audacious. Duke understood the problems of the marketplace. He knew White Burley and Bright, and his early cigarettes had been created from these tobaccos. The Bonsacks worked best with granulated American leaf, and Duke's own future appeared linked with that of the machine. He accepted the situation with good grace, and then went on from there.

By 1884 Duke had dealt with the growing, purchasing, and blending aspects of the business, or at least he no longer worried about them. With the Bonsacks he had taken care of manufacturing. Now he altered packaging. American cigarettes were packaged in soft, wraparound containers, similar to those used today. These were inexpensive but did not protect the cigarettes, which often were crushed. In 1869 the Bedrossians had introduced a slide-and-shell box for their brands, and others had followed. Now Duke developed his own version of the hard container, which though more expensive to manufacture than the soft pack, added a touch of luxury to them. This done, he turned to that facet of the industry in which he was to excel—distribution.

Duke was the only important manufacturer who understood the implications of the cut in excise taxes. Like the others he planned to retain the existing retail price structure, but while the other manufacturers intended to pocket the extra profits, Duke used the tax break to expand his market. Immediately he cut the wholesale prices for his brands by up to 50 per cent, even before the tax cut went into effect. Thus, dealers would make up to twice as much profit from the sale of a Duke brand as from that of most others. They snapped at the opportunity, and the Duke smokes doubled and redoubled their constituencies. While the others realized higher profits per unit, they found themselves selling fewer packs. As for Duke, his profit margin remained the same, but his total business grew enormously. As late as 1883, he was only one of many small manufacturers. Two years later Duke was a major factor in the field.

The Duke brands of this period—Duke of Durham, Cyclone, Cameo, and Town Talk—were similar to those put out by the other manufacturers. Pedro, which contained some dark imported tobaccos, represented a foray into the foreign field which eventually failed and was discontinued. Pin Head was more typical. Introduced in 1885 at ten for ten cents, it carried the inscription on the pack: "These cigarettes are manufactured on the Bonsack Cigarette Machine," and the brand became a big seller in New York and other eastern cities.

Like most popular American smokes, Pin Head came with cigarette cards. These were both a means of advertising and a lure
to purchasers as well as a stiffener for the pack, to prevent it
from crumbling. The "lure" had been pioneered by the English
manufacturer, P. Lorillard, who a generation earlier had placed
paper money in random packages of his tobacco and advertised
the fact, to encourage users to purchase his brands. American
News, which distributed several brands of smokes in the 1870s
and early 1880s, was the first to use picture cards in each pack.
Allen & Ginter combined the two ideas prior to Duke's arrival on
the New York scene. Their colorful cards came in series, with
each numbered to entice the buyer into additional purchases. In-
dian chiefs, famous battles, postage-stamp reproductions, baseball players, animals, and political figures were some of the series.
Leading actresses in enticing poses were particularly popular—
the soft pornography of the day. Allen & Ginter went further,
distributing booklets containing pictures of the cards, and Ginter
tried to sign famous actresses to exclusive contracts.

Duke learned the game quickly, and although he didn't introduce new ideas or techniques, he used the old as well as any of
the manufacturers. In the late 1880s he put forth an album of
"Sporting Girls" to popularize a new brand, Cross Cut Polo
Team, and he bid actively and aggressively against Ginter for
contracts and endorsements.

While on the road for Pro Bono Publico, Duke had demonstrated a good sense of marketing psychology. He rarely spoke to
retailers about tobacco, preferring instead to stress discounts,
sales potential, and inventories. Increasingly, however, his interests turned to finance and business organization, so that he had
little time to do more than plot sales strategy, while leaving tactics to others. Furthermore, he had few new ideas on how to
market his products. Duke was better employed at the New York
factory, and in any case he preferred to remain there, working a
ten-hour day and then touring the city's theaters and night spots
until after midnight. Needing a "road man," as well as one who
could come up with new concepts, he took on Edward Featherstone Small, the ambitious son of an impoverished southern family, who had Duke's tastes for the high life and wanted the
means to live it.

Small was given his first opportunity in the Atlanta market, which at the time was dominated by the Allen & Ginter brands. He began by discarding Duke's existing approach, one based upon price competition and rebates. None of the major cigarette companies had used pictures of scantily clad females on their cigarette cards for this market—such lures were reserved for the more sophisticated and racy northern cities. Small cracked this barrier. He created a cigarette card series based upon "Famous Actresses," and then flooded the city with free samples, pictures of one Madame Rhea, indicating that others could be had with purchases of Duke's cigarettes.

It worked. Atlanta became Duke territory and Small was given added responsibilities and a higher salary. While in New York for a conference, he came up with his most famous card series, called "Rags to Riches," portraits of leading businessmen who rose from obscurity. As Small had guessed, these cards appealed to the lower-class males who purchased American-made smokes. Sex and power, these were the hallmarks of many of Small's series, and they helped make Duke's cigarettes the best selling in the nation.

Of course, all of this was prior to the days of motivational research, depth psychology, and mass-media techniques. Madison Avenue still was a residential street at the turn of the century. Small did not develop a philosophy of advertising or ever attempt to reduce it to a science. But he clearly understood sales psychology as well as any person in the field. Just as Duke was developing business structure in the industry, Small was doing the same for advertising of cigarettes.

Duke gave Small an open purse and a free hand after becoming convinced he could manage the job, and Small was delighted to spend money and exercise his will. When several St. Louis merchants refused to see him, Small hired an alluring woman as a salesperson—a Mrs. Leonard—and called in reporters and cameramen for a press conference. As a result he got front-page coverage for the novelty, and at no cost to the firm. Duke cigarette sales picked up in St. Louis, and in no time the retailers were calling Small with orders—which he filled without the discounts he would have had to offer under normal conditions. Small, followed by reporters, went to their shops, accompanied

by the now-famous Mrs. Leonard and more stories appeared in
the newspapers. In this fashion, Small won the St. Louis market
for Duke.

Small may have been the first man to offer free signs to merchants with their names embossed in bright colors and advertisements for Duke brands on both sides and below. He would
underwrite the costs of cigar-store Indians and turbaned Turks
in whole or in part, if that was what the merchant wanted, so
long as the Duke name appeared in prominent places. What he
was attempting to do, of course, was to create brand loyalty
among customers by first instilling it in the minds of the merchants. And it worked, at least with the retailers. In many
markets they would feature the Duke brands to the detriment of
those of other manufacturers. These were local brands, to be
sure, and the loyalties were not as long-lasting as Small and
Duke might have preferred. Still, Small could boast of his
successes in this field. Others before him had made the effort; he
was the first to carry it off.

Small became wealthy and famous within the trade. With a
roll of his eyes he would explain the reasons for his success.
"The essential element in creating trade," he said, "is a few
grains of common sense, strategy and tact well sharpened, properly administered and rubbed with a little nigger luck." To this
Small added: "Above all, judicious advertising, especially if the
same is novel and astounding in magnitude."

Duke could not help but be pleased with Small's success, but
he did complain. "The fact that jobbers are getting calls from retailers is not sufficient proof that consumers are demanding very
many of them," he noted. "I want to know how the sales of
retailers compare on our Duke with other brands both with the
prominent retailers and the smaller ones." He felt that Small was
spending too much time with the shopkeepers, and not enough
on spreading the word to the general public. He began questioning Small's expense accounts, and rejecting some of his ideas for
card series. All of this may have been a blind for the real reasons
the two men were drifting apart. Now that he was successful,
Small began living in an extravagant manner and drawing attention to himself. Duke did not mind the extravagance, but he felt
that Small was making too much of a show of his success—

within Buck Duke there always remained the seed of a Puritan. Also, it was coming to appear that Small, and not Duke, was the guiding force at the firm, and Buck refused to share credit with anyone.

Finally, there was the matter of temperament. Small was a natural genius at advertising and sales, accomplishing both with ease and what to Duke seemed little effort. Duke did not trust people who put in less than a full day at the job. "I have succeeded in business not because I have more natural ability than those who have not succeeded, but because I have applied myself harder and stuck to it longer," he wrote toward the end of his career. "I know plenty of people who have failed to succeed in anything to have more brains than I had, but they lacked application and determination." True, Duke did enjoy periods of recreation, especially with attractive women, but only after all had been set right at the office. When in 1885 he cut prices once again in an attempt to drive competitors to the wall, some complained he would bring himself down as well. Duke responded by increasing his advertising budget, and this led to talk that he would be back in Durham before the year was out. Duke heard of this and said, "I don't talk; I work." His competitors could not have known that his profits could bear such expenditures—thanks to the efficiency of the Bonsacks, the rebates, and the efforts of Edward Featherstone Small.

Duke and Small had a falling out soon after. As Buck saw it, Small was doing more talking than working. In addition, he insisted on keeping his family in Atlanta and charging the company for trips home to see them. Duke picked upon this as an excuse to start an argument. In the summer of 1888 the two men went to Coney Island for a short vacation, and while there, Duke told Small he would have to move his family to Cincinnati, the heart of his territory. Small wouldn't hear of it. "The devil I will! I won't raise my children in that smoky town!" Neither man would give in. Shortly thereafter Small quit W. Duke Sons and took a similar position at Allen & Ginter.

This loss didn't faze Buck Duke. By then he had become the nation's largest cigarette manufacturer and had a personal worth of over $100,000. Thanks to Small, some of his brands were known regionally, though none had national acceptance yet. A

Duke partner, Richard Wright, had established Duke brands in the international market. The outlook was bright, or at least should have been. That year over 2.2 billion machine-mades were sold—only four years after the one billion mark had been passed.

Still, cigarettes were not the national smoke in 1888. More than 3.6 billion cigars were puffed that year. Gentlemen preferred the hand-rolled Havanas to the Russian and Turkish cigarettes and rejected the machine-fabricated American brands altogether. There were signs that cigarettes were cutting into the plug market, however. Sales of chew were down in 1888. Farmers who left the countryside for jobs in cities often turned to cigarettes on discovering that spitting was frowned upon in mixed company. In other words, the expansion of the American cigarette market was due more to the winning of converts from among the poor than from their acceptance by wealthy and influential Americans.

Duke had mixed feelings about this. He had succeeded in broadening the market for cigarettes among the lower classes. As he had set out to do, he demonstrated that cigarettes need not be an alternative kind of paper cigar, but could be viewed as a completely different product from any other using tobacco, with its own clientele, methods of production and distribution and promotion. His profit statements were fine, but Duke was unhappy regarding prospects in other areas. A social climber and something of a snob, he remained unenthusiastic about the goods sold by his company. E. H. Harriman could ride on his own railroad and J. P. Morgan own stocks underwritten by his banking house. Duke could not smoke his own cigarettes in public—they were not for people of his social class. Finally, Duke had ambitions to be known as more than America's cigarette king. So he was in a bind. How could he expand his market while at the same time changing it to please his ego?

III

The Trust

Buck Duke turned thirty in 1886, and already was hailed as leader of the cigarette industry. Business was going well, and Duke spent more than three quarters of a million dollars a year to see that sales continued to advance. Still, cigarettes weren't as important as plug or cigars in the total tobacco picture. Duke was restless and ambitious and dreamed of taking leadership of these industries as well as his own. More modest individuals such as Kinney, or those close to retirement like Ginter, would have been overjoyed had they achieved as much in an entire lifetime as Duke had in less than a decade. But they lacked his acquisitive instincts and cravings for social respectability.

In order to satisfy these drives, Duke set out to dominate all aspects of the tobacco business. For starters he would engulf the other cigarette firms. Then he would expand into plug and, finally, take command of the premium end of the industry—

cigars. In the process Duke would rationalize production and distribution, end inefficiencies, lower unit costs, and so increase his profits.

Such visions were not unusual in the late 1880s. All the nation's big businesses appeared headed in the direction of uniformity, and there seemed no reason to exclude tobacco products from the mainstream of industrial advance. The hundreds of plug, cigar, and cigarette brands seemed destined to be reduced to a bare handful. The day of the standard brand hadn't arrived, but its eventual outlines could be discerned—by Duke in particular—in the last decade of the nineteenth century. And this, too, would transform the habit and help make cigarettes more popular than might otherwise have been the case.

This was the dawn of the great era of trust-creation, which would culminate with the fashioning of United States Steel shortly after the turn of the century. Already John D. Rockefeller had shown others the way. There is no evidence that Duke tried to imitate Rockefeller—by accomplishing in tobacco what the older man had done in petroleum—yet both men searched for stability and security as well as empire, and both succeeded. Before he was through, Duke would rule his industry more thoroughly than any man before or after.

Duke began by intensifying his selling campaign in 1887, pouring fresh funds into promotion and lowering prices to retailers. These actions puzzled the other manufacturers. Surely Duke must have realized that any additional business he might obtain in this fashion would not compensate for razor-thin profit margins. They did not know about his arrangement with Bonsack, of course, or fully appreciate his strategy. Duke was not the kind of man to risk all on a single gamble, but this was what he did in 1887–89. He believed he could hold out longer than the others, and that once they became convinced of this, they would bow to his will.

Some leading manufacturers went to see Duke late in the year to discuss the possibility of industry peace. It was then that he told them of his plan for a giant enterprise to dominate the cigarette field. His rivals had a choice to make. Either they could join with him by selling out, or taking shares in the new corporation in return for their businesses, or be crushed by continued price cuts. They rejected the first alternative and didn't take the second seriously. Duke continued his campaign, and the other manufacturers returned the following year with their counteroffer: they would buy him out in order to rid the industry of a disruptive element. Duke's reply was yet another price cut; retailers were able to realize 50 per cent more profit by selling W. Duke Sons brands than those of some of his competitors.

At this point some of the other firms were forced to the wall. Kinney, then the third largest factor in the industry behind Duke and Allen & Ginter, was one of the first to accept the offer, and several smaller firms followed. Lewis Ginter held out. "Listen, Duke, you couldn't buy us out to save your neck. You haven't enough money, and you couldn't borrow enough. It's a hopeless proposition." Duke disagreed. "I make $400,000 out of my business every year," he claimed. (Probably a vast exaggeration, but how was Ginter to know?) "I'll spend every cent of it on advertising my goods as long as it is necessary. But I'll bring you into line." Then Duke initiated his massive spending program of 1889 and indicated to Ginter and others that a still larger one would be mounted—complete with higher retail discounts—the following year.

Was Duke bluffing? His opponents weren't willing to test the man. Ginter conceded defeat late in 1889, and the other major firms followed suit. Duke's lawyers set to work, and their product was the American Tobacco Company, proclaimed on January 31, 1890, with Duke its president.

The company was capitalized at $25 million, meaning that that much stock was issued to the participating firms. American Tobacco's tangible assets at inception were only $5 million, and of this, close to $2 million was in the form of notes issued by shareholders. W. Duke Sons and Allen & Ginter received $7.5 million each, in the form of common and preferred shares. Kinney got $5 million, while W. S. Kimball & Co. and Goodwin & Company each received $2.5 million. The new firm produced nine out of every ten cigarettes in the United States.

Duke moved quickly to consolidate and rationalize his new firm, which was necessary before he could expand into additional areas. That such was his goal never was in doubt. As one of his vice-presidents put it the following September, "The company is

organized for the purpose of curing leaf tobacco, to buy, manufacture and sell tobacco *in all its forms* [emphasis added]," and
later on Duke said, "We wished to manufacture a full variety to
make every style of tobacco the public wanted."

Within a year Duke had closed down the Goodwin factory
and other small operations, transferring their brands to the Allen
& Ginter facility in Richmond. By 1892 most of the American Tobacco domestic cigarettes were being produced in the South.
The Kinney facility on Twenty-second Street in New York continued to turn out the handmade Russian and Turkish smokes, a
variety Duke thought soon would be on the decline as a result of
continued price pressures.

Now that he had what amounted to a monopoly position,
Duke was able to extract even more favorable terms than before
from Bonsack. Not only were the royalties cut, but American Tobacco was granted sole use of the machines and any others that
might be produced by the company. Simultaneously he eliminated some advertising and promotion campaigns, which he felt
were no longer necessary. But Duke maintained prices to retailers, in order to keep the cost of American-style smokes low in
comparison to all other forms of tobacco and to encourage impulse buying, and in fact he tried to lower the prices regularly
over the next three years.

By 1893 Duke felt the time right to begin the second stage of
his program. He increased American Tobacco's capitalization by
$10 million and used the new stock to purchase several medium-
sized plug producers, which he refashioned into the National Tobacco Works. Then he approached the major producers—Liggett
& Myers, P. Lorillard, Drummond, and Brown—and "invited"
them to join National through an exchange of their assets for
shares. In order to make his point, Duke lowered the prices of
his brands, in effect warning the plug people that unless they accepted his offer, he would force them to the wall, as he had Allen
& Ginter and the other cigarette manufacturers a few years
earlier.

The plug group would not be cowed into submission. All of
them made cuts in prices, increased advertising expenditures,
and some even entered the cigarette business to fight Duke on
his own battlefield. Thus began what came to be known as the

"Plug War," in which Duke poured his cigarette profits into the battle and his rivals emptied their treasuries. Within a year and a half the price of major plug brands had fallen by half, and the decline continued into 1895. Together with the economic depression, this disrupted the tobacco business in all of its aspects. Many cigar smokers continued to switch to cheap cigarettes. Simultaneously, large numbers of cigarette users, some only recently converted from the chew, returned to plug once more due to its low price.

As had been the case in the cigarette battle, Duke was able to outlast his rivals. Some of the small companies approached him and granted National options to buy. Brown capitulated and Drummond followed; between them these two firms dominated the valuable St. Louis market, and their concession broke the ranks of those who remained. Lorillard gave National an option with the understanding that it could function as a separate unit with some autonomy. In the end, all but Liggett & Myers agreed to come under the Duke umbrella.

Aided by his investment bankers, Duke organized the Continental Tobacco Company in 1898, capitalizing it at $75 million. Into Continental went all those firms that granted Duke the options, exchanging their assets for shares of stock. American then sold National to Continental for $1.1 million in cash and $15.2 million in stock—a highly inflated price, but in those days that was the norm—and so became the directing force for the new trust. Naturally Duke was named its president. Now he controlled both the cigarette and plug industries. The only firm that had escaped his reach was Liggett & Myers, and Duke was certain it too would fall into line after a while—or be crushed. And so it did. After a brief scuffle with some Standard Oil millionaires who hoped to use L & M as a vehicle around which to create a rival tobacco trust, Duke forced them from the field. In 1899 he swallowed Liggett & Myers and with it the long-coveted Bull Durham.

With strong backing from the financiers, Duke ousted the old cigarette men from his boards, revamped operations, and prepared for the final push.

He began by gobbling up all the independent cigarette, snuff, and plug firms whose leaders could be persuaded, bullied, or beaten into submission. In 1900 he organized American Snuff around the Lorillard operation and soon had command of that branch of the tobacco business. Then Duke invaded the British market in force, and when the companies there united to form Imperial Tobacco, he retaliated with a burst of price cutting. In the end he came to an agreement which in effect divided the world between the two giant combines, in part through the creation of a jointly owned firm, British-American Tobacco, with Duke taking two thirds of the stock. By then antitrust sentiments were being heard in Washington, but Duke pushed forward, organizing Consolidated Tobacco as an umbrella for American and Continental, and in 1904 the bundle was reshaped once again, with a new American Tobacco Company taking control of the entire industry.

All of it, that is, except for one area—cigars. American Cigar, organized in 1902, obtained only a small part of that market. Cigars still were handmade, brand loyalty was strong, and the cigar companies were closely held and their leaders capable of withstanding financial pressures. No amount of price cutting and advertising could alter the situation. Given time and the invention of a cigar-making machine, Duke might have been able to take command of that last stronghold of the independents, but he had neither. He did continue to expand, however, buying companies that manufactured boxes, cigarette machines, pipes, tinfoil, tobacco stores, and even urban real estate on which new stores could be erected. American Tobacco dominated the market for additives and was a major force in the tobacco fields in the South. Duke even influenced Cuban politics in attempts to win favored treatment when he purchased leaf there.

In all of this Duke had demonstrated his abilities for acquisition and expansion. Newspapers and magazines carried stories of his feats, his growing power, and how American Tobacco had come to control the industry.

Impressive though his creation was, however, it was flawed. Duke was without peer in taking over companies, but he didn't know how to digest them. Most were able to function independently under weak corporate umbrellas. In many cases the old premerger company leaders remained at their posts, where they soon learned they could challenge Duke without much fear of retaliation—the president simply didn't know how to deal with such dissent from within his own ranks, or if he did, lacked the heart for a head-on confrontation. Duke failed to rationalize production and distribution, especially for cigarettes. His trust-building masked the fact that he had no new ideas to offer in this area. At the very least he might have cut down on the number of brands turned out by his various subsidiaries; at the most, Duke might have attempted to market a national smoke.

He did neither and so several brands continued on long after their useful economic lives had ended, because division managers had some affection for them. In some markets more than a dozen American Tobacco cigarettes competed for the same consumers, and consequently the company had to forego profits and actually accept losses on occasion. Duke's admirers and critics looked at the raw numbers and saw the vast scope of his enterprise. Few realized how deficient the man was in fashioning a viable business operation after he had acquired the various components for one. Duke had changed the face of the tobacco industry, but he had little impact upon the products themselves. One might go so far as to say that Duke actually prevented change, especially the production of a nationally advertised cigarette. Such a development would have to await the demise of American Tobacco.

Duke's enormous power did not mean he was content or even secure. Throughout this period he felt hemmed in by those who were out to destroy him and shatter his empire. He did not fear competitors; they could be handled with ease. He ignored critics within his companies. Rather, Duke had to confront two external threats, neither of which was susceptible to control. One of these emanated from Washington, where the antitrust movement that the Standard Oil group had feared was coming to a head. Even if this could be side-stepped, the other challenged his new empire at its very foundation, and Duke didn't know how to handle it. In this he would not be unique, for no cigarette man ever discovered an effective method for dealing with this particular enemy.

An anticigarette crusade which began in the 1890s was driving forward and winning new converts. The movement would not die. Nor could it be killed, though the tobacco people used all

their substantial power to do so. In the first years of the new century this movement seemed capable of bringing the entire industry to its knees, and doing so more effectively than would its
counterpart crusade of the 1960s. All Duke appeared able to
do was to watch it, wait, then pour money into lobbying
efforts, and finally hope the crusade would die.

No sooner had tobacco been brought to Europe than opposition to smoking appeared. The antipipe and cigar people
claimed users created clouds of noxious fumes wherever they
went, to the annoyance of nonsmokers. According to various critics, tobacco smoke corroded the lungs, befuddled the brain, and
irritated the innards. Smoking destroyed taste for food and drink.
The habit was addictive and, in general, a sign of weak character. It was the cause of impotence and sterility—though some
would only go so far as to say that children born of smokers
would be sickly and soon die. A London poet of the early seventeenth century put the thought well. He saw the fad spreading,
and it annoyed him:

> As I walked between
> Westminster Hall
> And the Church of Saint Paul,
> And so thorow the citie,
> Where I saw and did pitty
> My country-men's cases,
> With fiery-smoke faces,
> Sucking and drinking
> A filthie weede stinking.

Another poet of the period put the matter bluntly:

> Tobacco, that outlandish weed,
> It spends the brain and spoils the seed.
> It dulls the sprite, it dims the sight,
> It robs a woman of her right.

And, of course, there was King James I and his famous *A
Counterblaste to Tobacco,* inspired as much by hatred for Sir
Walter Raleigh, who sponsored smoking in England, as by the
habit itself. According to the monarch, smoking was "A custom
loathsome to the eye, hateful to the nose, harmful to the brain,

dangerous to the lungs, and in the black, stinking fume thereof, resembling the horrible Stygian smoke of the pit that is bottomless."

That these and similar antitobacco statements had little permanent effect is obvious, and in time those favoring the habit— lovers of tobacco as well as businessmen and politicians who profited from the culture and the trade—responded with poems and essays defending the pipe and the cigar as soothing, an aid to digestion, and the perfect companion to good talk and fine wines. In the England of the seventeenth century one found a preview of the great American cigarette debate of the 1960s and 1970s.

There was little in the way of antitobacco movements during the colonial period, though some Puritan leaders spoke out against smoking and chewing as being harmful to one's character. As has been mentioned, opposition to smoking did exist in the reform era of the 1840s and 1850s, but it was not as important or powerful as that directed against slavery and the saloon. The abolitionists, who might have weighed in against the leaf as being a product of slave labor, either refused to do so, made a point of noting that they smoked and chewed only Midwestern-grown leaf, or rejected outright the notion of an antitobacco crusade. Somehow the cigar, pipe, and even the plug were acceptable on this side of the Atlantic, even to reformers, as the movement against tobacco continued to grow in Britain.

Why was this so? One reason might have been the nature of the social structure in America, especially during and after the Jacksonian era. Tobacco was cheap and plentiful, and while no statistics on its use were kept at the time, it appeared that almost all adult males (and many adolescents) used the weed, at least occasionally. Many leading abolitionists themselves were smokers and scarcely could have supported a movement to eliminate a habit they enjoyed in their own drawing rooms. Then too, unlike alcohol, the harmful effects of smoking or chewing were not evident; one did not become blind drunk from smoking too many cigars. Finally, the crusade against smoking seemed rather trivial when set beside battles opposing slavery, for women's rights, and against alcohol. In other words, it was shunted aside, shoved to the bottom of the reform agenda in America, by individuals who knew they never would get around to challenging tobacco and perhaps didn't even care to do so.

Whatever the cause, this situation changed after the Civil War. Slavery had been ended, and the women's rights movement lost some of its early fervor. Alcohol prohibition remained an important issue, but those active in this crusade were battling the old and familiar enemy. Reform crusades require novelty in order to remain fresh, and there was little of this in the prohibitionist movement. The antitobacco forces suffered from none of these liabilities. Having never mounted a major crusade, the leaders could recruit followers eager for a new banner. And there was a new product to destroy. The opponents of tobacco in the 1880s and 1890s tended to ignore cigars, pipes, and plug. Instead they concentrated on banishing the newcomer—the cigarette.

Without meaning to do so, they had selected the proper target. Not only were cigarettes becoming increasingly important, but their prime markets were effete Easterners in large seacoast cities, the lower classes, and young people in all parts of the nation. Midwestern reformers of this period, who saw their enemies as being the urban dwellers—foreigners in particular—and who in time would unite to form the People's Party, were prime candidates for recruitment into the anticigarette leagues of the 1880s and 1890s. So were cigar smokers and users of plug and pipes, who looked upon the cigarette as being an improper use of a fine product, a damnable piece of esoterica. Adult males who used cigars could excoriate the cigarette as trapping youth into a bad habit at the wrong time of their lives. It was a mighty coalition which, interestingly enough, was not recognized as such at the time.

The key figure in this crusade—a person who never really understood how much potential power she controlled—was Lucy Page Gaston of Illinois. An interesting, colorful, and lively reformer, she is almost always overlooked by historians, even those concerned with the major reform efforts at the turn of the century or with the impact of women on the nation's development. Lucy Gaston belongs in both categories. For a while she seemed on the brink of bringing down Buck Duke's cigarette empire. Though he never conceded as much, one of the reasons

Duke was so anxious to expand into noncigarette areas might have been the general fear within the industry that Lucy Gaston and others like her might succeed in their lobbying efforts to end the production and sale of cigarettes in the United States. She was to the antismoking campaign what Carry Nation became to the prohibitionist movement and, in many ways, was more successful in her work—at least during the early years of the century.

Lucy Gaston was born in 1860, to parents who were active in several reform movements, especially abolitionism and temperance. Both her mother and father were known for their work in Illinois, and prominent leaders in the movement often stayed at their home when work brought them to the Midwest. As a child, Lucy Gaston's table talk was of the rights of Negroes and women, the evils of alcohol, the rewards for clean living, and assurances that God would provide for those who followed His dicta. Since the antisaloon forces managed to retain a semblance of organization during the 1870s, she joined them, probably through the influence of Women's Christian Temperance Union leader Frances Willard, a friend of the family. In addition, she taught Sunday school and read all the journals on reformism that came her way.

Lucy Gaston was not particularly attractive physically. She was tall, ungainly, and rather bony, both in face and figure. She had a high forehead, large upper lip, and mouse-colored hair, which gave her a rather masculine appearance. Throughout her life she would talk of her resemblance to Abraham Lincoln, physically as well as ideologically. Lucy Gaston never married. Instead, she devoted her life to what she called "The Cause."

While teaching, Gaston used to see young boys sneaking around to the back of the schoolhouse to puff on cigarettes. Invariably these were her worst students, she later said, and Gaston became convinced there was such a thing as "cigarette face," which anyone could spot instantly after having had training in the matter. Those who suffered from the malady eventually took to drink, became diseased, turned to crime, and in the end died horribly.

Cigarette face was caused by drugs found in the kind of tobacco employed in cigarette manufacture. (Interestingly enough,

Gaston rarely spoke out against cigars, pipes, or snuff, perhaps because she felt it futile to do so.) There were twenty such drugs, and nicotine was not the most harmful. Rather, Lucy Gaston warned against furfural, which she said was produced by the burning of glycerine.* According to Gaston, the furfural-producing agent became more concentrated as the cigarette was smoked, so that those who consumed only half the white tube and threw the butt away did not suffer major damage. Her children scoured the streets looking for these butts, and they were the basis of their smokes. Thus, they were inhaling a great deal of furfural, which produced cigarette face and its harmful consequences.

For a while Gaston confined her reformist zeal to work in the WCTU, but her fascination with the evils of cigarettes increased. Why fight against booze, she thought, when one cigarette had the kick of two ounces of whiskey? If alcohol was poison, what of furfural, which was fifty times as toxic by her reckoning? So she quit the WCTU—though remaining dedicated to its goals— to work full time for the abolition of cigarettes. Gaston started a newspaper in Harvey, Illinois, and used it to lobby for anti-cigarette legislation in the state capital. It was a slapdash affair, noted more for zeal than content, and consisted mostly of testimonials to the evils of smoking and benefits to be derived from quitting the practice. Apparently Gaston went through many newspapers looking for items pertaining to cigarettes, which she then rewrote for her own purposes. One of these, which she claimed came from the Denver *Post,* read: "*Daffy:* John Jones, aged 19, is very sick and at times acts very queer; caused by the excessive use of cigarettes." And another: "*Murderer:* Charles Burton, aged 17, is to be hanged for murder. He was a cigarette fiend," this from the New York *Telegram.*

Lucy Gaston founded the Chicago Anti-Cigarette League in 1899. Reformism once more was in vogue, and the League attracted an active group of members. Similar organizations appeared in other cities, spreading from the Midwest to both

---

* In fact there is such a compound; today it is employed in the manufacture of plastics, and can be produced by distilling bran with sulphuric acid. Furfural indeed can be lethal, but only traces of it can be found in cigarette smoke.

coasts, with Gaston the spark behind most of them. Two years later the National Anti-Cigarette League was organized, and its first convention held in 1903. With the exception of Carry Nation —who in January, 1901, entered a Wichita, Kansas, saloon, hatchet in hand, and within a few minutes smashed it to bits— Lucy Page Gaston was the leading female reformer in America.

Her zeal was rewarded. Most large cities had clinics to which cigarette smokers could go for a cure. Dr. D. H. Kress, the League's general secretary, patented a mouthwash that contained a weak solution of silver nitrate. Gargle with it after every meal for three days, said Dr. Kress, take warm baths and switch to a bland diet. By the end of the third day your craving for cigarettes will be over. Other remedies appeared. One of them, No-to-bac, was supposed to work for all kinds of tobacco use, and not cigarettes alone. Its motto was direct: "Don't tobacco-spit your life away."

The campaign was effective and, as was to have been anticipated, did best in the Midwest. Several cities there banned the sale of cigarettes in the late nineteenth century. Cigarette production peaked at 4.9 billion units in 1897, and then started to decline. By 1901 fewer than 3.5 billion were being turned out, and it seemed the small smoke was on the way out.

There were some within the industry who made light of Lucy Gaston's impact. The plug war, and not the ravings of this eccentric spinster, had caused the decline in cigarette sales, they said. Others thought the development of an economic boom—the return of prosperity after a generation of hard times—had encouraged smokers to switch back to cigars. Statistics seemed to bear them out. Cigar sales had been low during the 1890s, with between 4 and 5 billion the limits. Then the 5 billion mark was breached in 1900, and the following year, over 6 billion were produced. By 1906, the number was over 7 billion.

Buck Duke admitted to having mixed feelings about this situation. For a while Lucy Gaston's crusade may have harmed American Tobacco, but it all but destroyed his competitors. In 1896, the Trust had been able to account for slightly more than four out of every five packs sold; at the turn of the century, nine of every ten cigarettes carried the Duke label. For a brief moment,

it seemed Gaston's work had enabled Duke to tighten his grip upon the industry.

This was not to be. Several small companies increased production of Turkish and Russian blends, which had been less affected by the movement than the domestics—their upper-class eastern purchasers would hardly be influenced by Lucy Gaston's kind of crusade. Even Lorillard and Liggett & Myers put out some Egyptian blends, contrary to Duke's expressed desires and orders. But American Tobacco as a whole did not cultivate this market. By 1904 the Trust was in trouble; the sales ratio was back to where it had been in 1896.

Had cigarette users returned to plug and cigars? This might seem plausible, but at the same time evidence indicated the contrary. While the population increased in this period, the amount of tobacco consumed on a per capita basis declined. Sales of plug and cigars leveled off, a matter of some consternation at Trust headquarters.

Duke remained at a loss as how best to deal with this forceful, unbending, humorless woman and her legions of antinicotine converts. Duke tried lower prices and increased advertising budgets, more alluring cigarette cards and new brands, replete with testimonials. Nothing worked. It was this fear of Lucy Gaston as well as the craving for new outlets and profits that impelled Duke into the foreign markets. The head of the most complete trust in the nation feared a woman crusader would destroy the base of his business.

Not that Lucy Gaston was Duke's only problem. Ever since he had emerged as head of the tobacco empire, Duke had been the target of criticism from many sides. Part of this was the result of his cold and harsh manner. Ginter never made a secret of his dislike for Duke, and Richard J. Reynolds, whose firm was within the Trust, openly criticized the president and called for his ouster on several occasions. But a good deal of the hatred resulted from the kind of enmity any leader of a major industry is bound to attract, and the reformist atmosphere of this period added to the heat of the crusade. North Carolina editor Josephus Daniels claimed that Duke used bullying tactics against his rivals and those farmers who co-operated with them. The faculty of Trinity College in North Carolina contained several firebrands who

wrote and spoke against Duke's power in the state. Southern growers complained that American Tobacco dominated the auctions, forcing them to sell at knockdown prices that all but eliminated profits. Reforming journalist Ray Stannard Baker charged that "the tobacco trust keeps the price just high enough to tease the grower into continued production, but not high enough to yield him any appreciable profit beyond the bare payment for his labor." *McClure's* editorialized "The Tobacco Trust is the Scourge of the South." All of this disturbed old Wash Duke. "I wish Buck had never put us in the company and that we could carry on our business like we used to do it," he said, recalling the days when the firm sold Pro Bono Publico and a few other chews.

The facts did not bear out these charges. Even while tobacco use was declining, the price of leaf held firm; Duke did not take advantage of the situation to force farmers to the wall. After bottoming out at 5.5 cents a pound in 1896, the price began to rise, and in 1904 stood at an average of 7.8 cents, this at a time when accusations of price rigging were being made in Washington and in the fields. If anything, Duke's earlier success in popularizing cigarettes and developing new markets benefited the growers, and charges that he used strong-arm methods in the South never were proven, even after several extensive state and federal investigations. Yet Duke continued to receive a bad press in the South. Again, some of this was the result of his power, but there were other reasons as well. At a time when the section was solidly Democratic, the Dukes remained Republican. And old Wash Duke never had made a secret of his hatred of slavery and his sympathy for the plight of the freed Negro, while in a much quieter way, and with less conviction, his son seemed to agree.

Nor would Duke eliminate enemies within his own camp. He could have cracked down on Reynolds, not only by forcing him out of his company but also by destroying the man financially. This he did not do. Perhaps it was fear of the aggressive Reynolds, or this reticence might be explained by nonbusiness problems, the most important of which involved his marriage.

Duke had been one of the city's social lions at the turn of the century, hosting lavish parties and being free with his money. In the process he had acquired a mistress, a gorgeously voluptuous redhead named Lillian McCredy, who as the saying of the time went, had many friends besides Buck Duke. They had entered into a stormy relationship, with Lillian playing Duke like the fish he was, and in early 1905 she reeled him in. The two were married, though the new Mrs. Duke kept a lover on the side, one Frank Huntoon, president of a local mineral-water company. They kept in communication even during the honeymoon, with Lillian referring to her husband as "the octopus" and arranging meetings through advertisements in the newspapers.

Duke learned of the situation but did nothing to bring matters to a head. This would have been difficult, for shortly after the marriage he had taken up with Nanaline Holt Inman, the widow of a Georgia cotton merchant, and was angling for an annulment or divorce. The four of them—Buck, Lillian, Nanaline, and Frank Huntoon—played at the game in 1905–6, during which time Duke had little time to spare for his business. To further complicate matters, Duke had had an argument with President Theodore Roosevelt and because of it had worked against his renomination in 1904. Teddy won both nomination and election and was out to settle the score after his inauguration the following year.

In 1907 Duke was just settling down after his marital complications. A divorce had been granted in 1906, and Duke had married Nanaline soon after. But there was the attack from Washington to worry about, and the Lucy Gaston crusade, and troubles within the company, and difficulties with the cigar business, and the complexities and frustrations of directing a worldwide venture. It was too much for one man, even Buck Duke. He became morose and matters drifted.

It was then that the Circuit Court for the Southern District acted to simplify his life. In April 1890, three months after Duke had fashioned the American Tobacco Company, the state of North Carolina had initiated an antitrust suit aimed at curbing the firm's activities there. Other legal actions followed, and in 1897 the state of New York began an investigation of Duke's activities. Four years later the United States Industrial Commission did the same. Still, Duke was able to block litigation at that level, perhaps due to his then-friendly relationship with Teddy

Roosevelt. But the success of the Northern Securities decision of 1904, in which the Supreme Court ordered the dissolution of a railroad combine, and the growing enmity between Roosevelt and Duke, indicated that action against American Tobacco would be forthcoming.

It came in 1907, when the Circuit Court found the Trust's MacAndrews and Forbes subsidiary guilty of criminal violations under the terms of the Sherman Antitrust Act. Fines were imposed, and the decision resulted in several private suits being instituted. The following year, the Court found the parent company in violation of the Sherman Act. Appeals followed, with the case reaching the Supreme Court in 1910. In May of 1911 the justices decided that American Tobacco would have to be dissolved. Duke then was asked to prepare a plan for dismembership—his help was necessary, for no one else knew the ins and outs of the Trust as well as he. The task was complicated, but the eventual division was straightforward and "clean."

The American Tobacco Trust was succeeded by four large firms—Liggett & Myers, Reynolds, Lorillard, and American—plus many smaller ones. Since the first three companies had entered the Trust against the desires of their leaders, they welcomed the decision and offered little opposition to the way Duke sliced the pie.

Liggett & Myers received a third of the plug business and close to half that in snuff and was expected to become the leader in these two areas, as it had been prior to the takeover. Lorillard would be a more balanced though smaller firm, with a major stake in cigars, just behind L & M in snuff and second to American in pipe tobaccos. As had been the situation prior to 1890, American would lead in cigarettes, with such major brands as Pall Mall, Sweet Caporal, and Mecca. L & M, the industry's new number-two company, received Fatima, American Beauty, Home Run, and several others. Lorillard's brands all had a foreign tinge —Turkish Trophies, Murad, Helmar, and the like.

Richard Reynolds received no cigarette brands. Instead, his firm would consist of the old plug business with a minor stake in pipe tobaccos. His was to be the smallest of the "big four" successor companies. Reynolds was undisturbed by his prospects. In fact, he relished the idea of a direct confrontation with Duke.

There would be no such competition. Duke always had avoided head-on clashes with his divisional chiefs, and the habit died hard, even now that Reynolds was on his own. Also Duke disliked all contacts with the man, whom he considered a primitive boor. In any case he had become subject to fits of deep depression. Duke would lock himself in his room where he drank heavily, brooded, and contemplated the wreckage of his personal life and business empire. Occasionally he would go to the office, but rarely stayed until noon. He had lost interest in the Trust, and early in 1912 severed all relationships with American Tobacco, though continuing on as chairman of British-American.

Then his spirits revived. Nanaline was pregnant, and Duke prayed for a son. He was despondent when a daughter was born, but then became entranced with the infant, and spent most of the day playing with her. This revived interest in people spilled over into business. Shortly thereafter, Duke became involved with electric power, and he helped fashion a major utility, Duke Power & Light. He saw the potential of hydroelectricity and thought coal a dirty fuel which would befoul the air and, in any case, cost more than water power. After familiarizing himself with the technology, he set about making his new company the leader in that field. Next he searched for a proper monument, and his eye fell upon Trinity College, whose faculty had so criticized him during the period of the Trust. Duke promised the trustees a huge bequest if they would transform the school into Duke University. The faculty bridled at the idea, but in the end the trustees accepted and so Buck Duke had become a major philanthropist.

These were the kinds of things that occupied his last years. He died peacefully in 1925 at the age of sixty-nine, a relatively happy man at the end.

As for Lucy Gaston, she had welcomed the idea of state and federal investigations of the Trust, but understood that mere divestiture would not remove cigarettes from the mouths of American youths. An outright ban was the only way this could be accomplished, and she made complete prohibition the goal of her National Anti-Cigarette League.

Gaston recruited many allies to her cause, the first and most successful drive to banish cigarettes from the land. Lecturer and writer Elbert Hubbard told audiences that "Cigarette smokers are men whose futures lie behind them," while David Starr Jordan, Chancellor of Leland Stanford Jr. University, thought "Boys who smoke cigarettes are like wormy apples that fall from the tree before they are ripe." Ben Lindsey, deemed the nation's leading expert on juvenile crime, blamed its rising incidence upon the cigarette. "The cigarette habit not only had a grip upon them [youthful offenders] in boyhood, but it invited all the other demons of habit to come in and add to the degradation that the cigarette began." Lindsey and others despaired at convincing adults to stop smoking; perhaps they could do better with children. And Elinor Glyn, who later on would be considered an exponent of sexual freedom, thought it robbed people of their virility. "Every smoke is a tiny drop of old age, so small that for a long time it is unnoticed."

Gaston pressured several railroads into banning cigarette smoking on their lines. Many companies refused to hire women who smoked; the mere hint that a schoolteacher smoked—including in private—might lead to her dismissal in even the large eastern cities. Men under the age of twenty-one who smoked cigarettes could not find employment at Wanamaker's department stores, Montgomery & Ward, and Sears, Roebuck. Of course females of any age were expected to be nonsmokers. In 1908 New York City passed the Sullivan Ordinance, which made it illegal for women to smoke in public, and other municipalities followed suit. Toward the end of the nineteenth century the states of Iowa, North Dakota, and Tennessee had enacted laws prohibiting the sale and use of cigarettes; now they were joined by Arkansas, Indiana, Kansas, Minnesota, Nebraska, Oklahoma, South Dakota, and Wisconsin. As had been the case in the 1880s, the anticigarette movement was strong in the Midwest, important in the Far West, but lacked vigor in the East. When the Illinois Supreme Court declared that state's anticigarette law unconstitutional, Gaston initiated a campaign for an amendment to the Constitution permitting the recall of judges and came within a hair of having it passed. But she remained silent when similar laws passed by small towns in western New York were voided.

Most of this legislation had little effect, even where it was in place. Tobacco manufacturers retaliated by selling "makings" and including paper in the package—the laws banned cigarettes, and not the materials from which they were fabricated. In some states the sale of the smokes was illegal, but there was no reason the dealers could not give them away. So they did—with the purchase of matches for twenty cents.

In those areas where the laws were enforced, cigarettes were bootlegged, and the fact they were forbidden fruit may have encouraged some people to try them. Certainly Lucy Gaston hadn't intended to do so, but she had managed to provide cigarettes with a more romantic aura than might otherwise have been the case.

Cigarette sales reached their nadir in 1901. Three years later, for the first time since 1899, over 4 billion of them were sold. The 5.5 billion mark was breached in 1906, and then sales accelerated. In 1911, when American Tobacco was ordered dissolved, sales were at the 11.7 billion figure.

Needless to say, the rise in sales dismayed Lucy Gaston. At the same time there was a revival of the movement for prohibition of alcohol; Carry Nation reigned supreme among women reformers. Clearly the anticigarette movement was all but dead.

But Gaston continued her work, even after the National broke up in 1917. The American entry into the war had boosted the sales of both alcohol and cigarettes, but the absence of the men enabled the women reform movements to have a new burst of vigor. State organizations pressed for anticigarette laws, and they were passed in Idaho and Utah in 1921. In that year alone, close to one hundred measures affecting the use of tobacco were introduced in the legislatures of twenty-eight states. But the tide was turning, for in the same year, Arkansas, Idaho, Iowa, and Tennessee repealed their laws on the subject, and others would follow.

Lucy Gaston saw this coming. She knew that once the soldiers returned from the front—where she believed they smoked and drank whenever away from the fighting—they would work against her movement. So in 1920 she announced her availability for the Republican presidential nomination and told reporters that she could defeat any Democrat in the field. After all, she said, there was that physical resemblance to Abe Lincoln, and Gaston pledged to imitate his career—by emancipating the nation from smoking. Also, she made a point of reminding the newsmen that she had no husband to worry about, and so was free to conduct a strong campaign. The good, moral people of America wanted her to run—to save the nation from smokes and Bolshevism (she saw the two united; after all, cigarettes had first appeared in the United States as a foreign vice, and the early ones had been imported from Russia). In any case, women were more God-fearing than men, and should be elected to high office. Finally, Gaston told the reporters that she had more campaign experience than any other figure in the Republican Party.

She did enter the South Dakota primary, but received only a handful of votes. Soon thereafter she joined with the Prohibitionists when that party tried unsuccessfully to draft William Jennings Bryan. Then she retired from politics, though announcing her intention to return at some future date. Lucy Gaston was crushed when Warren Harding—a cigarette smoker—was elected. She said that Harding had a cigarette face and would come to no good. In fact, she thought his administration would be laced with corruption, and Harding would die before the end of his term.

In 1921 Lucy Gaston organized a new National Anti-Cigarette League, but conceded defeat as far as the nation's male population was concerned. Her new motto was "Save the Girl," and her goal was clear: "The Abolition of the Cigarette in America by 1925." After a term with a smoker in the White House, she reasoned, the nation would be ready for a spell of Lucy Gaston —especially since the women had the vote.

In June of 1924 the sixty-four-year-old reformer was struck down by a trolley car while crossing the street on the way to a rally. She was rushed to a hospital, where the broken bones were set. But Lucy Gaston did not respond to treatment, and her general physical state was poor. The doctors were puzzled and gave her a complete examination, in the course of which they discovered she had a fatal malady.

Lucy Gaston died on August 20, 1924. A quarter of a century earlier, when she had started the National Anti-Cigarette League, 4.4 billion cigarettes were consumed. In the year of her death, more than 73 billion cigarettes were sold.

To make matters worse, Lucy Gaston died of throat cancer.

IV

The Match

At no point in his career did Buck Duke do, or say, anything to indicate that he believed cigarettes would completely dominate the tobacco industry. Of course, he thought the small smokes would have an important role to play in his business, but so would plug and cigars. Habit, tradition, and circumstance would see to that. Some men never would abandon chewing, and the aroma of an expensive (and profitable) Havana would remain the sign of success and manliness. After all, Woodrow Wilson's Vice-President, Thomas Marshall, was supposed to have said, "What this country needs is a good five-cent cigar" and not "I'd like a quick smoke" or "I'm fresh out. Anyone here have a cigarette?" Gentlemen savored cigars, and offering one to a friend was a sign of comradeship, and not the almost automatic gesture of a cigarette smoker (furthermore, one "sneaked" a cigarette—the word was out of place when used in connection with fine cigars). Cigars had ritual, cigarettes convenience and low cost. As for plug, its use implied simplicity and even virility. At the turn of the century, the cigarette remained the smoke of the foreigner and of poor people, especially criminals, many of whom had what Lucy Gaston immediately would have spotted as bad cases of cigarette face.

Horatio Alger and other popular writers of the time appreciated this. So did playwrights and makers of silent films. When a young cigarette smoker appeared in a novel—always assuming he was an American—the reader knew he had been introduced to the villain. Audiences at plays and movies recognized the symbol as well. Members of the gang would sit around puffing at the small smokes. At one point they would discard them and move out, up to no good. William S. Hart and other motion picture heroes in Western films might take a shot of booze, but in the earliest films they rarely would smoke, while their archenemies—the fellows with the black hats—lit up between evil deeds.

In addition to this, cigarettes and cigars still were looked upon as indoor habits, while plug could be chewed either within the home (given spittoons) or in the fields and streets. Middle-class wives of this period insisted their husbands confine their smoking to designated areas—such as the den, or preferably the outdoor porch. Their smoke was supposed to leave a bad odor in the drapes, as well as in clothing—the smoking jacket was worn so the suit jacket could remain fresh, while some men donned the Turkish fez when smoking, perhaps to recall the romantic oriental origins of cigarettes or in deference to style.

Then, too, cigar smoking in the home was supposed to be done in the afternoons and evenings, though stogies and even Havanas were puffed throughout the day and night in offices and clubs. Urban wives might object to the use of plug in their homes—the spittoons hardly were attractive—but there is no indication that this form of uncleanliness was looked upon as being worse than the smell of stale cigar, cigarette, or pipe smoke. This feeling grew stronger when Lucy Gaston was in her heyday and would not disappear for another generation.

It was not unusual for a man to keep an unlit cigar in his mouth while walking through the streets on weekdays. In this way he managed to combine some of the benefits of plug with that of cigars. He would chew and regularly expectorate in the gutters. Then, when going indoors (and assuming the cigar was in halfway decent shape), he would light up. Cigar smoking out-of-doors was looked upon as ostentatious, boorish, and even affected. It implied that the individual could afford to smoke while going from place to place, and not just in repose, or that he wanted to draw attention to himself.

If the cigar went out, it would be chewed upon or, more likely, discarded. It would not be relit, and for an obvious reason: the practical, inexpensive, dependable, safe—and more to the point, healthy—match was yet to be invented. Matches were used to ignite cigars, to be sure. But those who did so considered their fumes even more harmful than those of tobacco. Men who scoffed at the idea that nicotine was dangerous, or that furfural caused cigarette face, were convinced that the inhalation of white phosphorus—the kind used in matches at the turn of the century—was most dangerous and could cause a variety of fatal diseases, including tuberculosis.

Cigar smokers lit their stogies with an ember from the hearth or a taper from an oil or gas lamp. Cigar stores maintained small lamps where impulse buyers could light up; men having their own cigars might drop into a cigar store for a light, for it was considered a courtesy item in middle-class neighborhoods. On such occasions they might inhale the smoke. But when they used matches, they would take care to keep the smoke in their mouths, and not in their lungs. Gentlemen in the 1890s did not carry matches on their person, no more than they would a dose of poison. The match box was maintained in the home, used to light stoves and gaslights—but rarely cigars or cigarettes.

In that decade the growth of the cigarette depended upon the number of smokers who could be weaned from cigars and pipes and those chewers who could be persuaded to make the switch from plug—along with the general increase in the male population. The development of the free and truly harmless match made it possible for smokers to light up out-of-doors and in any kind of weather. This may not have been of major importance to cigar smokers, who were accustomed to indulging while under some kind of roof, protected from winds that would carry away the smoke before it could be savored. But, the enjoyment of ciga-rettes depended more upon inhalation than aroma; the weather would not interfere with the ritual. In addition, the shorter, cheaper cigarette lent itself to the craving for that quick smoke on impulse that developed at about the same time the free and safe match was created. The decision to light up a cigar required some thought and reference to the calculus of pleasure. Was the time sufficient, the mood correct, and the place right for the consumption of tobacco that cost between a nickel and a quarter? And should everything fall into place, was there an open fire handy?

The modern match enabled cigarette smokers to overcome obstacles of time, place, and mood. Use, of course, would still have increased and eventually surpassed that of cigars without this kind of ignitor. What matches did was to alter the *way* cigarettes were smoked, encouraging their consumption during odd moments in the day; in effect, transforming their use from a thoughtful exercise into an almost unconscious habit.

A moderate user of cigarettes in the 1880s might burn up as many as ten a day—a pack. Those who switched from cigars to cigarettes merely lit the paper smoke instead of the more expensive variety. Cigarette users doubled their consumption in the era of the safe match. Those who lit up twenty or more times a day were not unusual, and the manufacturers made the change; before the end of the century, Buck Duke's Coupon, Sunshine, and Home Run came twenty to a pack. This was one of the side effects of the match. Its invention and popularization were more important for the industry than anything since the Bonsacks. It can be compared in significance to the conversion of women to smoking in the 1920s—open, habitual smoking, that is—for the growth of cigarette use.

Matches were known long before the end of the nineteenth century, but those that had been developed could not be considered cheap, durable, or practical. The Greeks and Romans, for example, used tapers tipped with sulfur and animal fats which on occasion—if the temperature and humidity were just right— could be ignited by friction. Other experiments followed. By the early seventeenth century, "tinder pistols" utilizing flints and gunpowder appeared in France and the Germanies, but the correct priming and use required time, patience, and skill. Slips could result in explosions and general conflagrations.

It was in this period that the first true match was created. In 1669 a German alchemist, Hennig Brandt, discovered phosphorus. Ten years later another German, Godfrey Haukwitz, and an Englishman, Robert Boyle, sold sheets of paper coated with a white phosphorus compound together with wooden splints tipped with sulfur. The splints were to be drawn through the paper and, after a few passes, would burst into flame.

Other experiments followed. In the late eighteenth century some French inventors used what were called "phosphoric candles" or "ethereal matches," consisting of phosphorus-soaked paper sealed in a glass tube. The paper would burst into flame when the tube was crushed. The Italian "pocket luminary" was an inexpensive though dangerous version of the ethereal match. This was a bottle lined with phosphorus oxide and kept tightly sealed. When fire was needed the bottle would be opened and a sulfur-tipped splint introduced and rubbed against the interior, and then quickly removed. If all went well, the person had a burning splint; if not, he had an exploded bottle, glass fragments imbedded in his hand, and first-degree burns.

A similar problem existed with "oxymuriated matches," which appeared in America during the early years of the eighteenth century. In this instance, the bottle was filled with sulphuric acid and the splints tipped with a composition of potassium chlorate, sugar, and gum arabic. Under the brand name of Empyrion Matches, they sold for two dollars a box of fifty, far too expensive for cigars. But in the right hands, they were useful for starting the morning fire.

Clearly a different approach was needed.

In 1827 John Walker, an English chemist and apothecary, created a match consisting of the familiar wooden splint dipped into a mixture of potassium chlorate, antimony sulfide, sulfur, and gum arabic. These were dried and, when a fire was required, rubbed between sheets of sandpaper for friction heat. More often than not they ignited. Walker did little to capitalize upon this invention. Instead, the idea was taken up by another chemist-apothecary, Samuel Jones, who obtained a patent for what he called the "Lucifer Match" in 1829. Other versions followed, which were mostly used in homes. Some daring and reckless individuals might have used the Lucifers to ignite cigars and pipes. Jones and other manufacturers warned that the gas that escaped from the match might cause grave harm, and that "persons whose lungs are delicate should by no means use the Lucifers."

To carry the story to the end of the century, the firm of Bryant & May came out with the still-popular Swan Vesta matches in 1850, which, despite warnings, were used to light tobacco. The formula for these matches was changed over the years, and today of course they are completely safe for smokers and indeed are used by them almost exclusively. Originally, however, the Vestas contained several poisonous ingredients, as did all matches of the period.

In 1855 a Swedish inventor, John Lundstrum, created the first true safety match, which also was used by some smokers who defied warnings. These and others were sold for a low price—around five for a penny. To this day the English pay for their matches, a tradition which in the nineteenth century was of little concern to wealthy cigar smokers who ignored the dangers but came to mean more for poor people who used a pack of cigarettes a day in the early years of the new century, and so required a handful of matches.

The development was different in the United States, due in part to the way the industry evolved, but even more to the fact that, in the end, Americans adopted the matchbook rather than the wooden match. Alonzo Dwight Phillips, a Massachusetts powder maker, patented a phosphorus match in 1836, and six years later another inventor, Anton von Schrotter, came out with a safety match which, however, was unreliable. Both matches, like the others produced in the next half century, contained white phosphorus and sulfur and were dangerous unless used carefully. In fact, the ingestion of match heads in quantity was one way to commit suicide in this period.

Matches became big business in the post-Civil War era, and in 1881 the so-called "Match Trust" was organized, when several leading manufacturers united to form Diamond Match Company, which immediately dominated the field. Diamond lowered unit costs and was an aggressive merchandiser, but showed little interest in technological innovation. The company did come out with a "drunkard's match" in 1882, a splint so treated as to be self-extinguishing at midpoint. Beyond that, Diamond appeared content to remain within the established markets. No attempt was made to appeal to smokers. Around this time several antismoking groups argued that matches as well as tobacco constituted a health hazard, and Diamond had no desire to draw additional protests from this group. Besides, Diamond's executives were more interested in expanding into overseas markets with their existing product line than developing a match that was both safe and inexpensive.

In 1892 a young Lima, Pennsylvania, lawyer named Joshua Pusey began experimenting with a new kind of match. Instead of wooden splints, he used cardboard, which was contained in a "book," each of which had fifty matches, and was somewhat similar to today's matchbooks. Pusey wanted to lower the unit cost of the match, and so he did. Unfortunately, his invention proved a failure technologically, and for a simple reason: the striking surface was on the inside, and the sparks created by the friction often ignited the remaining matches. Discouraged, lacking capital, and for some unknown reason incapable of seeing how simply his problem could be solved, Pusey sold his invention to Diamond in 1895.

The Match Trust did little with these books, except to place the striking surface on the outside to prevent flare-ups and accidental ignition. Some of them were produced, but they were unpopular and generally unknown outside of the Midwest. Then, in 1896, an unknown executive at a forgotten brewing company decided that matchbooks would provide an excellent advertising vehicle. He purchased some of them, had their covers embossed with the name of the beer, and his salesmen gave them free to saloonkeepers, who in turn kept them on hand for customers.

These matchbooks were a huge success, and other orders followed. Diamond was obliged to develop an entirely new technology to produce sufficient matchbooks to meet the demand. By the turn of the century hundreds of companies provided them to their salesmen, who in turn gave them to retailers, and the stores and shops would distribute them as a good-will present to customers. Doubtless some of the matches were used to light pipes, cigars, and cigarettes, but the practice still was not common. Fear of lung disease remained stronger than the desire for a free light. But half the problem of cigarette ignition was solved by the advent of the free match.

The other half came soon after. Around this time the movement for progressive reform began to escalate. Occupational safety was one of the period's manias, and several states passed legislation regulating conditions in mines, packing houses, construction sites, and factories. The match industry came in for a large share of the criticism, more perhaps than any other field with the exception of meat packing. For years, industry officials had been aware of the dangers of white phosphorus. The incidence of tuberculosis and various bone diseases among match workers was common knowledge, but nothing had been done about it. Many match workers came down with an ailment known as "phossy jaw," due to accidental ingestion of the element and its compounds. Now the manufacturers were obliged to make changes. Safety devices and practices would not resolve matters. What was needed was a new chemical mixture for the match head.

Diamond's chemists came up with a new formulation that was far less toxic than the old, while at the same time the technicians altered the manufacture of safety and book matches so as to protect the workers. In the process, both groups decided to place more of the chemicals on the striking surface and less on the match itself. Thus, the flame was far less dangerous than it had been. Diamond made its new formulation available to independent manufacturers without charge. By 1912, the truly safe match not only was being produced but, in the form of books, had become ubiquitous.

And they remained free, in that the matchbooks didn't cost the customer anything save perhaps a glance at the advertising. On the eve of World War I, most purchasers of a pack of cigarettes received a book of matches with which to ignite them. Cigarettes were cheaper than ever before, accepted in more circles than at the turn of the century, and were easily obtained. Fire was portable, dependable, safe, harmless, and omnipresent. This combination gave impetus to smoking in general and cigarette consumption in particular. Along with the fading of the Lucy Gaston crusade and the breakup of the American Tobacco Trust, the creation of the viable match formed the background for the next and crucial development, the formulation of the standard American cigarette.

V

The Coming of the Camel

If Buck Duke was the father of the American cigarette industry, Richard J. Reynolds was responsible for the development of the modern smoke. He did so not through preference, for like many of his generation he disliked this form of tobacco. Rather, Reynolds was consumed by a hatred for Duke, and this passion led him to try to beat the leader at his own game.

Reynolds was the major force in cigarettes from shortly after the breakup of the Trust in 1912 until his death six years later. In this period he turned the smallest of the big four companies into the fastest-growing and most-promising entity in the industry. In 1912 Reynolds had two small factories, no sales force of importance, and a bundle of debts. At the time of his death he was worth $10 million, most of which was derived from the cigarette, which he refused to have in his house.

The Reynolds family originally came from the area near Critz, Virginia, where Dick's father, H.W., was a middle-class farmer.

The boy was fifteen years old in 1865 when Union Army soldiers invaded the region. What they didn't steal or destroy they burned. Thus, Dick Reynolds' wartime experience was somewhat similar to that of Buck Duke. Unlike Duke, however, Reynolds came to hate the North and would have nothing to do with those Southerners who spoke well of the Yankees. He despised Duke, who in addition to preferring New York to the South, came from a family that worked for Negro rights and, on top of everything else, was a Republican. The industry contained no two people as dissimilar as the cool, methodical, unimaginative Duke and the temperamental, erratic, and often brilliant R. J. Reynolds. On the other hand, Duke became a rather worldly individual, while Reynolds rarely stirred from Winston, North Carolina, where he relocated after the war. Too, Duke attracted a great deal of publicity—most of it bad—and the outlines of his life and career are quite familiar. Very little is known of Richard Reynolds. When he died the news was covered in the Carolina press, but only one New York newspaper, the *Times,* published an obituary, and that only twelve lines long. There is no biography of Reynolds; he is afforded a short mention in most histories of tobacco, and even lacked a Who's Who entry. Many articles have been written about his company, but none on the man who created it. Finally, the corporation claims it possesses no in-house material on the founder.

In all probability H. W. Reynolds produced and sold plug and pipe tobacco before the war and tried to pick up the pieces of this business afterward. There are allusions to young R.J. taking to the road in the late 1860s, attempting to sell the product directly to retailers, trying to avoid the high commissions most Carolina producers paid to bulk salesmen under the consignment system. This was a period when Union Army veterans demanded the sweet Bright plug they had found in the South, and Reynolds and others—including Buck Duke—catered to their tastes. Using native Bright and then adding licorice and rum, he produced Oronoko and Reynolds' Bright 7, rather cloying mixtures that caught on in northern cities. In 1873 Reynolds opened a small factory in Winston, and then expanded upon it in 1875. By the end of the decade, he had the largest establishment in town. Soon after, however, the national taste turned to White Burley, which Reynolds came to view as a renegade and alien leaf. Determined never to use it in his plug, Reynolds began turning out a series of new brands, continually seeking sweeter mixtures to please the Northerners. Finally he and others in Winston turned to saccharin, which when blended into Bright produced a plug that had a candylike flavor.

Reynolds disliked his new brands—he always chewed Bright "straight," without any additives—but in this instance he bowed to public tastes. There only were three things he vowed never to do: Reynolds would never co-operate with Buck Duke, he refused to produce cigarettes (which he considered a prostitution of fine leaf and which catered to the decadent tastes of the worst elements in society), and R. J. Reynolds & Company would never market a brand containing White Burley.

Reynolds did need money to expand operations, however, and was obliged to sell shares in his company to several groups of private investors. These were purchased by Duke, who hoped to use Reynolds & Company as the base for his plug business. Shortly after the turn of the century, American Tobacco owned two-thirds of the outstanding stock and legally at least was in a position to dictate company policy.

Dick Reynolds refused to bow before Buck Duke, and due either to fear or a willingness to let matters rest, the Trust leader did not press the issue. Reynolds would accept American Tobacco accountants in his offices in Winston, but he insisted they keep out of his way. Nor would he travel to New York to meet with Duke or any other figure at company headquarters. When American Tobacco asked him to open new facilities outside of Winston, Reynolds not only refused but sent back mail unopened. In the end he did build a new factory in the nearby town of Salem, but he swore that no plant of his would be farther than a short ride from his central office.

So great was Reynolds' hatred for Duke that he openly co-operated with government trust busters, those reformers at Trinity College who claimed Duke was guilty of unfair practices, and journalists who demanded the smashing of the empire. In fact, he went so far as to help finance some of the reformers, and he leaked company documents to newspapermen, especially Josephus Daniels. At one point he admitted to Daniels that more than anything else, he wanted to be free of Buck Duke. "You will never see the day when Dick Reynolds will eat out of Buck Duke's hand," he told Daniels. "If any swallowing is to be done, Dick Reynolds will do the swallowing."

Reynolds hardly seemed in the mood for expansion in 1912, when American Tobacco disgorged his company, or at least this was the impression one would have received from reading the New York newspapers. Rather, it was generally believed that the sixty-three-year-old recluse would do his best to restore his company to the position it occupied prior to the Trust, as one of the leaders in plug and, in the process, purify it of the Duke taint.

This could not be, and Reynolds understood it. He now appreciated the need for compromise in some things. He had failed to prevent the American Tobacco takeover. He had said that he never would use White Burley in his plugs, yet he did so in 1905. Two years later Reynolds formulated a new pipe blend, Prince Albert, which was based upon that tobacco. By 1912, Prince Albert had become a national favorite, with close to 15 per cent of the market. Reynolds was capable of adjusting to new circumstances, and just as he had been able to sell to the Yankees and develop an appreciation for the non-Bright tobaccos, so he would enter the cigarette field. He hoped for profit and power, to be sure, but also relished the idea of "swallowing" his archenemy. As Reynolds boasted to Daniels on learning of the dissolution decree, "Watch me and see if I don't give Buck Duke hell."

The cigarette industry following the dissolution decree offered many opportunities for entry. The problem was deciding which opening to exploit. The Trust had covered the market, offering cheap brands at ten cents a pack and more expensive ones at fifteen and twenty cents. It produced Turkish as well as domestic smokes; in fact, Duke had made certain no market, however minor, had been overlooked. With the breakup, Lorillard had a strong position in lower-priced Turkish and domestic brands and was expected to formulate a premium blend. American Tobacco had Pall Mall, a premium foreign brand with a sophisticated constituency, along with a wide variety of the medium- and low-priced smokes. Liggett & Myers' Fatima was the leader among fifteen-cent Turkish smokes, and the industry anticipated that company would move into domestic blends in both the ten- and twenty-cent markets. Of course, Reynolds had an open field, since he had been awarded no brands at all.

There was a "brand explosion" in 1912–13, as the successor companies simultaneously moved on three fronts: they would buttress their strong points, fill gaps in their lines, and seek new markets at the price of competitors. L & M came out with Vafiadis, a high-priced Turkish cigarette, and experimented with Chesterfield, which was supposed to be an English smoke with American overtones—a lower-priced competitor for Pall Mall. Lorillard moved up with Hassan and Mecca, seemingly making a major push into the Turkish market. American advertised Pall Mall as a premium English smoke, and complemented it with Omar, a high-priced Turkish cigarette.

Reynolds made several false starts. He lacked the financial base and distribution system of American Tobacco and the staffs of experienced cigarette men possessed by the three other major firms, and so had to start from scratch. The market for Turkish blends was strong, as it had been since the turn of the century, and Reynolds felt a cigarette constructed primarily from sweetened Bright would find a market. So he purchased additional Latakia and other foreign leaf and turned out Osman, which he sold twenty for ten cents, while the Bright-based Reyno went for five cents. Neither brand made much of an impact on the market, so Reynolds had to reassess his position.

Unlike the others, he could not afford to maintain a large stable of brands, each with its own advertising campaign, workshops where the blends were created and then stored, special lithographing problems, and the like. He had a strong position in plug, while Prince Albert continued as a national pipe blend. Given this situation, Reynolds decided to create additional brands one at a time. The entire effort of his new cigarette department would be directed toward making it profitable. This done, he would add another brand, or discard failures and replace them with others. There is no indication that at this time Reynolds had hopes for more than that. So, while others employed a shotgun approach to the market, he hoped to use a pistol.

It was a prudent policy, and not the least bit daring. Had he failed, Reynolds still would have a thriving enterprise, and could make new efforts in the field. Success could establish him as a major force in cigarettes. Anything in between would be marginally profitable, or at least so it appeared.

Reynolds created a new cigarette, Red Kamel, a Turkish cigarette with a cork tip that went out at ten for ten cents. It wasn't a good seller, but the name struck Reynolds as being just right. He discarded Red Kamel in 1909, but four years later came out with Camel, whose blend was based upon Carolina Bright, and a highly flavored White Burley, to which was added some Virginia leaf and only a touch of imported tobaccos. Reynolds had come to appreciate the absorbent qualities of Burley and knew it could be made to resemble the more expensive Turkish leaf. In taste, appearance, and even name, it seemed like a premium blend, the kind that sold for from fifteen to twenty cents. But it wasn't Turkish, although Camel certainly did not seem like the traditional American brands, most of which were primarily Bright. It possessed a unique blend and in this represented a gamble.

The Camel package looked like those used for the premium brands. The smokes came twenty to a pack, and the wrapper had a picture of a camel, with palm trees, sand, and two pyramids in the background, and the legend, "Turkish & Domestic Blend." Reynolds priced his new entry at ten cents, knowing that he could turn a good profit due to his use of cheaper mixtures. Of course, none of this was known outside of the trade. Then he developed a switch on the conventional sales and promotion campaigns. Most of the other brands still used cigarette cards and other lures. On the back of the pack, in clear letters, Reynolds warned smokers: "Don't look for premiums or coupons, as the cost of the tobaccos blended in CAMEL Cigarettes prohibits the use of them."

Camel was introduced in Cleveland, Ohio, in the autumn of 1913, and was an instant success. Smokers noted its different flavor; Camel tasted like Turkish blends, but had a lightness due to the presence of the Virginia leaf. Some noted that the smoke was heavier than that found in most domestic brands—this was not surprising, since Reynolds had based the mixture upon the Prince Albert formulation.

Sales figures caused Reynolds to reconsider his situation once again. Now he decided to scrap plans for several new brands and concentrate on Camels, which he felt had the potential to sweep the country, to the point of taking sales from American's aristocratic Pall Mall, which sold for a quarter. He had spent $680,000 in 1913 for the advertising and promotion of all his products. Now he earmarked $1.3 million for sales efforts in 1914, with most of it going to Camel—an unprecedented sum to wager on a single brand. Reynolds established an in-house advertising department whose work he closely supervised. For one city, his copywriters sent forth the message, "Camels! Tomorrow there will be more Camels in this town than in all Asia and Africa combined!"

The effort worked. That year Camel became one of the nation's top sellers. Reynolds sold almost half a billion of the smokes, around 3 per cent of the national total. Now he poured all of his funds into new machinery, even to the point of cutting down on plug and pipe tobacco expenditures. The advertising and promotion budget went to $1.9 million, and by the end of 1915, Camel had become a truly national brand, being offered in all the states. Sales were 2.4 billion, 13 per cent of American output, and R. J. Reynolds Tobacco reported earnings of $4.7 million.

Advertising expenses were cut to $700,000 in 1917, and further to $400,000 in 1918 since the established brand needed less promotion and sales were soaring without it. One out of every three cigarettes sold in 1918 was a Camel. By 1919, when 21 billion of them were sold, the figure was two of every five, and Reynolds Tobacco reported earnings of over $11.2 million. It also had 23 per cent of the pipe tobacco market with Prince Albert and several minor brands, while the plug business, though declining, continued to add to profits—Reynolds had 16 per cent of this business.

Dick Reynolds died in 1918 knowing he had succeeded in besting Buck Duke in every way, at least insofar as tobacco was concerned. But he had done so by accepting White Burley and cigarettes, something he had vowed would never transpire. As for Duke, he appeared unconcerned—around this time he was dabbling in aluminum and textiles as well as planning new additions for his electric company.

Duke's successor at American Tobacco, Percival S. Hill, appreciated the nature of the Reynolds challenge and the Camel sales figures. In a matter of months American cigarette smokers had indicated their preference for flavored White Burley blends and were switching away from foreign-style smokes and those based upon Virginia and Bright leaf. He could see the effectiveness of a national advertising campaign and the profits to be derived from mass distribution. The Reynolds factory and office complex in Winston-Salem was the most efficient in the industry, and Reynolds also had taken the lead in the introduction of the most modern machinery. There may have been time for American to retake the lead, if only by imitating Reynolds. But Percy Hill was not the person for that kind of job. A gentle and effective staff man, he had been a perfect assistant, who had come to the Trust when it swallowed Bull Durham, and then came to be known as Duke's detail man. He performed well in that position, seeing to it that Duke's ideas were translated into action, and in general overseeing operations. But Hill had few notions of his own, and those that he had weren't presented forcefully. From the time of his accession to his death in 1925, the company drifted and declined, with vice-presidents taking power and operating without a major co-ordinating effort from the top. A company-sponsored, written, published, and distributed history, *Sold American!* (New York, 1954), stated his contribution as generously as possible, but even there could be found hints of Hill's failure. "For the first ten years of Percy Hill's presidency, both the sales and manufacturing departments were on a kind of shakedown cruise."

George Washington Hill was one of his father's vice-presidents, having come to the company to take command of a subsidiary, Butler-Butler, where he helped make Pall Mall a major brand. He was named vice-president in charge of sales for American after the dissolution, where he often clashed with others of his rank. George Hill urged them to imitate Reynolds; he wanted a smoke to pit against Camel and was certain he could make it the nation's leading seller. At the same time he continued to work with Pall Mall, in what turned out to be a mistaken notion that the White Burley fad might pass, and that the quality cigarette might be able to overtake Camel.

Meanwhile Charles Penn, the vice-president for manufacturing, experimented with Burley blends. Just as Reynolds had based Camel upon Prince Albert, so Penn turned to an American smoking brand for starters. Lucky Strike had done moderately well as a pipe tobacco since its introduction in 1871. Now Penn took the formulation, added new flavoring, and transformed it into a cigarette. Then he took George Hill to the factory to show it off. According to the company history, Hill was entranced by the cigarette, but even more so by the aroma in the mixing room, which he thought unusually pleasant—somewhat like that of morning toast.

With great fanfare and an expensive and imaginative campaign, George Hill introduced "Luckies" to the public in 1916. The slogan was "It's Toasted." According to the advertising copy, "The Burley tobacco is toasted; makes the taste delicious. You know how toasting improves the flavor of bread. And it's the same with tobacco exactly." Like Camel, Luckies was priced at ten cents. It too was offered without cigarette cards, so as to underline the idea that modern cigarettes were so expensive to formulate that the manufacturers had to eliminate giveaways so as to maintain a low price. Camel struck hard at the card business; Luckies all but killed this phase of the development of cigarettes in America.

The new smoke was an instant success. Penn gleefully ordered construction of a new factory in 1917, as the cigarette captured more than 10 per cent of the market. Hill was delighted, of course, and predicted that Luckies would lead the industry within a year. He was wrong. By mid-1918, the American Tobacco cigarette had only 6 per cent of the market, and Penn sadly cut back on his construction program.

One of the major reasons for the decline might have been the departure of George Hill, who went to France as a Red Cross major and later on served in Washington with the Motor Transport Corps. He would not return to American Tobacco until early in 1919, by which time Luckies had lost most of its early momentum.

The importance of Luckies in this period had less to do with its success than with the fact that American Tobacco had been obliged to introduce it in order to compete with Camel. The trend in the United States was toward national brands selling for ten cents. The cigarettes that boasted of their foreign mixtures were on the decline; not only were they already too expensive, but the coming of World War I made the importation of foreign leaf difficult and caused their prices to rise still further. Besides, given the right additives, Burley could do just as well. To be sure, the large manufacturers bowed to the sentiment that Turkish meant quality. Hill advertised Luckies as "A blend of Burley and Turkish tobacco (based on the original Lucky Strike Tobacco formula)" and of course Reynolds indicated the foreign connection with the name and wrapper for Camel.

A third major new brand, Chesterfield, introduced by Liggett & Myers in 1912, was less interesting and innovative, but it too helped establish the new pattern for American cigarettes. It was based upon Burley and used some foreign leaf for spice, perhaps because the company feared reaction if it utilized much additive. At first it had only limited success; like so many other brands, it tried to do too many things at once and obviously was imitative. With an English name, a Turkish blend, and American tobaccos, it was able to appeal to no large constituency, but merely cannibalized from others. Then L & M initiated an advertising campaign, clearly based upon the one that Reynolds had created for Camel. Chesterfield was labeled as "a balanced blend of the finest aromatic Turkish tobacco and the choicest of several American varieties." It did well, capturing 10 per cent of the market by 1917. Even then, L & M tried to play down the Burley base. "The Chesterfield blend contains the most famous Turkish tobaccos—Samsoun for richness, Cavella for aroma, Smyrna for sweetness, Xanthi for fragrance, combined with the best domestic leaf." Of course, most of the tobacco was Burley and Bright. Still, Chesterfield did contain fewer additives than the other new brands, and this may have helped it win a following.

Camel, Lucky Strike, and Chesterfield dominated the American market by 1917. It seemed evident that Burley blends, manufactured on a mass scale and sold nationally, would continue strong, with all other brands and varieties declining in popularity. Within a few years such once popular Turkish brands as Fatima, Murad, Mecca, Omar, Mogul, and Egyptian Prettiest—many produced by Lorillard—would become exotica. The old Virginia-Bright blends—Sunshine, Home Run, King Bee, and even Sweet Caps—also would decline. Buck Duke had created a new kind of organization, and Dick Reynolds had fashioned a revolution in cigarette preferences.

Still, the cigar continued to be the smoke preferred by gentlemen and those who were successful in business and the professions. American cigar production passed the 7.5 billion mark in 1917, a record. Havanas and other imports could not be dislodged as the proper smoke after a fine meal at an expensive restaurant. Such people kept their smokes in leather or gold cases, replenished from an expensive humidor; the cigarette was found in a garish soft pack.

But the situation was changing. Those Americans who wanted to affect "advanced" European manners smoked cigarettes, which also became the mark of intellectuals—especially those critical of cigar-smoking businessmen. Most important, the vast American middle class was taking to the cigarette in this period, and even some women were beginning to "come out of the closet" to smoke them in public places—though not in front of their families and friends. It appeared that given time, additional promotion, and the general tendency of American life, the cigarette would triumph over the cigar. A fast-moving civilization called for a quick smoke, and the pace of change was accelerating in the United States in 1917.

Then the tobacco companies received a bonus of sorts, in the form of a phenomenon which always had worked to boost sales in the past, and would do so in the future as well. The United States entered World War I in 1917, and the doughboys went off to fight cheerfully—and with cigarettes dangling from their lips, and cartons of smokes and matches in their duffel bags.

VI

After the Battle

The message was bold, simple, and direct. Americans of a half century later might have found it crude, shocking, and even unfeeling, but it suited the atmosphere of that period. Featured was a drawing of a doughboy, leaning wearily against the side of a trench, probably in France. His clothes are crumpled, his face smeared with grime. But the helmet is at a cocky angle, signifying spirit and resolve. There is a knowing smile on his face, as if to say the American can take anything thrown at him, and then return for more. The reason is also clear; between his lips is a freshly lit cigarette. The message was placed beneath the picture. "Murad—After the Battle, the Most Refreshing Smoke is Murad 20¢-20."

This particular advertising campaign began during the summer of 1918, and was at its height around the time Dick Reynolds died. It was typical of the genre. Bull Durham contracted to sell its entire output of cigarette tobacco and paper to the U. S. Army and told civilians that they would have to make the great sacrifice for the duration. But they could reflect that "When our boys light up, the Huns will light out!" The Bull Durham people implied that they were making a significant contribution to the war effort. "The Makings for US, the leavings for the Kaiser." It was the same for other advertisements. General Jack Pershing was asked what Americans could do to help his brave boys. "You ask me what we need to win this war," he replied. "I answer tobacco, as much as bullets."

A patriotic nation—and industry—responded promptly. Fewer than 18 billion cigarettes had been produced in 1914. When America entered the war in 1917, the figure was over 36 billion. Two years later close to 54 billion cigarettes were turned out by the nation's tobacco companies. Per capita consumption went from 134 in 1910–14 to 310 in 1915–19.

Tobacco sales tend to rise during wars. However in the nineteenth century, during the Crimean, Boer, and Spanish-American conflicts, it was the cigar and plug that captured much of the new business. But in 1914–18 cigar sales actually declined from what they had been in the previous five-year span (they went from 77 to 73 per capita), and the same was true for plug and pipe tobaccos. In contrast, cigarette sales increased; the war accelerated the switch to that form of tobacco.

These smokes were not considered "classy" in 1914. The companies had done all within their power to sell them to the middle classes and to sell American males on the virtues of cigarettes, but with limited success. Dramatic imagery didn't help. For example, the news that those who remained on the *Titanic* had gone to their dooms puffing on cigarettes was advertised by the companies, but sales did not increase, perhaps because Americans attributed this behavior more to English stoicism than an excess of bravery. In World War I the cigarette came to be identified with all the positive values—quiet dignity, courage, and dedication above all. Consider this story, published in the New York *Globe* in January 1915, concerning the sinking of the British battleship *Formidable*.

THE CIGARETTE OF COURAGE

Captain Loxley of the *Formidable* went down with his ship, standing on the bridge calmly smoking a cigarette. A survivor of the disaster tells how he rushed up on deck, borrowed a cigarette from one of his comrades and a light from another, and then dashed below to get more cigarettes. We often hear also of other heroes who go to their doom lipping a cigarette between their teeth. It never is a cigar or pipe, but always a cigarette.

In moments of severest tension few men can preserve a complete semblance of composure and control without something to finger or munch, some little means of muscular occupation, of nervous discharge. Talleyrand, the classical example of the undismayable, had no need of a cigarette between fingers or lips, but his *sang-froid* is said to have been literally physical, derived from a pulse down in the forties.

A singer facing the dread ordeal of a new public may handle a piece of music to which he never refers, a slip of paper bearing words, or, if the singer be a woman, a fan or a flower. The men dying for country and faith are going to death with the solace of the cigarette. A neat revenge that makes this snare of youth a white badge of courage.

There is no evidence the cigarette companies planted such stories or paid reporters to write them; in any case, this was not the style in the industry at that time. Rather, the gallant Edwardians who led and wrote about the war appeared to relish the picture of a brave man, inhaling a cigarette as though still on the Strand in London or lounging in the vestibule of a Broadway theater between the acts, while awaiting his doom on the forecastle of a battleship or in the Flanders trenches.

Americans who followed the war in the newspapers during the neutrality phase in 1914–17 would see pictures of English, French, German, and Russian soldiers at rest in the backlines, more often than not smoking cigarettes. There were photos of the Kaiser lighting up and offering one of his cigarettes to a passing grenadier—the comradeship of war. Not to be outdone, important French and Belgian politicians trekked to the front lines to be photographed handing out packs of cigarettes to men coming off the line. Americans started the Belgian Soldiers' Tobacco Fund, to raise money for cigarettes that were distributed gratis to soldiers in that army. This transpired after a news story that some Belgians sent an appeal to their minister of war. "Give us worse food if you like, but let us have tobacco." Not to be outdone, the small French colony in Mexico started a fund, which eventually sent thirteen tons of cigarettes to that army. Then the movement caught on in other countries, where civilian groups organized cigarette funds on a local basis. According to one report, the Red Cross chapter in Westchester County dispatched ten million of them to Allied soldiers during the neutrality phase. These were passed through the lines by the governments, which waived tax and import restrictions, so that the soldiers could have as many cigarettes as they wished, to be smoked whenever they chose to do so.

The crusade to provide free cigarettes intensified once America entered the war in 1917. Any man in uniform in 1917–18, in almost any part of the United States or France, could be certain of finding a canteen where he could get free coffee, doughnuts, and cigarettes. Enormous quantities of all three were consumed.

The antismoking forces bemoaned this situation, but did not criticize private individuals and groups, or even governments, for their actions. Such opposition might be construed as an affront to the fighting men and a lack of patriotism. Lucy Gaston and her followers shied from this. (The same was true for prohibitionists who, while continuing their lobbying activities, called a halt to forays against saloons that catered to soldiers and sailors.)

"Cigarettes are just as bad for small boys as ever," said a Lynn (Massachusetts) *Evening Post* reporter. Approval of their use in wartime did not signify acceptance once the fighting was ended. "The case of the soldier on service under modern conditions is very different. Nothing can well be more trying to the nerves of man as such service as millions have been giving in turn in the trenches." A narcotic was needed "to soothe the nerves somewhat, to deaden the loneliness." Indeed, smoking well might have saved lives by preserving sanity. "Whatever may be the effect under normal conditions of living, they help soldiers at the front endure the strain," the article went on to say. "All anticigarette crusades must recognize this fact and be governed accordingly."

And of course, there was the admonition to civilians as well as soldiers to "pack up your troubles in your old kit bag and smile, smile, smile," which was possible "while you've a lucifer to light your fag." (This was British usage, and the terms weren't picked up by Americans. The lucifer was the familiar wooden splint match, such as the Swan Vesta, and the "fag" a cigarette composed primarily of Virginia leaf and Bright, and not the White Burley that was sweeping over America in this period.)

The old anticigarette crusaders naturally were dismayed by all of this. During the war outdoor smoking became acceptable, with even some women appearing in public with cigarettes in hand. Flint and wick cigarette lighters and wrist watches replaced humidors and watch fobs as gifts for departing officers— the quick and simple were replacing the ornate and measured. The nation was being barbarized, so the reformers thought. As a sign of this, per capita use of cigarettes in America reached 426 in 1919. Contrary to the hopes of reformers and expectations of those who believed cigarette smoking would decline with the arrival of peace, the habit grew. By 1925, the per capita figure was slightly below 700.

During the war, several prominent public figures warned against the evils of inhalation, noting that what might be won on the battlefield could be lost at the tobacconist. Thomas Edison wrote that cigarette paper when burned released "acrolein," which when inhaled could destroy brain cells. "I employ no person who smokes cigarettes," he wrote in a letter to Henry Ford. Yet Edison did smoke cigars and, in between, chewed on strong plug. As for Ford, he issued several diatribes against the "little white slavers," which he was convinced contained the vilest poisons known to man. Clarence True of the Methodist Temperance and Moral Board argued that the cigarette makers had conspired to "hook" soldiers on their product by distributing them free or at low prices. The most pressing problem of the postwar period, said True, would be dealing with a returning army of drug addicts.

Yet little was done beyond talking. Percival Hill rightly noted that "millions of American men have convinced themselves that cigarettes are good for them," and American Tobacco said it would continue to help the boys at the front, no matter what men like True said and did. By wrapping themselves in the flag, the tobacco men were able to silence all but the most vociferous and least effective of their opponents. But as the Eighteenth

Amendment moved closer to ratification and the war to its conclusion, reformist interests began to turn toward the cigarette.
"Prohibition is won," cried Billy Sunday when the Amendment
was added to the Constitution. "Now for tobacco."

The manufacturers assumed some sales would be lost as a result of the reborn antismoking crusade, but this wasn't as important to them as was the switch from giveaways to sales. The distribution of free smokes to servicemen ended shortly after the
Armistice. Now the doughboys had to pay for their cigarettes,
and so they did. The companies were troubled by what these
men would do after they left the service. Would the impulse
smoking that had become endemic among lower- and middle-
class men in 1917–18 continue into the peacetime period? These
people were being mustered out, presumably to live in a less
tense environment and one in which they would have to pay
from ten to twenty cents for a pack of smokes. Manufacturers assumed sales would suffer, but none of them dared guess how far
they would decline.

The industry did well in 1919, but the following year, for the
first time since 1905, the consumption of cigarettes as a percentage of total tobacco output declined, going from 19.6 per cent to
19.3 per cent, while cigars recaptured some of the ground lost
during the war.

In anticipation of just such a problem, the industry had organized the Allied Tobacco League for the general promotion of
smoking and defeat of legislation aimed at hindering the growth
of cigarette consumption. State chapters stressed the League's
belief in freedom of action for all citizens. If a person wanted to
smoke, let him, they said. All infringements upon personal liberty had to be opposed. First it was liquor, and now the
"reformers" wanted to deny cigarettes to Americans who wanted
them. What would be next? The reformers spoke of their desire
for a better and healthier America; the Allied Tobacco League
responded that in fact they were in the process of creating a
police state, in which individual freedoms would be lost.

Coming as it did at a time when the Justice Department had
initiated an anti-Bolshevik crusade, these appeals struck a strong
note of civil libertarianism and won the support of such diverse
individuals as philosopher John Dewey, former President Wil-

liam Howard Taft, and film director D. W. Griffith. A Kansas procigarette group presented President Harding with a carton of smokes after learning that Lucy Gaston had urged him to give up the habit to set a proper example for youth. Harding replied that "I think it is fine to save the youth of America from the tobacco habit," as he accepted the carton. "I think, however, the movement ought to be carried on in perfect good faith and should be free from any kind of hypocrisy or deceit on the part of those who are giving it their earnest attention."

The President did stop smoking in public, however—he was a politician who believed in counting votes—and during the rest of his life confined his smoking and boozing to behind closed doors. Others did bow to anticigarette pressures. Mme. Ernestine Schumann-Heink, the famous opera star, had endorsed cigarettes. The crusaders talked several recital halls into canceling her appearances on moral grounds. She relented, withdrew from her endorsement contracts, and issued a strong blast against smoking.

As it happened, both sides had wasted much time and effort; there is no indication that pro- or anticigarette propaganda had much effect. The returning doughboys had no intention of giving up their smokes, and neither did the civilian population, which during the war had taken to cigarettes. The slight decline in cigarette sales in 1919 and the rise in cigar consumption had been due to the return to cigars of those soldiers who couldn't get them in the trenches. Cigarette sales resumed their upward march in 1921, when over 52 billion smokes were produced, 8 per cent more than in the previous year. Henry Ford and Thomas Alva Edison continued their crusade against "the little white slaver," but in that year cigarettes accounted for 22.4 per cent of all tobacco sales.

By then it had become evident that the anticigarette laws could not be enforced, and a movement for repeal gathered strength; by the end of the decade all the state laws had been wiped from the books. But the Gaston forces and their allies counterattacked, and did so on what they perceived of as being the weak point in the armor: price.

The price of a pack of cigarettes depended upon a number of variables, the most important of which were the efficiency of

manufacturing; overhead charges for distribution and advertising; the cost of raw materials, especially tobacco; and taxes.
In periods of great demand and limited supply of smokes the
price could rise sharply, but most of the time the manufacturers
simply would increase their output. Too, brand loyalty never was
so strong as to lead a Camel smoker, for example, to purchase
that cigarette if Luckies were more than a few cents cheaper. In
general, the Big Three of that period—Reynolds, American, and
L & M—tried to keep the selling prices of Camel, Luckies, and
Chesterfield on the same level. This was not collusion; it was
good business practice. Finally, by tacit agreement, Reynolds
was permitted to lead in the alteration of the price structure, because of its industry position and the unwillingness of the others
to mount a serious challenge.

The costs of producing cigarettes advanced early in the war.
White Burley prices doubled from 1913 to 1918, as farmers
reaped the bonanza of higher demand. Federal taxes, which
were $1.25 per thousand in 1916, went to $2.05 the following
year and $3.00 in 1919. The need to expand production facilities
resulted in higher capital outlays at Reynolds, American, and
L & M, and so a temporary increase in costs per unit. Advertising
and distribution charges did come down, but this was a minor
consolation in the face of other costs.

The Big Three were obliged to raise the price of their cigarettes on a wholesale level, to which the new taxes had to be
added. Clearly the ten cents per pack price could not hold. In
1917, Reynolds suggested that retailers might charge thirteen
cents for a pack of twenty Camels. American and L & M experimented with a sixteen-cigarette pack, in an attempt to keep the
price at a multiple of five, but then followed Reynolds to thirteen
cents. The prices kept rising in 1918 and took a sharp jump when
the excise tax was hiked in 1919. By then a pack of Camels,
Luckies, or Chesterfields fetched as much as twenty cents.

There followed a major price break. The White Burley crop
for 1918 had exceeded all expectations, and so the price dropped.
Frightened, the growers expanded production in 1919, hoping in
this way to keep their total income constant; they would sell
more tobacco at the lower price in order to receive the same
money as before. This in turn caused the price to fall still lower,

and then the cycle repeated itself. By 1930, the White Burley price was little more than half that of 1918.

The manufacturers rejoiced, thinking this would mean larger profits. They would expand advertising, but given a stable tax level (all but promised by the federal government) and their new plants, costs per unit were bound to decline. Part of this would be passed on to the consumer; packs of standard brands would go to fifteen cents, perhaps two for a quarter. The rest would be pure profit.

However, lack of agreement among the Big Three and a bout of price cutting prevented this. By 1921 Luckies were being offered at great discounts—for a few weeks the retail price of a pack was as low as eight cents—but then it stabilized. The industry settled back into the ten-cent mold.

It was at this point that the anticigarette forces launched their new attack. If Americans wouldn't respond to appeals on moral, legal, and health grounds, perhaps they would refrain from smoking—or at least cut down—because of price. In alliance with other groups, they lobbied for state and local cigarette taxes, and it was their pressure that was partially responsible for the hike in the federal rate in 1919. In this way, they forced a rise in prices.

The manufacturers responded by fighting the taxes, and then they tried to hold the line by accepting lower profits. The Big Three experimented with new packages—the "flat fifties" for example, fifty smokes in a tin container that resembled a cigarette case festooned with advertising. The ten-cent pack remained the standard, however, and soon the price went up.

To the delight of many industry leaders, there were few customer complaints, and no indication that a two- or three-cent price increase harmed sales. Within a few years Camel, Luckies, and Chesterfield were back to fifteen cents and two packs for a quarter.

By then it was evident that in this industry at least price competition would be wasteful, and in fact there was little of this in the 1920s. The manufacturers would try to increase sales in other ways, most importantly through advertising. The marketing men at American, Reynolds, and L & M kept their eyes on demographic statistics, while the sales people took note of the cult of

youth that developed after the war. And all were deeply interested in the female smoker, the largest untapped market in the
nation.

This was in marked contrast to the approaches used by the
cigar, pipe, and plug sales forces. In this period none of these
types of smokes and chew attempted to win young people to the
habit, and in fact their ads—especially those for cigars—tended
to feature older men. Of course, none thought women ever
would be lured to pipe, plug, and cigar, or for that matter
whether it would be desirable for them to do so. Would a "real
man" want to use a form of tobacco enjoyed by women? Not in
the 1920s. If women ever took to cigars, then the men who
smoked them might be considered somewhat effeminate. It had
taken cigarettes many years to overcome this kind of prejudice;
manufacturers of other kinds of smokes hardly would take the
risk of such a change.

Some cigarette men were dubious regarding this shift in
emphasis, but most knew it had to come. Before the war the cigarette manufacturers had spent most of their time trying to lure
cigar and plug users to their brands. This fight was over by 1920.
Cigar production reached the 8 billion mark that year and then
declined, not rising above 7 billion for the remainder of the decade. In the early 1930s, cigar production fell below 5 billion for
the first time since the turn of the century, while the figures for
plug and smoking tobacco were equally dismal. Thus, the cigarette companies could turn to a new battlefront—women—and
the prime weapon here was advertising.

As one adman of the decade noted, you don't sell the steak,
you sell the sizzle. That was what transpired within the cigarette
business in this period. Buck Duke and others of his generation
had used cigarette cards, coupons, and the like to attract buyers.
For the most part these were gone by 1922. The companies used
the money saved by their elimination in the creation of expensive
advertising campaigns.

In early 1929 George Washington Hill commented that only
three people in the world possessed the secret formula for Lucky
Strike. Presumably he was one of them. Hill refused to name the
other two, implying strongly that once their identities were made
public, the individuals would be subjected to intense pressures

and even dangers. One was left with the image of an American Tobacco vice-president chained to the wall, with L & M and Reynolds thugs trying to beat the information out of him, or of a seduction by a Clara Bow-type vamp, offering any and all of her favors, for a list of the ingredients in a Lucky Strike.

Of course, this was pure hyperbole and self-advertisement. George J. Whelan, the onetime cigarette manufacturer, and in the 1920s a leading figure in the distribution and sale of tobacco products, scoffed at the idea. "There is no secret about cigarette making," he said. "Anyone can analyze a Camel and manufacture it." That was not the point, said Whelan. "The users would say it was not the same. Such is the power of advertising."

The weight of evidence and experience was in Whelan's favor, but this did not mean Hill was engaging in deception. Certainly a competent tobacco man could have duplicated the formula for any cigarette. The granulated leaf in the white tube was not homogenized, and each variety could have been isolated with ease. All the major companies had executives who could identify additives by taste alone, while their chemists could have refined the information in their laboratories. There were no manufacturing secrets. Furthermore, most long-time smokers had a difficult time distinguishing between similarly blended cigarettes of that period, and the occasional smoker was at a loss to pick one brand out of several when given blindfold tests. Indeed, when such tests were given, some smokers were unable to tell whether the cigarette was even lit, at least on the first puff.

Hill must have understood this, though he would never have conceded the point. But the question really wasn't that important. For years advertisers and manufacturers had recognized they were selling dreams and status as well as patent medicines, soap, clothing, and other consumer products. The nameplates of Packard, Rolls-Royce, and Duesenberg carried a cachet in automobiles that far outweighed their real and supposed advantages over less prestigious makes. The same was true for whiskies— even then "house brands" sold for lower prices than advertised ones, though the liquor was identical, and only the bottle and nameplate separated the $5.00 booze from the $3.00 variety.

Such was the case with cigarettes. The person who smoked Luckies more often than not had been lured by the images put forth by Hill's campaigns, and the same was true for the other brands. American Tobacco's blenders and chemists provided the formula, the production people put it into a package designed by artists, and then the product was advertised by an agency. How much did each contribute to the enjoyment realized by the smoker? There is no way of answering, at least in a "scientific" sense. But the experience of the industry in the 1920s and afterward indicates that advertising was as important as any other factor.

Hill became the master of this phase of the business, just as Buck Duke had shown others how to organize and Dick Reynolds led the way with national brands and the White Burley mix. He was as single-minded in his sphere as they had been in theirs. As one of his associates put it, Hill became so devoted to Luckies that the cigarette eclipsed all other interests; it was akin to "a missionary's devotion to Jesus."

Hill was a small, vain, arrogant man, who was rarely seen without a huge cowboy hat, dark blue suit, and a Lucky between his fingers. His company limousine was festooned with packs of Luckies, which were hung down the windows and lined the windshield, while the car was manned by bodyguards, more to attract attention than to protect the passenger. As Hill got older, he became more eccentric, taking to an open convertible to be better seen, and placing fishing flies on his hat. Hill had two residences, a penthouse on the East Side of Manhattan, and an estate in Irvington, New York, complete with lake on which there were swans and a "forest" where he kept deer. Hill had two special pets—dachshunds, whom he named Mr. Lucky and Mrs. Strike.

Hill, and the lesser men who imitated him, dominated the cigarette scene for the next generation. This is not to say he "reinvented" the cigarette, as had Reynolds, for this not only was impossible in the 1920s, but unnecessary. Rather, he showed that the image precedes the product, and that concept can and should dictate not only how an item is sold, but what the company will produce. In other words, Hill would come upon an advertising idea, and then create a product it would fit.

Also, he showed the rest of the industry—and businessmen in nontobacco areas—how the public could be swayed to accept or reject an idea or product. In this regard he was more than a manufacturer or corporation executive; he was a dream merchant.

Hill was credited—unjustly, as shall be seen—with popularizing public smoking for women. Together with one of his advertising men, Edward Bernays, he devised some curious ways to plant the idea in the heads of middle-class females. Bernays hired a psychoanalyst, A. A. Brill, in his search for a proper theory to go with his ideas, and Brill provided one. "Some women regard cigarettes as symbols of freedom," said Brill. "More women now do the same work as men do. Many women bear no children; those who do bear have fewer children. Feminine traits are masked. Cigarettes, which are equated with men, become torches of freedom." To this, Brill added the familiar Freudian idea then sweeping sophisticated America. "Smoking is a sublimation of oral eroticism; holding a cigarette in the mouth excites the oral zone."

Whether because or in spite of this, Bernays hired a group of attractive models whose job it was to smoke Luckies in public. Later he enlisted leading debutantes for the job, after convincing them that by smoking they would be striking a blow for freedom.

The plan seemed to work; at least, it garnered a great deal of free newspaper space for cigarettes in general and Luckies in particular. "Of course you benefit yourself more than the other fellow," said Hill about such promotion. "But you help the whole industry if you do a good job. . . ."

Doubtless women would have smoked openly even without such a campaign—the 1920s was a period of female liberation, in this regard at least, and the atmosphere of the "Jazz Decade" encouraged what in an earlier time would have been seen as an aberration. Still, Hill was not satisfied. True, women were smoking in increasing numbers, but not enough of them were using Luckies. Why?

According to Bernays, the green color of the Luckies pack clashed with the clothes women were wearing. Bernays foolishly suggested that Hill change the design of the pack and was treated to an explosion. "I've spent millions of dollars advertising the package. Now you ask me to change it. That's lousy advice."

Together with Bernays, Hill set out on a different kind of

crusade—he would make green the color preferred by fashionable people, and in this way encourage women to purchase and display his smokes. Bernays worked it out with friends in the fashion industry. For example, Philip Vogelman of Onandaga Silk gave a Green Fashion Luncheon (paid for by American Tobacco) with green menus, which featured beans, asparagus salad, pistachio mousse glacé, and crème de menthe. With company support, psychologists discussed the implications of the color in the area of mental health (all good) and artists the use of green in the works of great masters (they approved). Mrs. Frank Vanderlip, a prominent socialite, sponsored a Green Charity Ball—paid for by American Tobacco—at which all who attended had to wear green gowns. Green did become the "in color" that year. Hill was pleased. Bernays received a bonus.

For all of his energy, inventiveness, and even brilliance, Hill was unable to focus his attention upon details and tactics. Like many other powerful men, he liked to amaze others with new concepts, and he always thought in grand terms. Hill would manipulate assistants, associates, and division heads, and, after steering them into new paths, remain on the sideline to criticize and intervene to correct what he believed to be mistakes. No one at American really had a free hand. Hill was there to claim credit for successes and blame others for failures. He liked to believe that only George Washington Hill could carry out the grand plans, but he lacked the patience for such work.

For this reason he needed men like Bernays—clever tacticians and resourceful aides. And he knew how to get them. Hill's method of winning Bernays is illustrative of how he worked. Once he saw a particularly effective Chesterfield ad—one that ridiculed Lucky Strike's use of opera stars in testimonials. He learned that Bernays had been responsible for its inception and presentation. Armed with this knowledge, Hill had one of his friends, David A. Schulte, the cigar-store magnate, hire Bernays on condition that he drop all other tobacco clients. The retainer was attractive, and so Bernays accepted. A year later he was called into Hill's office and told that his work was good, and that the contract would be extended. "I don't understand," said Bernays. "I've never worked for you." Hill roared with pleasure. "The hell you haven't!" and then told Bernays what he had done.

"You've been on the American Tobacco payroll for nine months. You were working for Liggett & Myers, weren't you? And we got you from them, didn't we? And you didn't know anything about it. That's why Lucky Strike is on top."

Years later, Bernays had lunch with Ivy Lee, perhaps the nation's top public relations man—he was the one who suggested John D. Rockefeller give shiny dimes to children to "humanize" his image—and learned, almost by accident, that Hill had retained Lee's company for public relations. Why should American Tobacco want two such highly priced PR men? And why was the matter kept a secret? Confronted with this, Hill seemed quite pleased with himself. "If I have both of you, my competitors can't get either of you."

Public relations men like Lee and Bernays were there to provide ideas and make contacts. The day-to-day advertising, and most of Hill's basic ideas, came from the Lord & Thomas advertising agency, the most powerful and famous in the field, headed by Albert D. Lasker, considered the father—or at the very least, godfather—of modern advertising. Among Lasker's clients were Kleenex, Pepsodent, Palmolive, RCA, and Sunkist—and at election time, the Republican Party. Lord & Thomas dominated radio advertising—Lasker all but invented soap operas—and was responsible for more new ideas in the field than anyone else of the period. Lasker did not seek clients in the 1920s; they came to him for interviews, and if he thought the conditions and price were right, he would take on the product. Otherwise, he might recommend a lesser firm.

Percy Hill approached Lasker in 1923, seeking his aid in making Luckies the nation's number-one cigarette. Lasker liked the idea and the challenge, as well as the fee—15 per cent of all bookings above the retainer—and asked whether he was to deal directly with Hill. He was told that George would have that responsibility, and Lasker knew of the son's reputation. "That's fine, Mr. Hill," he said. "But if I'm to deal with George, and not you, I cannot accept your account unless George and I get to know each other better." George Hill had to go to Lord & Thomas' main offices in Chicago and see how Lasker handled his business. This was crucial; their initial encounter was made on Lasker's home ground, and Hill had to make the journey, thus offering the symbolic bow to the new advertising man at American Tobacco. Lasker never would be an assistant, employee, or even a mere consultant. The relationship between Lasker and Hill would be that of equals, and it was fixed from the start. Lasker would accept Hill's ideas, but he then would add his own touches and have full responsibility and power for their implementation. "It isn't hard to work with Hill," said Lasker later on. "All I have to do is let him be the agency and pretend that I'm the client." This meant that he would plant an idea in Hill's mind, and soon thereafter George would burst into his office and demand a campaign based upon what he now claimed was his own concept. Then Hill would have to sell Lasker's own thoughts to their originator, and Lasker always allowed himself to be swayed. In this way, Lasker got the program, and Hill the credit for its origination, and both men were content.

It was Lasker who created the campaign that lured women into public smoking. He was supposed to have gotten the idea from a casual remark by Paul Hoffman, the head of Studebaker. "Get women to smoke, and you'll double your market," said Hoffman. Soon thereafter, Lasker's wife told him that she smoked a cigarette before meals, on the advice of her doctor. It seemed to soothe her nerves and enhanced digestion. More important, it helped kill her appetite and so cut down on calories. Once, when they were dining in a fashionable restaurant, Flora Lasker lit up, and was told by the manager that she would have to extinguish the smoke; women were not allowed to puff away in his place of business. Enraged and at the same time seeing an opening for a new campaign, Lasker set to work.

Other cigarette men and their agencies had the idea long before Lasker began his campaign, but they didn't know how to capitalize upon it. Women wanted to seem glamorous, and the delicate sex would prefer a mild smoke—that seemed to be the pitch. Prior to World War I, women rarely appeared in cigarette advertisements, and when they did, it was usually as background figures. The companies knew that many more women had taken to cigarettes during the war, and that as always was the case at such times, a general loosening of morals was underway. How could this be capitalized upon?

Lorillard tried the waters first. Its Helmar cigarettes already were quite popular among men, and some women had taken to them too. In fact, Lorillard dominated the Turkish market in America with such brands as Egyptian Deities, Gods of the Nile, Mogul, and Murad as well as Helmar. Now Lorillard made its pitch for the female market. Someone at the company decided to gear the ads to upper-class, liberated women, the very kind that used cigarettes before the war. And it proceeded timidly.

Starting in 1919, the company began using women in many of its magazine and newspaper ads. All the presentations featured oriental settings, or at least what Americans of that day would take for such an atmosphere. The women were pictured as lounging on divans, settees, or plush cushions, always looking languidly out at the reader. In no case did the model have a cigarette in her hand or mouth, and in fact few ads contained even pictures of the cigarette or the pack. Furthermore, all the models clearly were occidental—calm Edwardian beauties. Thus, the American woman, seeing such an ad, might be able to project herself into it. As one critic noted, the ladies looked as though they had "never been East of Brooklyn Borough Hall." There was the brunette beauty in the Murad ad, reclining against a rich silk-covered wall, her right arm behind her head as though to cushion it, with a look on her face that in 1919 signaled refined sex, but today appears somewhat drug induced. Her fine right leg is crossed—but encased in harem pants so as to only hint at the form. And close by the toe is an open box of Murad. The message was simple enough: "Be Nonchalant. Light a Murad Cigarette."

The Lorillard campaign fizzled; sales didn't rise, and so it was abandoned within a few months. That marked the end of this approach. But during the 1920s Player's, an English smoke, used women in its ads in a similar fashion. This time they were society belles who looked as though they were lounging after a party at Noel Coward's.

In 1926 L & M tested the water. In a newspaper ad that year, Chesterfield portrayed a man and woman seated by a riverbank at dusk. The man is lighting up, and the woman looks at him with admiration mixed with wistful envy. "Blow some my way," she coaxes. Does he offer her a cigarette or doesn't he? In a preview of the Tiparillo ads of the early 1970s—in which it was

suggested that women might want to begin smoking small cigars
—the reader never finds out. One writer noted, "They are all link-
ing up the woman and the cigarette, yet none of them offers her
a package for sale." Chesterfield wouldn't go that far.

Neither would the Philip Morris company, whose Marlboro of
that era was a high-priced English smoke. In a 1927 ad, the company showed women and cigarettes together, with the slogan:
"Women, when they smoke at all, quickly develop discriminating
taste." The idea clearly was that Marlboro was the kind of cigarette women might like. Also, Marlboro was "Mild as May."
There is no evidence this ad had any important impact, and in
any case it didn't last for long. Perhaps Philip Morris feared that
any gains to be made among women would be more than offset
by those men who would stop buying the cigarette for fear it
had acquired a "sissy" image.

Clearly the idea was in the air. All that was required was the
proper approach.

At first Lasker took the conventional road. There were the
usual testimonials from actresses and sports personalities, as well
as public figures like aviatrix Amelia Earhart, who had a somewhat masculine appearance in flight regalia. Then, in 1928, he
set out on a new tack. Recalling his wife's words and the inci-
dent at the restaurant, Lasker decided to show that cigarettes
could be a substitute for candy. Apparently Hill had thought of
the concept at the same time or, at least this was the tale at the
office, perhaps planted there by Lasker so as not to take credit
from his employer. Hill told Lasker that he had met a woman
who said she was seventy years old, but looked forty. The reason
for this, she claimed, was her use of cigarettes, for by using them
she avoided candy. Hill had his slogan ready: "Reach for a
Lucky Instead of a Bonbon." Lasker suggested a minor alteration: "Reach for a Lucky Instead of a Sweet." This would include cakes and pies as well as candy. Hill readily agreed, and
the campaign was initiated.*

"I Light a Lucky and Go Light on the Sweets. That's How I

* Another story was set forth in the official American Tobacco history.
According to this version, Hill saw a fine-looking woman in a taxicab
smoking a cigarette, shortly after eying a stout lady chewing gum. "But
right there it hit me: there was the lady that was stout and chewing, and
there was the young girl that was slim and smoking a cigarette. 'Reach for
a Lucky instead of a Sweet.' There it was, right in front of you."

Keep in Good Shape and Always Feel Peppy." That was the first ad, which featured Al Jolson. An Amelia Earhart ad of 1928 read: "Lucky Strikes were the Cigarettes Carried on the 'Friendship' When She Crossed the Atlantic," and in smaller type, "For a Slender Figure—Reach for a Lucky Instead of a Sweet."

As the general outline of the campaign became evident, several rival ad agencies tried to belittle the Lasker-Hill approach. There was nothing original about the idea, they said. In 1891, for example, Lydia Pinkham's tonic asked women to "reach for a vegetable instead of a sweet." But the impact was obvious in 1928, and also effective.

The candy manufacturers were outraged, and retaliated. Schrafft's removed Lucky Strikes from their counters. Candy ads featured a turnabout. Sweets "fixed" saliva, they trumpeted, which not only deadened appetite, but lessened the urge for cigarettes. Which were more dangerous? The candy and smokes people had different answers. In any case, Lasker and Hill were delighted at the counterattack, which only served to fetch additional publicity.

The next year Lasker unleashed a new campaign and attack against candy. It featured pictures of athletic-looking individuals, followed by fat ones in the same pose. The slogan: "When Tempted to Overindulge, Reach for a Lucky Instead." The implication was clear. Not only was it better to smoke than be fat, but cigarettes were actually health-giving. "For years this has been no secret to those who keep fit and trim. They know that *Luckies* steady their nerves and do not hurt their physical condition. They know that *Lucky Strikes* are the favorite cigarette of many prominent athletes who must keep in good shape. They respect the opinions of 20,679 physicians who maintain that Luckies are less irritating to the throat than other cigarettes." Toward the close of the campaign Lasker went all out. There was a picture of actress Constance Talmadge, in which she smiled and said, "Light a Lucky and you'll never miss sweets that make you fat."

Luckies still employed opera singers in some ads, but since they tended to be robust, if not actually fat, the message was different. Luckies protected their throats; other cigarettes did not.

The Lucky Strike campaigns were classic examples of the

"hard sell," in contrast to which those for Camel and Chesterfield appeared somewhat bland and washed out. Camel ads featured pleasant, contented people with cigarettes in mouths or between fingers, in addition to the usual collection of celebrities. Reynolds' counterpart to "Reach for a Lucky Instead of a Sweet" was "I'd walk a mile for a Camel." While graphic, it became memorable only after years of constant repetition. The Chesterfield ad was soothing: "They Satisfy." It was simple enough, but as one critic asked, "What the deuce does that mean?" The answer was, "A NEW thing in cigarettes, that does for your smoke hunger exactly what a drink of cold water does for your thirst."

Lorillard took a different path by introducing its new cigarette. By the mid-1920s it was evident that the company's oriental brands were dying. Lorillard had ignored the Burley standard market for a decade, in part due to interests in plug and smoking tobaccos, the mistaken belief that Turkish blends would stage a comeback, and poor corporate leadership. Lorillard had stable earnings, but the company clearly was declining in relation to the rest of the industry. It finally came out of its torpor in 1926 when after selling $15 million worth of securities to obtain a war chest, it introduced Old Gold, taking the name from a nineteenth-century plug.

Like the other standards, Old Gold contained Burley with a small amount of Virginia and Turkish leaf along with flavoring elements. The differentiation came in advertising, often clever responses to the appeals made by others. For example, an early "O.G." slogan was, "Eat a Chocolate. Light an Old Gold. And Enjoy Both! Two Fine and Healthful Treats!!" In response to the Chesterfield slogan, Old Gold had "Not a Cough in a Carload." O.G. prepared large ads featuring cartoons by John Held, the most popular illustrator of the Jazz Age, which were humorous as well as informative. But its most important campaign featured the "Blindfold Test." Smokers were masked, and asked to puff on an Old Gold, a Camel, a Chesterfield, and a Lucky. Then they were asked, "Which cigarette is *really* the most appealing?" Old Gold did well in such contests—or at least, Lorillard publicized those in which it was the clear victor.

Lorillard was reluctant to abandon its Turkish blends, and for a while tried to mount campaigns for them too. Murad in particular was publicized in 1926–27, but in the end the ad budgets for all cigarettes save Old Gold were cut drastically. In an age of standardization, one entry per firm was the limit. The costs of advertising and promotion would not permit more than that.

This was the contribution of men like Dick Reynolds, George Hill, and Albert Lasker. Reynolds started the change, and Hill and Lasker made certain it would take hold and become the norm. In 1925, when Hill took over as head of American Tobacco, Camel sold 34.2 billion cigarettes while Luckies with 13.7 billion was in third place behind Chesterfield, which sold 19.7 billion. That year, Reynolds spent close to $10 million to publicize its brands, with most of the money going for Camel. American Tobacco's outlay in 1925 was $8.7 million, and Luckies received approximately half that sum.

The Big Three slugged it out for the next five years, and in 1930, Hill realized his dreams. Lucky Strike was in first place, with 43.2 billion in sales, against Camel's 35.3 billion and Chesterfield's 26.4 billion. Old Gold, coming up fast but clearly not in their league, had 8.5 billion sales. As for ad expenditures, Hill had poured $75 million into Lasker's campaigns from 1925 to 1930, with $19.7 million in the victory year of 1930 alone. Still, Reynolds had spent even more money in this period—$92.9 million. This made the victory seem even sweeter—though Hill would not have used that word.

From 1925 to 1930 American cigarette production rose from 82.7 billion cigarettes to 124.2 billion, for an advance of over 50 per cent. In this period, while Camel stagnated, barely holding its own, Lucky Strike sales went up by 215 per cent.

Hill was hailed as an advertising genius, and he accepted such compliments. Lasker said little, but clearly he felt he merited the applause, which he received within the industry. "Hill was a particular pain in the neck because he thought he was an advertising genius, and he wasn't," said Lasker to a friend, and referring to his client's flamboyant behavior, he added, "Take that monkey business of wearing a hat all the time, and spitting on the desk."* On another occasion he said, "I made Lucky; I could

---

* Lasker was referring here to the story that once, at a board meeting, Hill spit on the table, shocking his associates. "That was a disgusting act," he said, "but none of you will ever forget it." This was what he wanted from his ads—impact. Later on the story was used by Frederick Wakefield in his novel about the industry, *The Hucksters,* in which the villain clearly was based on George Washington Hill.

unmake it too," and also, "There is no advertising man in the world but me!"

There is no method of determining whether Lasker or Hill contributed more to making Luckies the nation's leading cigarette in the 1920s; certainly both were important in the advertising campaigns. While it is obvious that these campaigns induced people—especially women—to purchase Luckies, we cannot say how many would or would not have smoked were it not for the messages in the printed media and on the radio.

Interestingly enough, neither Hill nor Lasker knew very much about tobacco, and what knowledge they possessed came second hand. Hill rarely visited the fields and auctions after he became president of American Tobacco in 1925, while Lasker felt out of place in anything but the most manicured rural or suburban environment; both were men of the cities, just as the cigarette was the urban smoke. In this respect they differed from Dick Reynolds, who always considered himself a tobacco man and remained in North Carolina. Even Buck Duke had roots in the Carolina soil, and he knew as much about leaf as any of his vice-presidents.

Between them, Hill and Lasker induced more people to smoke cigarettes than had any other individual in history; at the very least they managed to popularize smoking—open smoking, that is—for middle-class women, a sizable slice of the population. Most of their pioneer work was completed in the 1920s. By the end of the decade, adolescent females as well as males were signaling their independence by smoking cigarettes—usually Luckies, Chesterfields, or Camels—in public. To many Americans in their forties this seemed shocking, but then, so were other aspects of the Jazz Age. Cigarettes went with youth and beauty. The cigar seemed stodgy and middle-aged, an Edwardian remnant in the modern age, while plug was deemed antediluvian. The cigarette manufacturers were secretly pleased when elderly reformers launched broadsides against their product, correctly concluding, in mock-Newtonian terms, that every action on their part directed against cigarettes had an equal and opposite reaction on the part of young people in favor of the smokes. Switch a middle-aged person from cigars to cigarettes and you might sell him the product for another twenty years.

But when a teen-ager took to cigarettes, he might be a customer, of the same brand, for a half century. Figured at a pack per day, that came to 17,800 in a lifetime, and at fifteen cents each, $2,670, or close to three years' salary for the average worker of that decade. It was a pleasing prospect.

Hill and Lasker made millions from the business, and their work enabled other executives to become quite wealthy and prominent. Hill remained in the industry for the rest of his life, despite setbacks and stormy confrontations with other American Tobacco executives resulting from his imperious ways, high salaries, and enormous bonuses. Hill was convinced that he possessed genius and never allowed anyone, including Lasker, to challenge him on that score. Perhaps he was right. But after a Federal Trade Commission ruling against him, he was forced to change that famous slogan, which now became, "Avoid Overindulgence If You Would Maintain That Modern, Ever-Youthful Figure. Reach for a Lucky Instead." It didn't have quite the same ring, and soon was replaced by others, such as "L.S./M.F.T.—Lucky Strike Means Fine Tobacco" and "Lucky Strike Means Fine Tobacco. So Round, So Firm. So Fully-Packed." These too lacked the original zip, but by then it no longer mattered; the important work had been done.

Hill died of a heart attack in 1944, at the age of sixty-one. Two years earlier he had successfully repelled an attempt on the part of American Tobacco's board to have him step down. "I am the company," he told reporters, "and those bastards better not forget it."

While George Hill was fighting his last major battle at American Tobacco, Albert Lasker decided to retire. He was sixty-two at the time and wanted a more relaxed life. Besides this, his son Edward showed little interest in advertising, and for the past decade Lasker had held on only in the hope of handing the business to his heir. He would liquidate Lord & Thomas and sell the assets, as well as transfer his accounts to three associates, Emerson Foote, Fairfax Cone, and Don Belding, who promptly formed Foote, Cone & Belding. Most of Lasker's accounts decided to go to this new entity, which really wasn't much different from the old. Foote, the New York partner, was named president —in large part because he was to service the Lucky Strike account, and Lasker thought it wise to flatter Hill by assigning the top executive to American Tobacco.

Lasker spent the rest of his life dabbling in art and politics. And charities, especially those relating to health. At one point he helped reorganize and refinance the American Cancer Society, at a time when it was close to dissolution. Lasker died in 1952, at the age of seventy-two. Of cancer.

VII

Cheapies, Loosies, and Kings

In 1930 the nation's tobacco companies turned out more than one thousand cigarettes for every man, woman, and child. Per capita consumption had more than doubled since 1920, while total industry production had risen by 150 per cent in the decade.

This remarkable growth had resulted from a number of factors —habits acquired during the Great War, the looser public morality of the 1920s, the benefits of standardization, imitation of screen idols who smoked, the growing emancipation of women, and of course the large-scale advertising campaigns. By 1930 America had become a nation of cigarette smokers.

More often than not the ubiquitous cigarette was one of the standard brands produced by the "Big Three plus One" American, Reynolds, Liggett & Myers, and Lorillard, the principal successors to the old American Tobacco Trust. By 1930 Luckies, Camel, Chesterfield, and Old Gold accounted for nine out of every ten packs sold in the United States. The major manufacturers continued to produce their old pre-World War I brands— L & M, for example, marketed Fatima, Home Run, American Beauty, and Imperial—but these were for older people, usually those living in small towns or rural areas not reached by intense advertising campaigns. Most urban Americans who came of age in the 1920s were expected to make their choices from among the leading brands.

The major tobacco firms had only minor competition. Brown & Williamson, which in 1930 became a wholly owned subsidiary of the giant British-American Tobacco, had a small representation with two brands, Raleigh and Wings, which together had less than 1 per cent of the American market that year. Philip Morris & Company Ltd., which had been formed in 1919 to acquire the American business of the English Philip Morris & Company, imported several brands into the United States, and in addition had a marketing arrangement with Stephano Brothers, a Whelan Drug Store subsidiary with a few minor nonadvertised brands of its own. Philip Morris also owned Continental Tobacco, a manufacturer of a variety of English-style smokes for the American market, including English Ovals, Marlboro, and Dunhill. Axton-Fisher of Kentucky had an important position in the plug business and also was in cigarettes in a minor way. Lloyd "Spud" Hughes, a racing-car driver had tinkered with tobacco in his spare time and had developed a method of impregnating leaf with menthol. Lacking time and losing interest in this innovation, Hughes sold it to Axton-Fisher for $90,000. Spud cigarettes went for twenty cents a pack in 1927, when it was advertised as the perfect switch smoke for those who ordinarily used standard brands but had sore throats. In 1930 Spud had less than 1 per cent of the market. Larus & Brother, a manufacturer of pipe tobaccos, also ventured into the cigarette field. Its Edgeworth pipe tobacco was said to be Joseph Stalin's favorite. Larus put it out as a cigarette, and in this form it had a minor vogue among trendy intellectuals. In 1930 the company sold only 26 million of them, however.

The major firms tended to ignore these small fry and, in 1930, concentrated upon taking customers from one another. That year, at the beginning of the worst depression in American history, the manufacturers appropriated record amounts for advertising. Reynolds had a $15 million budget for Camel, up from less than $10 million the previous year, and American set aside $19 million in an attempt to break out of the number-three slot. Lorillard did not release its budget figures that year, but in the summer initiated a major billboard campaign for Old Gold.

The companies would later claim that heavy advertising charges militated against cuts in the prices of cigarettes. There is no indication the major companies ever considered such a policy. Instead, the firms would continue to compete on an advertising and distribution basis alone, though new wrinkles were being added. Camel would talk of its superior tobaccos, while Reynolds' agents would spread rumors that Luckies used dangerous chemicals in the formulation. Then Luckies would retaliate. In 1931 Lasker ran a series of ads that talked about the use of sheep-dip in tobacco cultivation. These implied that the substance was present in all cigarettes—except Luckies, which removed it with the toasting process. And at the same time, American Tobacco people started rumors that several workers in Reynolds factories had come down with dangerous communicable diseases. Neither firm appeared to have thought such tactics unethical, but Reynolds and American never would have considered a price war, though one might have been anticipated in the first stage of a depression.

The reason was simple: Demand for cigarettes continued high in 1930; apparently many Americans would give up food before cutting down on their consumption of smokes. So the incentive was missing. The companies would not deviate from their standard—in most parts of the country, two packs for a quarter. Instead, in early 1931, the Big Three plus One prepared for an across-the-board price increase.

As had become the custom, Reynolds gave the signal. The company had developed a method for wrapping packs in moistureproof cellophane. Production was switched from the old glassine wrapper to what Reynolds advertised as the "humidor-pack." The necessity of spreading the word was one reason

Reynolds required a large ad budget that year. In late June, the price of Camel to retailers went from $6.40 per thousand to $6.85, and Luckies, Chesterfield, and Old Gold followed suit. Now a pack sold for fifteen cents in the stores.

Sales fell slightly in July, the decline continued throughout the summer, and prices remained firm. There was no organized consumer protest and no public pressures for a return to the old two-for-a-quarter price. But a tug of war had developed between the major producers and their customers, with the companies betting they would win. The nation's smokers had been hooked; now they would be reeled in.

George Washington Hill put the matter bluntly, as was his custom. "I naturally saw the opportunity to make some money," he later explained. "At the same time I realized that if it was not the right thing to do, it was within my power to change it." James Andrews of Liggett & Myers, who had been responsible for creating Chesterfield, and was close to retirement, said as much, while conceding that his brand "might have a tremendous increase in business" had it held to the old price. As he later observed, "The inertia of custom, plus extensive advertising, tend to assure a well-established manufacturer his existing share of the market provided he does not permit his competitors to do anything drastically different from himself." Benjamin Belt of Lorillard was not about to break the cake of custom; Old Gold went to fifteen cents.

Of course, the industry leaders considered themselves to be proprietors of the only shops in town. There was no serious thought that a new company would enter the field, or that any of the minor firms could mount a serious challenge to the four established standard brands.

In retrospect, the price increases of 1931 can be seen as a blunder, born of arrogance, greed, and shortsightedness, which in turn had been created by the closed nature of the industry during the 1920s. While it was true that advertising budgets had risen in 1930, and Reynolds had additional expenditures resulting from the change in wrappers, costs were declining throughout the industry. All the major producers cut wages at the onset of the depression. Furthermore, the prices of raw materials—especially tobacco—were far below that of the late 1920s. (In

1928, for example, Reynolds paid slightly more than 32 cents per pound of White Burley; by 1931, the price was down to 11.3 cents. In this same period, the cost of Bright fell from 28 cents to 14 cents.) The tobacco companies had record profits; their balance sheets were in excellent condition; executive bonuses actually rose in 1931. Prices were not hiked because of higher costs or greater demand; rather, the manufacturers thought they could extract an extra two and a half cents or so per pack from the public.

The move backfired. In 1931 for the first time in a decade, sales fell, going from 124 to 117 billion. Some decline was in order, given the deepening economic depression, but the price increases served to exacerbate the situation. More important insofar as the four standard brands were concerned, some customers began looking for substitutes. There was a move back to roll-your-owns. A bag of Bull Durham cost five cents in 1931, and together with some paper—a sheet of old newspaper would do— could be stretched to produce twenty smokes. Old-timers, and those willing to learn the technique, could cut their cigarette budget by three-fourths in this way. There was a burst of enthusiasm for roll-your-owns in 1931 and 1932, as sales of this form of tobacco remained firm, while several companies tried to market simple machines for those smokers unable to grasp the method.

By 1931 many urban smokers had begun purchasing "loosies." They would enter their neighborhood grocery, tobacco shop, or candy store, and ask the proprietor for one or more cigarettes, usually though not always by brand name. These went for a penny apiece. Since the retail price was around fifteen cents for a pack of twenty, the retailer did quite well with the loosie trade, while the customer, who lacked money for a full pack, at least had some of his favorite smokes. "The poor man's cigarette case" —an empty package of some leading brand into which the loosies were placed—made its appearance around this time. This kind of purchase continued throughout the depression and World War II. After the war, when prosperity had returned and cigarettes were up to twenty cents a pack, some retailers continued the practice, catering to adolescents who were just starting on the habit. Not until cigarettes went to a quarter a pack did it come to a halt, though in some parts of the country loosies still are sold to teen-agers—for a nickel apiece.

The tobacco firms never acknowledged the existence of this loosie trade, which would have spoiled the respectable image they were trying to maintain for their products. They sponsored radio programs featuring swing bands, comedians, variety artists, and even a handful of dramas. Always the ads were upbeat and cheerful. Cigarettes were rewards for hard successful efforts, in sports or business. The advertisements in newspapers and magazines showed comfortable people at ease, in better than average surroundings, smiling, talking, laughing, or just relaxing, with a cigarette in their mouths or between their fingers. One such Camel ad had the slogan, "For Digestion's Sake—Smoke Camels," with testimonials from society women, at a time when some Americans hadn't much food to digest, and certainly had little in common with the New York Smart Set. Clearly the ads, as well as the prices, indicated that the major firms were out of touch with reality.

The movies tried to portray this reality, or at least a version of it, and as luck would have it, the images created on the screen benefited the industry. Early in the depression several companies, led by Warner Brothers, released films of social conscience in which the criminal or member of the lower class, portrayed by such actors as James Cagney, Paul Muni, Humphrey Bogart, and George Raft, smoked cigarettes, even while gunning down opponents. Given the quasi-revolutionary atmosphere of the time, these men were looked upon as heroes. After several protests made their way to Hollywood and the studios had time to react, the same actors were cast as FBI agents or policemen, but the cigarettes remained. Working women, often their consorts or wives, played by Ann Dvorak, Ann Sheridan, Bette Davis, and others, also smoked cigarettes. In time it seemed that most heroes and heroines were addicted to them. In this way, the most important and effective entertainment medium of the 1930s served the interests of the cigarette far better than did the paid ads put out by the Madison Avenue copywriters.

In one movie, the hero turned to a friend and asked to "bum a cigarette." Such a phrase would have horrified the tobacco people in the mid-1920s, but it caught on in the late 1930s and had a positive rather than an adverse effect.

Simultaneously, the image of the cigar smoker underwent a transformation. Several homely hero-villains chewed on cigars—Edward G. Robinson, for example. More often than not, when a "good guy" smoked cigars, he was a heavy-set, middle-aged, or old friend of the hero, often a comic actor. In the 1920s, cigar smoking was associated with success—bankers, brokers, politicians, businessmen would puff on Havanas. They continued to do so in the films of the early 1930s, but now they were the enemies of good and decent Americans. Just as the cigarette had become the symbol of tough proletarian vigor, so the cigar was the scepter waved by almost all "heavies," much to the distress of that segment of the tobacco industry.

Cigar production had declined throughout the 1920s, both in absolute terms and on a per capita basis. So it cannot be said that the depression and the negative image created by cigar smokers in movies crippled a thriving industry and killed a popular habit. Rather they sealed its doom, at least for a large majority of male American smokers. Many cigarette smokers would have taken to cigars prior to World War I, had they the income. Cigarettes were more acceptable after the Armistice, but the fine cigar remained the sign of one's arrival in the higher reaches of business, the professions, and society, and of aspirations for such rank. Cigars took on negative connotations in the 1930s from which they never recovered. President Roosevelt smoked cigarettes from a holder; he was never seen with a cigar. Of course, Winston Churchill seemed always to have a cigar in hand or mouth, but this did not help sales.

In 1930, cigars had the worst year since the turn of the century, with less than 6 billion sold. Eight years later the cigar makers turned out only 5 billion. Per capita consumption went from forty-eight to thirty-nine.

Habit, accident, and the forces of change—the decline of the cigar, images created in Hollywood, the loosie innovation, lower leaf prices—combined to make standard cigarettes more popular and unit profits higher in the early 1930s than they had been the decade before. But at the same time, radio and print ads and the price increases worked against the interests of the major manufacturers. It was as if the Big Three plus One were trying to commit suicide and were prevented from doing so by circumstances. As it was, the cigarette manufacturers were among the most successful businesses in the country in the 1930s, often posting record sales and profits. The figures could have been better, however. That they were not was due to the emergence of a set of competitors, both domestic and foreign, who had been encouraged to expand by the blunders of the leaders.

In September 1931, as sales of Luckies, Camel, Old Gold, and Chesterfield continued their slow decline, Larus & Brother introduced a new cigarette called White Rolls. In taste and appearance it differed little from the standard brands and, in fact, was a direct imitation. White Rolls contained the usual blend of White Burley, Bright, and flavoring elements. There was no major advertising campaign, but by using the distribution network created for Edgeworth, Larus was able to get its smokes into retail outlets. Demand was strong from the start, due wholly to price. White Rolls sold for ten cents a pack.

For several years Philip Morris had produced a ten-cent cigarette called Paul Jones, which was marketed in New England with little impact. Watching the progress of White Rolls, and recognizing the appeal of price, Philip Morris decided to go national with Paul Jones. In October the company entered into arrangements with chain drugstores to display the packs in windows and on counters, and the following month ads appeared in local newspapers. "America . . . Here's Your Cigarette!" There was a pack of Paul Jones, with the price—20 for 10¢. Later ads observed that prices of all essential consumer goods were too high and that Paul Jones had been marketed in recognition of this fact.

In March 1932 Brown & Williamson announced that henceforth one of its minor brands, Wings, would be sold at ten cents a pack. Up to that time, Wings had little appeal outside of the Chicago area. Within a month it was a national brand, without a major ad campaign, growing only by word of mouth. Wings carried messages on the back of its packs that were changed regularly. One read, "Many smokers say, 'A friend recommends WINGS! He's a real friend who enables you to save 33⅓% on your cigarette bill!'" and another, "ADVERTISE? YES!—we do—

by the best method—word-of-mouth of a satisfied consumer. 15¢ quality for 10¢"

Taken together, White Rolls and Paul Jones were producing 350 million cigarettes a month in March. Wings was gearing up for half a million, given its better distribution network and production facilities. Still, Larus ran its factory around the clock, seven days a week, and announced a major construction effort for 1932.

S. Clay Williams, president of Reynolds, told reporters there would be sharp cuts in advertising for Camel. He would not give reasons, but it was evident he thought the campaigns had become counterproductive, too ostentatious in a time of economic depression. But Williams did say, "Camel will not be disconcerted by the advance of a competitor so long as advertising is mainly responsible for it; but when a cigarette moves up without a maximum of advertising we will take serious notice." This was happening in 1931. Still, Williams would not lower his prices, a move that could have snuffed out the competition. With the exception of L & M, the other majors followed his lead. And all that L & M did was to take one of its brands, Coupon—the only cigarette put out by the large firms that sold for ten cents, and that in the 1920s—and pack it ten to a container to sell for five cents. But L & M did not attempt to go national with Coupon, which was sold only in the South. The company feared retaliation from the others and thought a popular Coupon would cannibalize sales from Chesterfield.

In June 1932, Axton-Fisher introduced Twenty Grand, which was an instant success. Within three months they were producing 700,000 a day, and at that could fill only 20 per cent of all orders. Like Larus, A-F embarked upon a major expansion effort, hoping to make Twenty Grand a national smoke.

The strategy worked, far better than anyone in the industry had anticipated. Cigarette sales declined only slightly in 1932, which was deemed a good showing considering the sorry state of the economy. The pattern of sales for individual brands had changed, however. In 1931 the four standards had accounted for 92 per cent of the total market; the following year sales of Luckies, Camel, Chesterfield, and Old Gold took 81 per cent of the market. Not one of the major brands was spared, with Camel suffering the most, its sales falling by 30 per cent.

Smokers throughout the nation were switching to the economy brands. Wings displaced Old Gold as the nation's fourth largest seller, this accomplished with next to nothing in advertising and in a startlingly short period of time. Little wonder then that the major firms began examining their advertising and price policies and planning a response.

The counterattack began in early January 1933. For the first time in years, industry leadership was taken by American, perhaps in recognition of Reynolds' blunder in raising prices. Vice-president Vincent Riggio announced that the price for Luckies would be slashed from $6.85 per thousand to $6.00, and promptly Reynolds, L & M, and Lorillard fell in line. Almost immediately some retailers lowered the price of standard brands to two for a quarter, where they had been prior to the 1931 increase, though some tried to retain part of the extra money for themselves, keeping at fifteen cents for a while, or dropping to fourteen.

Riggio claimed success, noting that sales for Twenty Grand and Wings seemed to be declining. He stated that these brands, and others in the ten-cent category, "will pass out of the picture." But price resistance continued, and so Hill and Riggio took the next step. In February, they lowered the price of Luckies to $5.50 per thousand. Once again the other major firms followed, certain this would destroy the ten-centers. Hill asked for and got a new advertising campaign, telling the public that Luckies henceforth would sell for two packs for twenty-three cents. Large-scale retailers, such as supermarkets, were encouraged to go to eleven cents a pack, and even to ten, while several were given rebates as well, if only they would "push" Luckies, Camel, Chesterfield, and Old Gold and either stop carrying the ten-cent brands or display them in out-of-the-way places.

This gambit had mixed results. Sales of Twenty Grand did not collapse in 1933—in fact, they went up, from 2.6 billion in 1932 to over 4 billion. But Wings was hit hard, undergoing a decline to 5.6 billion from 1931's 7.1 billion. White Rolls was almost eliminated as a serious competitor, and never again would sell as many as 100 million smokes.

Was this the result of the price cuts, or some other factor?

Reynolds wasn't certain, but in any case had lost its taste for the struggle. In January 1934, the company raised the price of Camel to $6.10, and the other firms followed. For the rest of the decade that cigarette, Luckies, Chesterfield, and Old Gold would sell for two packs for a quarter. It seemed, at the time, that the economy smokes had won their battle and would continue making inroads against the standard brands.

But the economy part of the market had its own troubles. Beginning in 1932, a flood of new brands came to the market, unlike anything that had been seen since Buck Duke began his crusade for cigarettes a half century earlier. Some lasted for less than a year, while others went on to become quite profitable. This too seemed like Duke's old strategy, and to old-timers, it appeared that a new age of uncertainty was about to begin. The new smokes included Ramrod—advertised as being "mild as a summer breeze"—and Bright Star—"nothing but the very best." Then came One-Eleven, Black and White, Sunshine, Golden Rule, Avalon, Revelation, Sensation, and dozens of others. These tended to rotate in popularity. There were so many of them, with new brands coming to market every month or so, that the consumer hadn't the time to become accustomed to a single brand. Too, the major firms had advertised glamour, while the economies stressed price. A Camel smoker might feel his cigarettes superior in one way or another to Chesterfields, and so keep buying them; the person who smoked Wings did so because of price more than anything else, and he easily could have taken to a Paul Jones or an Avalon if they were available. And this was another part of the problem. The smaller firms and the foreign companies lacked the distribution facilities of the majors; many of their brands were regional and unable to break out of the mold, while even in their "central areas" the economy smokes were not as easy to purchase as the big standards.

The result was uncertain leadership among the economy brands. White Rolls declined steadily after 1932. Wings "peaked" in 1935 and then declined until the end of the 1930s, while Twenty Grand reached a plateau in 1933 and stayed there for the remainder of the decade.

None of the economy brands ever mounted a serious challenge to Camel, Luckies, and Chesterfield, though throughout most of the 1932–40 period at least one such brand reported better sales than Old Gold. Furthermore, by the end of the decade it seemed evident that none of the small American companies would grow any more. Already Larus and Axton-Fisher were in financial difficulty, their new factories in danger of foreclosure. The successor companies of the American Tobacco Trust had been able to withstand their attack. On the other hand, the result of the ten-cent brands had opened the industry more than ever before. Reynolds, American, Liggett & Myers, and Lorillard would remain powerful, but now they were joined at the top by the two British firms, Philip Morris and Brown & Williamson.

Both firms had ten-cent brands on the market in the early 1930s. Stephano, a Philip Morris subsidiary, introduced Marvel in late 1932, and the following year sold 158 million units, far fewer than Twenty Grand or Wings. Still, Philip Morris had capital and a distribution network, while Larus and Axton-Fisher lacked both. Given these, Marvel sales began to climb. By 1939, they surpassed Old Gold, making it the leading economy smoke put out by the independents. As with others of its genre, Marvel couldn't command much brand loyalty, but it was profitable.

Avalon, the Brown & Williamson entry in the ten-cent field, appeared in 1933, shortly after American Tobacco had instituted its second price decrease. Apparently B & W thought the standards were going to a dime, and hoped Avalon would crack the circle. The cigarette grew in popularity, especially when it remained at ten cents while the others went to two for a quarter. Brown & Williamson expanded its territory and provided Avalon with a modest advertising budget. By 1939, their sales were slightly below Old Gold and their profits far better.

Led by the two British firms, the economy cigarettes did well during the Great Depression. By 1939 the ten-cent brands accounted for around 34 billion cigarettes, a shade less than 20 per cent of the market. Still, the British companies were not content with this. While seeking to consolidate their positions with the economy brands, they also pushed forward with standard brands of their own, hoping to challenge Luckies, Camel, and Chesterfield.

Shortly after having entered the economy field with Marvel, Philip Morris readied a smoke to compete with the standard

American brands. Philip Morris English Blend was to sell for
fifteen cents, but in taste, appearance, and advertising, resemble
the twenty-cent foreign smokes. The company created an elegant
brown package and a "high toned" ad campaign, geared to attract an upper-class clientele—and those who liked to think of
themselves as belonging to that group—and women. It was a
sensible idea. Philip Morris believed many Americans would
seek escapism from the dreariness of the depression, in this respect too the movies would help. In 1933 musical comedies and
light romances were quite popular; if James Cagney smoked a
Lucky, what did Fred Astaire extract from his silver case? Certainly not the same kind of smoke. Philip Morris hoped to attract
the Fred Astaire-Cary Grant-Adolphe Menjou-William Powell
set, and not the proletarians. Then, too, the cigarette was
different. Instead of Maryland tobacco, small quantities of which
were found in Camel, Chesterfield, Lucky Strike, and Old Gold,
Philip Morris used Latakia. Not only did it taste different, the tobacco was darker and had a stronger aroma and perhaps this
was more romantic as well.

Philip Morris was introduced soon after American Tobacco
had cut the price of Lucky Strike and the others had followed.
Thus, the new smoke sold for a slightly higher price than those
with which it had been intended to compete. In mid-1933 the
consumer could purchase Twenty Grand or Wings for ten cents,
Camel or Luckies at two packs for a quarter, or Philip Morris at
fifteen cents. Given the price differences, at that time, the new
smoke's future did not appear especially bright.

Still, sales were good, in large part due to an imaginative campaign built around the midget Johnny Roventini, a former page
at the Hotel New Yorker. "Johnny" appeared in most of the ads,
in full-page uniform—complete with pill hat—smiling and indicating by word and appearance that individuals who could
afford to stay at fine hotels should consider his smoke. Philip
Morris ads appeared in the daily press and popular magazines,
but the stress was placed upon such quality outlets as *Vogue* and
Town & Country. The radio ads were most effective. On such
programs as "The Philip Morris Playhouse," Johnny's distinctive
voice would be heard—above a minor bustle—with the words,
"Call for Philip Morris," as though he was paging an individual
at the Ritz or some other such exclusive place.

The campaign was effective, and despite the higher price, sales rose steadily throughout the decade. By 1937 Philip Morris took fourth place in the American market from Old Gold and, in 1939, sold one-third the number of Chesterfield. Not only had Philip Morris cracked the inner circle, but in the late 1930s its success caused the other manufacturers to reconsider their appeals.

Perhaps the best way to counter the economy smokes would be a blunt appeal to elegance, and not the kind of middle-class glamour portrayed in the Camel and Luckies ads, which still featured testimonials by sports figures and Hollywood stars. Johnny was a Philip Morris full-time employee, a living corporate symbol who made guest appearances (always in uniform) and clearly did more for his smokes than a baseball player could for Chesterfield. Philip Morris had combined a foreign smoke with a new form of advertising, and the mixture worked.

If Philip Morris seemed a throwback to the time when the market had been dominated by foreign brands, the Brown & Williamson entry in the standard field, Raleigh, was presented in a fashion similar to that used by Buck Duke in the late nineteenth century. Raleigh featured the giveaway, which had been ended by Camel in 1913.

In late 1932 Brown & Williamson decided upon a new strategy for the American market, one that might be described as the buckshot approach. The firm introduced a wide variety of cigarettes, each with a minimum of advertising, hoping that one or more would capture a small segment of the market, so that in total B & W would become a major force in the industry. The company had a menthol brand to compete with Spud–Kool. Viceroy, a luxury smoke with a filter mouthpiece, did fairly well in the New York market. As for the standard field, B & W "redid" Raleigh.

Raleigh had been introduced with a good deal of fanfare and advertising in 1929 as a twenty-cent brand. It was an English blend, with a Continental style, and, considering the competition, did quite well, with sales of close to a half billion that year. However, the depression killed expensive cigarettes and Raleigh's sales dropped. For a few months it seemed B & W would eliminate the brand, but instead in 1931 it was revamped, given a new blend of tobaccos and a price that made it directly competitive with the standards. To attract buyers, Raleigh offered coupons that could be exchanged for merchandise, one for each pack and four extras per carton. Retailers were given an incentive, then, with Raleighs; they would break open the carton, pocket the four coupons, and, if enough were sold, might turn them in for cameras, pens, cigarette lighters, and similar prizes.

Raleigh sales advanced smartly throughout the decade and in 1939 became the nation's fifth best-selling brand, behind Philip Morris but far ahead of Old Gold, Marvel, and Avalon.

The successes enjoyed by Philip Morris and Raleigh troubled the major firms. Reynolds and Lorillard, however, were content to stand pat, the former deciding to concentrate upon Camel and the latter busy reviving Old Gold and preparing to enter the ten-cent field with Sensation. American Tobacco did respond. By then day-to-day operations were being handled by Vincent Riggio, the vice-president for sales, and Paul Hahn, who was in charge of administration, advertising, and public relations.

Riggio was troubled by the decline of Lucky Strike, which had relinquished industry leadership to Camel in 1934 and showed no sign of regaining it, no matter how much advertising money Hill would pump into the stream. Such things as being in first place were of almost adolescent pride to George Hill, but Riggio and Hahn felt otherwise. Incremental sales that might be realized by further investment were too small to matter much. Luckies was profitable and could be sustained by momentum and consumer loyalty; a major new campaign made little sense, especially for a cigarette that old. What American Tobacco needed was a new product, one that would not compete with Luckies—why cannibalize sales from your own brand?—and was not a ten-center, since Hill would veto one. Riggio did not believe it possible to rival Philip Morris or Raleigh in their fields and, in any case, had little desire or inclination to follow the lead established by others. He needed a new approach, and in the end found one—by adopting an innovation introduced by his son in 1938.

Frank Riggio, Vincent's son, had been a salesman for American Tobacco in the 1920s, and was sales manager in the early 1930s. Chafing under Hill's control and also eager to get out from under his father's shadow, he left American in 1937 to form his own company, Riggio Tobacco. The following year he introduced his first and most popular cigarette, Regent, which sold for twenty cents. Regent claimed to be a "superior blend of fine tobaccos," but its acceptance was due more to two innovations. The cigarettes came in a handsome cardboard crushproof box, which really was more a paper case than anything else; users of other brands would buy one box of Regents and then slip their smokes into it to keep them fresh. Also, Regent was "king size"— 85 mm instead of the familiar 70 mm. There had been cigarettes of this size in the past, but Regent was the first to appear outside of esoteric markets since World War I.

Regent sales were sufficient to keep the company alive, but Frank Riggio lacked funds to create a major distribution network or advertise properly. Of course, his father took note of the cigarette, and decided to imitate it at American.

Riggio planned to base his king-size entry upon an established quality brand, Pall Mall, a Turkish smoke with an English name that Buck Duke had sold in the early years of the century. Pall Mall survived into the postwar period and was considered the class of the American line. But it was barely profitable; George Hill kept it on because he loved the "gorgeous" red package with the gold crest, and the idea that he had the "Cadillac of cigarettes" in his corral.

Hill and Riggio experimented with Pall Mall in the early 1930s, altering the pack's design and even toying with the idea of lengthening the cigarette. In 1936 they abruptly reformulated the blend, eliminating most of the Turkish leaf and replacing it with Bright, in what Riggio called the "modern blend." Pall Mall remained a high-priced, standard-size smoke, but now it was distinctively American in flavor if not in image.

In mid-1939 Riggio decided to take the next step. To the Bright mixture he added flavored White Burley, and the Pall Mall size was boosted to 85 mm. Then he took Pall Mall away from the parent company and placed it into a subsidiary, American Cigarette and Cigar, where it would receive special attention. Shortly thereafter Hahn was named president of Cigarette and Cigar, with a mandate to sell Pall Malls.

As had been the case with Camel in 1913, the time and the

product were right, and so was the man. The United States was coming out of the depression, and people had more money to spend. Pall Mall cost fifteen cents, the same as Philip Morris, but it clearly offered more tobacco. Thus, the buyer was able to obtain quantity along with quality, and perhaps thought the more than 20 per cent additional cigarette was worth the extra two and a half cents or so per pack. Hahn's ad campaign was most effective. "Something is Happening in the Cigarette Business" was one slogan accompanying a picture of distinguished people comparing the length of a Pall Mall with that of a standard brand. The ad went on to say that Pall Mall was produced by the "bulking method," which was never clearly explained, and was "extra mild," due to its length and the mixture. Another slogan was "Modern Design Makes the Big Difference," with pictures of beauty in design—buildings, aircraft, autos, and Pall Mall.

Whatever the reason, Pall Mall sales shot up to 1.5 billion in 1939. Elated, American transformed another of its standard-size brands, Herbert Tareyton, into a king, and saw its sales take off impressively. The other manufacturers followed suit; all planned to introduce kings into their lines during the early 1940s.

Clearly the shape of the industry and the nature of the market had been altered greatly during the 1930s. In part this had resulted from the blunders committed by the major firms in 1931. However, the emergence of the economy brands the following year, and the successes enjoyed by the higher priced cigarettes in the late 1930s, when prosperity was returning, also indicated that the American smoker would find some way to get smokes when he or she was strapped for money, and then spend more once incomes expanded.

It would never be the same as it had been in 1930. That year, Reynolds, American, and Liggett & Myers had 91 per cent of the market, with Camel, Luckies, and Chesterfield holding domain over the smoking world. In 1939, these three firms had only 68 per cent of the American market. Brown & Williamson accounted for close to 11 per cent and Philip Morris another 7 per cent, and both the English companies were ahead of the fourth successor firm to the old American Tobacco Trust, Lorillard, which came in at less than 6 per cent. Between them Axton-

Fisher and Larus had 3.7 per cent of the market, only slightly more than Stephano, which remained under the Philip Morris banner, though its sales were recorded separately. Clearly the insurgents hadn't been able to show stamina or any lasting power, and they would vanish from the scene within the next decade.

The 1930s witnessed the development of many new tendencies for cigarettes. There were economy brands of various kinds, depending upon where one happened to live. The mentholated Spud was joined by other menthol brands—Cigarette Time from Continental (another Philip Morris subsidiary), Menthorets from the small Rosedor Cigarette Company, Snowball out of Paul A. Werner of New York, and Brown & Williamson's Kools. The Winston Cigarette Company put out a smoke for women called Fems, which featured a red mouthpiece that wouldn't show up lipstick. It didn't catch on, and Winston went out of business in less than a year. Hed Kleer Tobacco tried to improve upon Spuds and the other menthols with Hed Kleer, an eucalyptus-flavored smoke. Then there were the cigarettes based upon pipe tobaccos, for those who wanted to switch from the briar—Cookie Jar, Barking Dog, Rum & Maple, and of course, Edgeworth. Lambert Pharmaceutical entered the field with Listerine, for those seeking a different kind of taste. Toward the end of the decade, the Health Cigar Company introduced Sano, which it claimed had 1 per cent nicotine, and Lincoln & Ulmer countered with O-NIC-O, which was supposed to contain even less of the substance.

The low-nicotine brands of that period were supposed to appeal to the same market as the menthols—smokers with sore throats, or those who for one reason or another didn't like the stronger tobaccos. They did not attract a particularly large following, perhaps because of their small advertising budgets, but more likely because in 1940, very few Americans knew much about the long-term health problems identified with smoking. The major fear in this period was loss of wind; athletes weren't supposed to smoke for that reason. Still, almost all the major firms used baseball- and football-player endorsements, and even track stars claimed to use one or another cigarette, some going so far as to swear it helped in their efforts.

With all of this increasing diversity, the industry remained under the control of the giants; only in 1940 there were six of them. This was the perception of several Justice Department lawyers. So in 1940 the tobacco industry was hit with another antitrust suit, which charged the major firms with having engaged in a conspiracy in restraint of trade. It seemed curious to industry insiders; they had been accustomed to such accusations, but the new ones appeared to have far less substance than would have been the case a decade earlier. On the eve of the king-size revolution and World War II, the industry prepared once again to defend itself against Washington.

In 1941 the major companies were convicted of violations of the Sherman Antitrust Act and fined, in total, a quarter of a million dollars. Appeals followed during the next five years, and in the end the Supreme Court sustained the verdict. In fact, the decision meant very little insofar as the industry and the public were concerned. The companies spent far more for legal aid than the sum of the fine, and the courts did not order the companies dissolved or reorganized, as with the American Tobacco Trust case a quarter of a century earlier. In fact, there was less competition in 1946, when the trials finally ended, than there had been six years earlier when the prosecution began.

In essence, the Supreme Court found that the major companies had dominated the industry by preventing the entry of new firms. "Prevention of all potential competition is the natural program for maintaining a monopoly here, rather than any program of actual exclusion," read the majority report. "'Prevention' is cheaper and more effective than any amount of 'cure.'"

The Court was referring to the maintenance of industry position in this last sentence. A decade later the same words would be repeated in a different context, and at that time the results would be far more threatening to the industry than anything the courts hoped to do in the mid-1940s.

VIII

Gone to War

Despite uncertainties about the antitrust suit, the major cigarette manufacturers were optimistic in 1940. The war boom that had commenced the previous year was providing the kind of economic stimulation required to end the depression. This is not to suggest that the nation was back to its pre-1931 prosperity; close to one out of six male adults was out of work in 1940, and double-digit unemployment would not end until mid-1941. Still, the direction of the economy had been altered. Those seeking work in 1940 knew that, given a continuation of war orders, jobs would be opening up.

Naturally, workers and their families were heartened by the prospect of full employment, high wages, and discretionary income. At the same time, however, they were troubled about the war. Hitler controlled most of the European continent and was threatening to invade Great Britain. A Germany victory there was bound to set off an American response in one form or another. During the 1940 presidential campaign, both Franklin Roosevelt and Wendell Willkie promised to maintain the peace, but few thought this possible if Britain fell. Late in 1940 the United States had its first peacetime military draft. In 1939 less than a third of a million personnel had been on active duty; by the end of 1941, there would be two million men in uniform.

Thus, the nation was elated at the prospect of prosperity, and tense regarding the future of peace.

Both sentiments helped cigarette sales, especially those of the major manufacturers. Perhaps an employed and confident work force would turn away from the economy brands and start buying the standards. Impulse smoking, often not possible during the depression, might become fashionable once more. Furthermore, smoking was deemed an acceptable way to alleviate tension; the more perilous the situation, the greater the per capita consumption of cigarettes. Finally, soldiers smoked more than civilians, or at least they did so during World War I, and there seemed no reason to think it would be different in a new war. Tobacco company executives knew the statistics by heart: Cigarette production went from 18 billion in 1914 to 26 billion in 1916, the last full year of peace before President Wilson's war declaration. Two years later, consumption was over 47 billion.

Would this experience be duplicated in another war? If so, the 180 billion cigarettes of 1939 could be a new springboard; by the conclusion of World War II, the industry could be turning out 400 billion smokes. This was the kind of talk in company board rooms during the summer of 1940.

As industry analysts saw it, costs were bound to rise, placing unbearable pressures on profit margins. Within a short period the standard smokes would have to go to fifteen cents a pack, and then higher. But the ten-cent brands would face the same pressures, and since their profit margins were slimmer than those for the standards, they would either have to increase prices or cut back on quality; perhaps the manufacturers would attempt a combination. These developments, occurring in a period of rising prosperity, would benefit the standards. A newly affluent population would not turn down Camel for Twenty Grand in order to save a few cents a pack. Also, their sizes and power would enable the majors to squeeze out the small firms, and in such a way

as to make it appear a natural development—as indeed it would
be—in the eyes of the courts.

This was pretty much the way it happened. While their lawyers prepared briefs for the antitrust suit, executives at the major
tobacco companies earmarked funds for new construction. Advertising firms were told to prepare war-related campaigns. Purchasing agents were ordered to lay in additional stocks of imported leaf, enough to last for the duration of the war. By early
1941, Camel and Chesterfield ads featuring soldiers and sailors
were commonplace. Luckies held back on this score, preparing
for what was heralded as a "surprise campaign" for later in the
year. Meanwhile, those small cigarette firms that used Latakia
and other imported leaf found that there was none to be had; the
majors had cornered the market.

The situation was more complicated for domestic leaf, but
here too conditions favored the major purchasers. Given the
greater demand, one might have anticipated American tobacco
growers would increase their production, but this did not happen. The farmers had learned an important lesson during World
War I, when they had expanded to meet demand, only to face
collapse with the return of peace. From 1914 to 1919, acreage under cultivation had gone from 1.3 million to close to 2 million,
while production rose from one billion pounds to 1.4 billion, and
prices from 9.7 cents per pound to 31.2 cents. Farmers had borrowed heavily in order to set these records. But while profits
were excellent in 1918–19, they provided an insufficient cushion
for the 1921 decline, when the price for a pound of tobacco at
auction fell to 19.5 cents. Declining demand resulted in an acreage cutback to 1.3 million, and production of slightly more than
a billion pounds.

There would be no repeat performance of this economic trag-
edy during and after World War II. Some 2 million acres of
tobacco land were under cultivation in 1939, and this yielded
nearly 1.9 billion pounds at an average price of 15.4 cents. The
farmers were better off than they had been during most of the
1920s. As a result of several New Deal reforms, especially those
involving marketing and production, farmers might receive payments not to produce crops, or at least to hold them back. New
Deal mechanisms were designed to raise the price of farm prod-

ucts. There were no price ceilings in 1940. Instead, the Commodity Credit Corporation functioned to support prices. Thus, the markets of this period were less free and open than those of 1914–15, and the change benefited the tobacco farmers. The growers had expanded production in response to higher prices prior to World War I. A quarter of a century later, the sons of some of these farmers knew they could cut back on production in the face of increased demand—which would cause prices to rise—and in this way make as much profit from a small crop as they could from a large one. Moreover, they could receive payments from Washington for so acting. There would be no repeat of the 1921 collapse, assuming all went as planned, for production would not rise during World War II.

The plan worked, though it took a while before the farmers received their rewards. The tobacco growers refused to increase their acreage in 1940, and instead let their fields lie fallow. The average price of leaf at auction went up to 16.1 cents from 15.4 cents the previous year, as a result of the smaller plantings and the increased tempo of company purchases for inventory. The farmers tightened the screws in 1941, planting 100,000 fewer acres and harvesting 200,000 fewer pounds. Prices responded by shooting to 26.4 cents. The Office of Price Administration came into being the following year, but by then the growers had their victory and were content to permit a modest increase in plantings and production. But the price, set just prior to the advent of the OPA, was 36.9 cents.

Assured of a high price by both government regulation and the nature of the market, the farmers sought to consolidate and strengthen their advantage. They lobbied for increases, with petitions accompanied by veiled threats of production cutbacks. For a while the government was able to keep prices in line, but in the end the OPA capitulated, and the farmers were better off than ever before.

In 1944 some growers revolted against increases in their costs of transacting business and asked for still further price adjustments. They closed their warehouses and refused to take leaf to market until and unless their wishes were satisfied. The government gave in—the demand for smokes during the war was such that they had no other choice. In 1944 production was close to 2 billion pounds, while the price reached 42 cents, both of which were records.

As was expected, all the manufacturers passed cost increases on to customers, always after having received necessary government approval. But the major firms were sensitive to the ways such advances would affect the antitrust suit, while at the same time seeing in the price increases a way to smash the economy cigarettes, and to do so within the context of law and the public good.

In mid-1940 the standards' wholesale price had increased little more than 4 per cent; in contrast, the economies rose over 15 per cent. In addition, the government increased its tax from $3.25 to $3.50 late in 1942, and this had a larger proportional effect upon the economies than it did on the standards.

The retail price of standard brands rose to fifteen cents a pack by early 1942, when the OPA attempted a freeze at current levels. Additional advances were permitted, however, so that by the end of the war Camel, Luckies, and Chesterfield sold for twenty cents a pack. In this same period the economy smokes went to fifteen cents, or around the same percentage increase as the standards.

The prosperity of the war years worked in favor of the standards. In addition, American, Reynolds, and the other major firms had excellent distribution networks and advertising, while the economy smokes lacked both. Finally, there was the matter of tobacco inventories. Stated simply, the smaller firms lacked them, while the major ones had enough tobacco by 1942 to last for the duration. Thus, Luckies, Camel, and the other twenty-centers tasted pretty much the same in 1945 as they had in 1941, aside from substitutions of additives. This was not so with the economy brands, some of which were forced to use scraps, stems, and leaves that in previous years they might have discarded. The standards used different flavoring elements to make up for shortages of sugar, licorice, anise, and the like; the economy brands employed additives to mask the taste of their inferior tobaccos.

Experienced smokers didn't have to be told what was happening; their taste buds provided all the information needed. When given the choice between Camel and Marvels, the latter selling at five cents a pack cheaper, the fairly affluent smoker usually selected the standard—providing it was available. This showed up in sales. Those for the three major brands rose by over 37 per cent in the war period. In contrast, sales of economy brands were cut in half.

From the time of the Japanese attack on Pearl Harbor to the end of the war, there were recurrent rumors that cigarettes would have to be rationed. While there were spotty shortages of some brands in late 1942 and early 1943, the vast majority of Americans not only had all the smokes they wanted in this period, but a full selection of brands. Part of the reason for this was the privileged position of the industry in wartime; as much as almost any other product, cigarettes were considered vital in time of emergency. Just as General Pershing had called upon Americans for tobacco in 1918, so Douglas MacArthur told the employees of Wright Aeronautical, who had raised $10,000 for the war effort, to use the money to purchase smokes for his troops. "The entire amount should be used to buy American cigarettes which, of all personal comforts, are the most difficult to obtain here." President Roosevelt declared tobacco an essential crop, and the draft boards gave deferments to tobacco growers, just as they did to wheat and corn farmers. The soldiers and sailors did get their smokes. Total industry sales went from 218 billion in 1941 to 257 billion the following year, but the military's share almost doubled, rising to 21.7 billion from 11.5 billion in the same period.

The major companies scrambled for this portion of the business, out of patriotism and self-interest. Military sales were tax free, and even while the companies shaved their profits, they still did quite well in this area. If one went by the raw figures—a dangerous assumption as will be seen—the military men smoked twice as many cigarettes as their civilian counterparts. So the major firms wanted this market, not only for what it could do for sales and profits while the war was on, but in order to create brand loyalty for after the peace was signed. It had worked in World War I, and there seemed no reason to think the sons of the doughboys would behave any differently than their fathers.

The major companies adopted the same strategies, focusing their advertising on military themes. "Keep 'em Smoking," read one Chesterfield blast; "Our Fighting Men Rate the Best!" Reynolds retaliated with "Camels are the Favorite! In the Army

. . . In the Navy . . . In the Marine Corps . . . In the Coast Guard!" To this, Chesterfield responded with an appeal to women, showing actresses in various service uniforms, and the slogan, "His Cigarette and Mine," which may have prompted Camel's picture of a flyer, smoke between firm lips. "You Want Steady Nerves When You're Flying Uncle Sam's Bombers Across the Ocean [Names withheld for defense purposes and national security]." But the most impressive effort was put forth by Hill, who still had control over what went into advertising at American.

For years, Hill and others at American had known the Luckies pack was a drawback. The dark green color did not appeal to women, and tests showed men didn't like it either. It lacked the "cleanliness" of the white Camel and Chesterfield wrappers, or the richness of the warm brown of Philip Morris. Earlier Hill had gone to great lengths to popularize the pack, even manipulating the fashion industry through Bernays and others. But he could not find a graceful way to alter it.

The war presented him with the opportunity. In 1942 the green pack was replaced by a white one of the same basic design, with a new slogan: "Lucky Strike Green Has Gone to War!" The implication was that American Tobacco had stopped using the color so as to make the ink available to the armed forces, perhaps for camouflage paint. In fact this was not the case; Lucky Strike green was not needed by any branch of the defense effort, but in terms of advertising impact it was a brilliant idea. Camel and Chesterfield might employ military themes in their ads, Hill seemed to be saying, but Luckies was making the real sacrifice, not only providing enjoyment for the boys in uniform, but actually helping them win the war by altering its wrapper. The Luckies appeal was highlighted by the previously mentioned slogan—"L.S./M.F.T.—Lucky Strike Means Fine Tobacco," to which was later added "So Round, So Firm, So Fully Packed. So Free and Easy on the Draw." The initials sounded like a military Morse code signal, and the description of the cigarette itself had vague sexual connotations geared at drawing nudges from the soldiers and sailors, with implications that a Lucky might do when women were not available.

All the major brands made plays for the post exchange market.

Early in 1942 Old Gold announced that henceforth every man in uniform would be allowed to purchase three cartons of the smokes for the price of one on paydays. If he smoked a pack a day, given the current post exchange prices—15 cents a pack in the continental United States—the serviceman would have enough smokes for a month for $1.50 out of his $21 salary. Of course, many smokers used more than a pack a day, and so Old Gold must have anticipated a few additional sales, at 15 cents on base and 20 cents in the civilian market. By late 1942 the other standard brands were making similar offers, but all were ended a few months later, perhaps because the firms thought it no longer necessary, or because servicemen could count on receiving free packs at canteens, and these were paid for by civilian groups. Some brands took to "adopting" an Army or Navy base for a week, providing a set number of free cigarettes for that period. Retail outlets did the same. Throughout the war, enterprising servicemen knew they could count on free, or at the very least cheap, standard smokes.

Soldiers received free cigarettes in their field rations. Along with the dehydrated soup and lemonade mix and the can of Spam was a small pack of smokes—four cigarettes in the K pack, three in the C—plus a matchbook. None of the major companies thought much of this market, so the way was open for a small producer and a new brand.

Larus had introduced Chelsea in mid-1941, with little fanfare or hope for market share. It was an economy brand, which sold at fifteen cents for a pack of twenty-four—the purchaser of Chelsea paid the same price as he might for one of the standards, but received four extra smokes per pack. Larus believed it would gain a small following in the upper South, enough to make the effort worthwhile. Along with other manufacturers, Larus put in a bid for military orders and was surprised when it was accepted. By mid-1942, all the company's efforts were being employed to create machines to package the C and K ration smokes. Larus developed a laminated glassine inner wrap to replace scarce foil, which later on was licensed to the major companies. Within a year of Pearl Harbor, soldiers were receiving their Chelseas in the field, and Larus had become the major supplier of smokes to the military.

When soldiers in the Pacific theater of operations complained their packs became soggy in the damp climate, Larus placed Chelseas in converted Planter's Peanuts cans—"seventy-fives" as they were known—and within one year had shipped close to 7 million of them. Larus began advertising the brand nationally as well, and civilian sales were surprisingly strong—2 billion in 1944, going to twice that in the following year. By then several industry analysts had observed that the major firms had committed a blunder in ignoring the military market and permitting Larus to accustom a generation of servicemen to its brand. A poll conducted in 1945 indicated that Chelsea would be around after the war had ended, and soon challenge the standards. This did not transpire. Instead, the large manufacturers increased their military sales, so that by the time peace was declared the soldiers and sailors were getting all the Camels, Chesterfields, and Luckies they wanted.

The Chelsea phenomenon was indicative of industry-wide caution in this period. Advertising expenses rose only slightly during the war, while marketing drives seemed to lack their old aggressive edge. In part this was due to the antitrust suit, but it also resulted from the kind of uncertainty that troubled most American businessmen.

How long will the war last? How dependable are our sources of raw materials? These were the two key questions. All the major firms had the need to stockpile tobacco in 1939–41, when they were buying heavily in the face of rising prices. But their commitments indicated differing views as to the nature of the war.

Reynolds, the largest firm with $277 million in sales in 1939, gambled on a short struggle, after which tobacco prices would come down sharply, as they had in 1920–21. The company purchased relatively little leaf for its stockpile, or at least much less than might have been anticipated given its size. American Tobacco, a close second with $271 million in sales, was much more aggressive, thinking the war would last for several years. Furthermore, the company wanted to have a good supply of leaf for Pall Mall if that new smoke turned out to be as successful as Riggio thought it might. Riggio made a large commitment to inventory in 1940 and 1941, so much so that the auctioneers noted that American was outbidding all others for White Burley and Bright. This provided Hill with one of the last of his advertising ideas. In 1942 he commissioned several famous artists to paint pictures of life in the fields, always featuring the leaf. These were reprinted in magazines and newspapers with the slogan, "Lucky Strike Means Fine Tobacco," which Hill later adapted for the L.S./M.F.T. campaign. He also helped create a radio campaign, designed to spotlight L. A. "Speed" Riggs, a tobacco auctioneer. Riggs would use his colorful auction spiel—which sounded like a jumble of syllables—as though to indicate a real auction, and would end with the words, "Sold American!" to indicate that the company dominated the bidding for fine tobaccos. Riggs also was featured in print ads, and soon became almost as familiar as Philip Morris' Johnny.

Liggett & Myers followed the American lead, perhaps in the hope that a long war would enable it to rise from its third position in the industry—$233 million in sales for 1939. Lorillard and Philip Morris entertained no such aspirations, with $80 million and $73 million respectively. Still, Lorillard did purchase heavily for Sensation and in the hope of an Old Gold sales revival while Philip Morris concentrated upon the stockpiling of imported leaf.

Thus, Reynolds went against the industry's drift, apparently willing to take the risk. Such action was not unusual at this company, which still turned out a single cigarette, refused to enter the economy field, or even consider king-size brands. Reynolds' fortune rode with Camel, in 1940 the nation's best seller.

This turned out to be a mistake. All the leading brands advanced in 1941, but Camel less than the others. Once again, for the first time in eight years, Luckies moved into the top position, while Liggett & Myers initiated new advertising programs for Chesterfield, and Philip Morris continued to grow more rapidly than any of the leading standards. In 1942 close to 60 billion Luckies were sold, against 56 billion Camels and 41 billion Chesterfields, while Philip Morris was in fourth place with 23 billion.

When Camel had engaged in its battles with Luckies in the early 1930s, fresh ad campaigns had been able to rectify the balance. The situation was different in early 1943, however. Demand for tobacco far outstripped production, and given the na-

ture of price controls, Reynolds couldn't bid the price upward
and so obtain additional supplies. Instead, the company had to
settle for its allocation and draw the rest from a meager inventory. The only alternative was to settle for waste tobacco, and
Reynolds hardly would do that. So in late 1942, the firm began
rationing Camels to retailers. At first this went unnoticed, but by
spring 1943, Camels were in short supply in most parts of the
country. This was not the case with the competing brands, so
smokers began making the necessary switches.

Camel did have scarcity value; but the OPA kept prices from
being adjusted upward, so as to mitigate the situation somewhat.
As it was, Camel sales for 1943 came to less than 58 billion, and
Reynolds' gross was $414 million. Now Luckies and American
were in first place by wide margins—68 billion for the cigarette,
$529 million for the company. Liggett & Myers posted $294 million in sales, while Chesterfield sold a record 50 billion units.

The situation worsened in 1944, when military sales reached
close to 85 billion, a quarter of total production and, given the
situation, a market that could not be cut. By late summer, retailers had to settle for from 60 to 80 per cent of previous shipments for Luckies and Chesterfield—and 40 per cent for Camel.
The newspapers were beginning to feature stories about "volun-
tary rationing" plans and of how some retailers were meeting the
problem. As expected, many broke the price barrier by selling
scarce brands for premium prices on a widening black market—
fifty cents for Camel, forty cents for Luckies and Chesterfield
were considered bargains in New York and Chicago. Others sold
only to old customers. A large number of stores would sell cigarettes for only one or two hours a day—long lines would appear
an hour or so before the sales period. One no longer could
purchase standard smokes by the carton; a kindly retailer might
sell three packs at a time to an old friend, but at a black market
price. In small towns loosies went for a nickel apiece.

Throughout most of 1944, Camel stood in third place, as
Chesterfield went to second and Luckies remained the leader.
But the combination of a bumper crop and the exhaustion of
L & M's reserves enabled Camel to make up some lost ground.

As it was, all the major brands suffered sharp declines in sales
to civilians, with Camel performing more poorly than the others.

Luckies reported 64 billion, Camel 49 billion, with Chesterfield at 48 billion. Due to shortages Philip Morris faltered, selling 28 billion, while Old Gold came in at 15 billion, despite the success of a new advertising campaign claiming that "apple honey" gave it an "edge on mildness." (In fact, the company used apple extract as a flavoring in a desperation move; the older and more conventional additives had become unobtainable or prohibitive in price.)

At the same time, the economy cigarettes continued to decline. Only 9.5 billion of them were sold in 1944, down from the 24 billion of 1941. At that, Marvel accounted for close to half the total. Still, sales for that cigarette were below those posted in 1942, and Stephano, its manufacturer, was in bad financial trouble, seeking a merger, preferably with a cash-rich firm.

Axton-Fisher, the leading independent in the early 1930s, had already taken that path. In 1942 the management sold out to the Giannini interests of California, which were closely associated with the Bank of America. The Gianninis had visions of making Axton-Fisher a major firm, by dropping Twenty Grand and Spud —the depression smokes—and creating a new brand that would compete with the standards. With great fanfare and a large advertising budget A-F introduced Fleetwood, which was designed to sell at fifteen cents a pack with the slogan, "A cleaner, finer smoke." Fleetwood never amounted to much, in part due to the nature of the market, a clumsy ad effort, and the simple fact that even had all gone well, one hardly could make cigarettes without tobacco—and A-F's warehouses were almost bare. The Gianninis held on for a year and then decided to give up on their dreams of creating another R. J. Reynolds. Axton-Fisher was purchased by Philip Morris in 1944 for what amounted to the book value of its assets with nothing for good will and trademarks. Philip Morris used what little good tobacco remained in the warehouses for its own brands. Whatever was left was used to produce Spud; the menthol flavoring would mask the inferior leaf, and there was a chance that this kind of cigarette might catch the public fancy some day. Fleetwood and Twenty Grand were discontinued.

The all-out boom of 1943 and the bust of 1944, the continued need to ship standard brands to the servicemen and the increasing demand in the civilian market, combined with the nature of

Office of Price Administration regulations, resulted in the creation of a large number of new brands in late 1944 and early 1945.

The OPA was firm in its insistence that cigarette prices not be raised. Thus, the standards retailed at twenty cents and the economies at fifteen, even while they fetched more than twice that on the black market, and while increases in raw materials and labor costs cut deeply into profit margins. Were it not for the antitrust suit, the leading firms might have attempted to innovate. As it was, they preferred to stand pat with what they had. This left the way clear for small companies to experiment with new products. For a while it seemed a replay of the early 1930s, when Axton-Fisher introduced its economy smokes, stealing the march from the Big Three plus One.

The OPA controlled the prices of existing cigarette brands, but was in a quandary regarding how to treat new ones. There was no difficulty with Fleetwood, the first of the new brands to appear during the war. Axton-Fisher set the price below that of the standards and in line with the economies, and this seemed antiinflationary and reasonable. What might have happened if the company had fixed the price at twenty cents? Was Fleetwood the equal of Camel in terms of quality? How would the OPA handle such a situation? For that matter, A-F might have pegged the price at forty cents, claiming that Fleetwood merited it, and then entered into a prolonged debate with the OPA over methods of determining quality. Were the costs of tobacco and manufacturing the keys? If so, how did advertising fit into the equation? What were the values assigned to brand names, distribution networks, and management? Clearly the matter never could be resolved, but in the case of Fleetwood, to the relief of the OPA, it did not become necessary.

Sol C. Korn of Brooklyn recognized the dilemma. He had entered the tobacco business in the days of the Trust, carving a small niche for himself in fine pipe blends. In 1944 he was the president of Cambridge Tobacco, Dover-Hall, and Stewart-Allen, all of which produced pipe tobaccos, and he also headed Fleming-Hall, a distributor for cigars and Ban, a mint used to mask "smoker's breath." Korn had a goodly supply of pipe tobacco, the market for which was stagnant and the prices fixed by

OPA decree. Korn knew this tobacco could be used to produce cigarettes; in fact, Axton-Fisher had turned out some Mapletons for him in 1942, prior to the Giannini takeover. Now he decided to go into production for himself. In late 1944 he transformed some of his pipe blends into cigarettes—Stratford, Jameson's Irish Mixture, Cambridge Arms, and Coffee-Tone (flavored with coffee extract), and others. All were priced to sell for nineteen cents, assuring an excellent profit for the smokes, which were made of cheap tobacco and strongly flavored additives. Korn then awaited an OPA protest. None came. By January 1945 he was producing 4 million smokes a day, and preparing to sell stock in his growing cigarette company to the public.

F. & E. Soter, another small New York firm, entered the field around this time. Fred Soter purchased three reconditioned cigarette machines and transformed his pipe blends into Lady Hamilton, which he priced at forty cents. Unlike Korn, who did not advertise and used his existing distribution company, Soter did place small ads in newspapers and later signed an exclusive contract with Gimbel's, which took all he could produce. Again, there was no protest from the OPA.

Other brands and firms followed. Alliance Cigar transformed some of its Havana leaf into two brands, Khakies and Puppies, each going for forty cents. The Tobacco Blending Company of Louisville sold Melody. G. A. Georgopolous of New York had Duo-Blend (sold exclusively at the Harvard Club and the Ritz-Carleton at a half dollar) and young Riggio added Air-Flow to his Regent line.

By early spring the OPA began serving notice on the manufacturers that an investigation was being planned. But one never transpired, for the war ended all such talk. The small firms went out of the cigarette business, having banked their windfall profits.

The Big Three plus One reported record sales in 1945, but were unable to translate these into profits. They might have been able to overcome the problems had they been willing to market inferior smokes at premium prices. This they would not do.

Their drop in profits had an impact upon marketing, in part resulting from the picture after the record sales push of 1943.

Short of tobacco and unable to meet existing demand, all of the leading firms decided to make drastic cuts in advertising.* From the $38 million spent for magazine, newspaper, and radio ads that year, industry outlays in 1945 fell to slightly more than $24 million, the lowest since the early 1920s by almost any measure.

Significantly—or it might have been interpreted as such—the decline seemed to have no appreciable impact upon sales or brand preferences. Industry leaders attributed this to shortages and related dislocations, and they prepared to return to splashy, expensive campaigns once the war was over. By 1949, ad costs were more than double those of 1945.

Was this necessary? By the early postwar period it might have been thought that brand loyalties were strong, especially for the three leading standards, which after all had been around for more than a quarter of the century. Furthermore, although shortages vanished in 1947, when some prices actually fell due to competitive pressures, demand for cigarettes remained strong; though advances hardly matched those of 1939–45, there was no decline such as had been experienced after World War I. Indeed, even without mounting a major ad campaign, Camel was able to recapture those smokers who had switched to other brands due to wartime shortages. It ran almost even with Luckies in 1947 and was back in first place two years later, followed, as usual, by Chesterfield, Philip Morris, and Old Gold, in that order.

One of the more interesting developments of this period was in the area of military sales. In 1945, when there had been more than 12 million men and women in uniform, these tax-free sales peaked at 65 billion, or over 5,400 when calculated on a per capita basis. The military man and woman, then, smoked fifteen cigarettes per day on the average. Then came disarmament. By 1947, there were only 1.6 million Americans in the armed forces, and that year the military took 34 billion cigarettes, for a per capita figure of 21,250, or fifty-eight smokes per person each day.

---

* It might have been worse. Early in 1944 there developed a shortage of cigarette paper, most of which had been imported from France prior to the war. Harry Straus of Ecusta Paper started a crash program to develop an American industry, and his work made possible the continued production of standard brands in 1944 and 1945.

Servicemen of the early postwar period did not develop a sudden craving for close to four times the amount of cigarettes puffed by their counterparts who experienced combat stress. In fact, there is every reason to believe that smoking among servicemen actually declined in this era, if for no other reason than that the tobacco companies stopped distributing free smokes with an open hand. Too, during the war, many men in uniform purchased cartons of standard brands to give to their relatives in civilian life, and this practice became less prevalent after the war when shortages were ended. Finally, calmer periods in the past always resulted in a cut in smoking, and this seemed to have happened in the second half of the 1940s, when the per capita figure for civilians fell somewhat.

How, then, is one to explain the high military sales, especially to soldiers who served in Europe as part of the army of occupation? The answer is both simple and quite memorable for those who were in Germany and other parts of the continent in those years. Cigarettes no longer were mere smokes, to be consumed in a habitual fashion. Rather, the major companies—American, Reynolds, and Liggett & Myers—were turning out a currency system for the liberated areas.

A quasi-barter economy had developed in Europe shortly after the D-Day invasion in June 1944. People no longer trusted their currency, which could become worthless in the event of an Allied victory. Nor were they confident that the American-sponsored scrip would have value—what if the Germans pushed the Allies back into the Channel? So they exchanged goods and services without benefit of currency, by barter arrangements.

Not even the simplest commercial dealings were possible under such an arrangement, as the Europeans soon realized. Some common currency was needed, and by early 1945, one was found in American cigarettes—Luckies, Camel, and Chesterfield in particular.

These smokes possessed all the basic qualifications for a currency. They were uniform, easily recognized, universally accepted, almost impossible to counterfeit and, in the beginning at least, had scarcity value as well. In fact, the cigarette currency in some ways was superior to one based upon the paper scrip, in that it had as its foundation a product with intrinsic value, and one that was self-liquidating.

At first there were few cigarettes in relation to goods, and so three or four smokes would purchase a fine piece of china, and a couple of cartons fetched a quality camera. After a while Europe would be flooded with the smokes, and cigarette inflation would set in. At that point the owner of a pack would be tempted to smoke his holdings, and in this way cut down on the supply of currency. Thus, there would be no need for the authorities to withdraw this form of money. Rather, it would go up in smoke, which, as will be seen, actually happened.

The cigarette currency might have been short-lived were it not for an action taken by Secretary of the Treasury Henry Morgenthau in early 1945, when he presented the Soviets with a set of engraving plates for Allied occupation money. The Soviets promptly printed the occupation marks in wholesale amounts, using them to pay off their troops, purchase goods from the Germans, and in some cases even to bribe Allied soldiers. In the early occupation period, Soviet troops would buy fountain pens from Americans for $400 in the scrip, while wrist watches fetched over $1,000. It wasn't long before the authorities cracked down on these practices. In mid-1945 the Army noted that occupation troops were sending home twice as much money as they received in pay. Clearly a good deal of the extra funds came from sales to the Russians and others. Such remittances were forbidden, and at that point the cigarette currency came into its own.

American soldiers stationed overseas could purchase a pack of standard-brand cigarettes for five cents; after a while the price went to two for fifteen, this at a time when American civilians paid between twenty and twenty-five cents for a pack. Ten or so cigarettes could purchase a good meal—or an evening with a woman. Waiters and taxi drivers preferred a two-cigarette tip to occupation scrip. There seemed to be nothing the Germans possessed that could not be had for cigarettes.

For their part, the Germans would exchange American cigarettes for shoes, lodging, or faked papers. Thus, the Americans poured their smokes into the German economy, and then the Germans used them, among themselves, to exchange for the goods needed to survive. In fact it was a one-way transfer on the American side; a German hardly would try to purchase a pair of army shoes from a sergeant for a carton of cigarettes. But once the smokes and the shoes entered the German economy, ratios between them were easy to develop.

The system worked well, but by late 1946 the military government considered it intolerable, especially after several congressional investigations. The Army acted on two fronts simultaneously, in the hope of bringing some form of regularity to the market.

First, the Army established official barter exchanges, to which soldiers and civilians could bring goods for which they would receive "barter units." The nature of the market did little to improve American-German relations. The Germans would bring their heirlooms and valuables to market, where they would be evaluated by military personnel. Thus, a silver tea service might be "priced" at 400 units, an offer the German might consider unfair. Since the Germans usually brought nonhomogeneous items to the market—one-of-a-kind valuables—such suspicions were created daily. As for the American soldiers, they traded standard products, such as toothbrushes, pens, and other post exchange purchases at the market, and knew the prices in barter units in advance. Cigarettes, of course, were a major item. By means that no one at the time understood or cared to explain, the price was set at twenty barter units a carton.

The GIs visited the exchanges to compare prices there with those on the black market. Clearly the latter was preferable, and so few traded their goods for barter units. Recognizing the problem, the Army made a stab at currency revaluation. The price of cigarettes was raised to forty-five barter units, and at this, some smokes came to market. Enthused, the military hiked the price to ninety-five. Now the soldiers fought to get into the exchange with their cigarettes. As for the Germans, they were irate, for now they were getting fewer smokes for their precious cameras, furs, porcelain, and the like.

The Army also noted a strange development: more cigarettes were being brought to market than were being sold at the PXs. This led to a new investigation.

The military government learned that once the price for a car-

ton went to ninety-five units, the PXs were inundated with soldiers seeking all the smokes they could get. The stores responded
by rationing the number of packs a GI could purchase—initially
to twelve a week. Thus, at a time when American civilians were
able to buy all the cigarettes they wanted, there were shortages
overseas, in a striking reversal of the situation of 1944–45.

The soldiers knew what to do. They would ask relatives and
friends to send them cartons of smokes on a regular basis. These
cost more at home than they did at the military stores, of course,
but, since they were destined for servicemen, did not require a
tax stamp. A pack of Camels obtained this way fetched a dime.
In Berlin, the same pack could be exchanged for almost five
barter units. A sterling silver tea service went for 500 units at the
Berlin Barter Market. By mid-1947 there was a continuous flow
of cigarettes from America to Europe, and tea services and the
like the other way.

Estimates vary, but the post office claimed that some 2.5 million pounds of tobacco products a month were being sent to Germany alone. Several small shipping companies appeared to cater
to this market, and they advertised openly in Army publications.
The government scarcely could object to shipments from home,
at least not before preparing the way in Congress. Not until late
August were postal regulations adjusted to prevent the companies from performing their services, and the cartons from
home were banned soon after. Enterprising Americans now
shifted to bulk tobacco shipments, which were not forbidden for
another year. Finally, in the winter of 1948, the Army lifted the
rationing system at the PXs, and the cartons and leaf stopped
flowing across the Atlantic. At the same time the barter market
in Berlin quietly closed its doors, signal proof of the failure of
fixed currency rates, even when based upon the cigarette.

By then the soldiers had developed new wrinkles in the system. Cigarettes would be sold for lira and francs, and these cur-
rencies would be sent home, to be exchanged for dollars at the
official rate. Soldiers would ship fine art—purchased with cartons
of cigarettes—to their families, who often sold them for hard
dollars. After a while the soldiers had to pay duty on the shipments. In all honesty they would declare that a small painting
had been obtained for twenty cartons of Luckies—at the PX rate

that came to little more than twenty dollars. In fact, the object's true value could be determined by the black market rate—many times that rate—or even the exchange rate established at the Barter Market.

Some of these ploys were unmasked during courts-martial in 1948 and after. Doubtless there were others, never discovered. Most were based upon that universal currency in the Europe of 1945–48, the American standard cigarette.

Other potential scandals were overlooked. While Secretary of State James Byrnes and Senator Tom Connally were meeting with the Russians in Berlin in late 1946, Mrs. Byrnes and Mrs. Connally were busily purchasing cigarettes at the PX, and then taking them to the Barter Market, to obtain antiques and other valuables at bargain prices. This was perfectly legal and legitimate. But the following year planeloads of senators and representatives set down in Berlin. Ostensibly, the legislators were there to obtain information for the purpose of framing new measures. But always there was the visit to the Barter Market, to exchange cheap cigarettes for works of art and antiques. The Germans saw this and were irate. Hermann Goering had plundered the galleries of Europe in the first half of the decade, they said. Now the Americans are trying to do the same in Berlin. Of course, the two developments were quite different, but the Germans did see a similarity. Still, they continued to use the cigarette currency as the best available. In February 1947 the Hamburg police offered a reward for information regarding the murder of a young man. Conventional money wouldn't do. Instead, the police set the reward at 1,000 standard American cigarettes.

It came to an end in 1949. By then the German economy was well on the way to restoration, while currency reforms provided that country with a stable paper money. American visitors to Germany in 1948 had noted that cigarettes still were used as currency, but they no longer were being "clipped" or "sweated," by which they meant that the smokes were not cut down or relieved of small amounts of tobacco, which were then used to create new cigarettes. Also, cigarette inflation had set in; the product was actually being smoked, not only by Americans but by Germans as well. A Chesterfield introduced into the system in early 1947 might have been smoked a year later, having passed through a score of hands in the interim. It had served a useful purpose, though one hardly considered by Liggett & Myers at the time of manufacture.

Tobacco had been used as currency by the Indians. Fine leaf was a prime barter item in Virginia during the seventeenth and eighteenth centuries. The Germans of the late 1940s would have understood the Southerners of the early 1700s, in this respect if in no other. For they were growing tobacco in flower pots—or at least trying to do so—and busily working at sweating and clipping.

Bella Spewack, the American writer, visited Germany in this period, and took note of the cigarette currency. "The American dollar is still loudly eloquent in a Europe which has little faith in its own currency," she wrote. But it was not supreme. "The American cigarette, which has intrinsic value and is therefore more stable, is the noisiest coin of the realm today."

IX

Hitchhikers for a King

By most measures the cigarette industry seemed back to what might be termed "normal" by late 1947. The military market remained an important aberration, but the tobacco companies knew what to anticipate from it and so could plan accordingly. More important was the fact that most of the men and women who served during the war were out of uniform and employed or in schools collecting payments under the GI Bill of Rights. They appeared to be smoking as much as ever.

There would be no depression following World War II, or even a return to economic uncertainties. In fact the economy was booming. Rather than worrying about declines and a return to the breadlines, Americans were troubled by accelerating inflation, a shortage of consumer goods, and forecasts of more of the same.

This had not been anticipated. Rather, industry and government economists had looked for a repeat of the post-World War

I experience, when the gross national product peaked in 1920 and then plummeted, with the old levels not matched for five years.

After the first war there had been fears of a new anticigarette campaign and a revival of the cigar and pipe, but there were opportunities too—more Americans to be won over to cigarettes, the fresh new female market, and the exploitation of the standard brands, which had just begun when the war erupted. In the end, the positive elements proved more important than the negative. The anticigarette movement fizzled, and the cigar and pipe continued to hold only limited appeal for smokers. The cigarette industry still was young and vigorous in the 1920s.

There would be no sales or production declines following World War II; the cigarette habit was too deeply ingrained to be altered. The blossoming economy worked in favor of a strong industry; so did a major alteration in the way people purchased their cigarettes. The old ways survived; loosies continued to be sold to youngsters just starting to smoke, and most people got their packs from the old outlets. But increasingly Americans purchased smokes by the carton. These sales took place in candy and drugstores, as well as at tobacconists. Also, supermarkets and department stores carried cartons, which were sold at discounted prices. The rise of carton sales was important, indicating not only a commitment to individual brands, but a rising standard of living. So was the increase of impulse buying from the nation's vending machines, of which there were over a half a million by the end of the decade.

These changes in distribution worked in favor of the habit. The open carton at home, the fact that smokers rarely were far from a fresh pack at work or play, and the economic strength of the nation made cigarettes as easy to acquire as a drink of water.

There were no external problems for the industry to overcome in this period. Cigar sales remained poor as they were increasingly identified with older people. Nor were there signs of a renewed antismoking crusade in the late 1940s. Instead, there was what might be termed a "cautious hedonism" in the air. Americans wanted to enjoy themselves after years of economic depression and war. Smoking was part of that enjoyment. So were families and children. The industry leaders looked at the economic and demographic statistics and liked what they saw. The baby boom of the late 1940s and early 1950s would be transformed into a smoking boom eighteen or so years later. America was a prosperous and growing nation. There seemed no reason to assume that cigarettes would not grow with it.

This was the problem. The manufacturers had no new markets to conquer, and so could not anticipate a repeat of the growth they had enjoyed in the 1920s. Middle-class teen-agers had been won over. Was the smoking age to be pushed back to fifteen or below? Perhaps, but it didn't seem probable. An estimated three out of every four adult males were regular or occasional cigarette smokers, and this percentage didn't seem capable of being increased. Further converts from the ranks of cigar, pipe, and plug users weren't likely. On the other hand, less than half as many women as men smoked cigarettes.

The per capita consumption of cigarettes in 1947 was 2,569—128 packs a year for every man, woman, and child. This was two and a half times the figure for 1929, the last peacetime year during which Americans enjoyed prosperity. How much higher could the figure go? Industry estimates were that the "average regular smoker" consumed a pack and a half a day. Could such people be won over to two packs or more? Might the light smokers—those who consumed less than a pack a day—be lured into using more than that amount?

Increases in these areas would be difficult to achieve. A pack of standard smokes cost around twenty-two cents in 1947, and so represented no great economic problem for most middle-class Americans. Individuals who wanted to smoke weren't prevented from doing so by price, but rather because they chose to maintain their own levels of consumption. There was no indication that price cuts would increase sales significantly or, for that matter, that small increments in the price of cigarettes would cause the vast majority of users to smoke less than they did.

Perhaps something could be done to make the product more attractive. No one in the industry seriously thought the standards could be challenged. Luckies, Camel, and Chesterfield were considered as much a part of the national scene and as solid, stable, and lasting as Ford, Chevrolet, and Plymouth. Their relative rankings might change, but these three standards seemed certain to lead the industry for the foreseeable future. Similarly, there appeared little chance that a new version of the economies would be developed, or that the Turkish and other foreign blends would make significant comebacks. In 1947 the small market for such esoterica as mentholated, low-nicotine, and filtered cigarettes appeared neither interesting nor capable of expansion. The industry expected little from these sources.

In contrast, the king-size smokes did offer possibilities for change, growth, and perhaps would enhance profits as well. The revamped Pall Mall had been selling beyond expectations as America had prepared to enter the war, more than 4.5 billion in 1941. The interest in the larger cigarettes spilled over into the other American Tobacco king, Herbert Tareyton, which was given a new package and an advertising campaign that stressed its elegance. But for whom? The answer was that Tareyton was redesigned to appeal to the purchaser of premium cigarettes. Like Pall Mall it carried a higher price tag than the standards, and the ad campaign stressed luxury, excellence, and quality, with a touch of the European flavor. American had expected Pall Mall to be the Cadillac of its line. As for Tareyton, it would stress the continental tradition: the trademark was a monacled gentleman with a hint of gray at his temples and dressed in evening clothes.

Both brands did well in 1942 and 1943; in the latter year American sold 7.2 billion Pall Malls and 3.2 billion Tareytons, dominating the king-size market which no other major producer seemed interested in entering. Despite this, the company considered both brands expendable. Were the sales due to cigarette shortages or actual preferences for the longer smokes? There was no way of telling. Furthermore, the kings required more tobacco than the standards, and so seemed wasteful in a time of national emergency. When leaf shortages were felt at the company, Riggio ordered production cutbacks at Pall Mall to channel the leaf to Lucky Strike. As for Tareyton, he suspended production of that brand for several months, allowing a rebirth only after becoming convinced that adequate tobacco would be available in 1945. That year, Luckies posted an 8 billion advance over 1944, while Pall Mall sales dropped by 200 million and Tareyton sold slightly more than half a billion. These declines were due more to cutbacks than a diminished demand, however, and American planned to pick up where it had left off when the war began. Sufficient king-size smokes would be turned out to satisfy demand. How great would that be, and from what source would it come? Riggio thought the premium-priced kings might possibly carve out a special niche in the urban upper-class market and, at best, hammer away at Philip Morris sales.

The company was both pleased and shocked by the 1946 market. As anticipated, Luckies sales were excellent, though Camel was rising rapidly as leaf inventories were being replenished. But Pall Mall rose to number six in industry sales, ahead of Raleigh and just behind Old Gold. Tareyton sales boomed, rising to 3 billion. Even so, these two smokes had only 4 per cent of industry sales between them, while the three major standards had eight out of every ten sales.

At the same time several leading advertising executives wondered how long the major companies could continue to sell old products with prewar images and promotional campaigns. Yet sales climbed during the next two years, rising from 352 billion to 397 billion in 1948. These seemed impressive gains to some, but they didn't understand that much of the growth had been accounted for by overseas sales, especially in occupied areas on the European continent. After 1948, post exchange purchases and shipments from the United States to the occupation troops sharply declined. These losses were compounded by spotty declines in American sales resulting from strikes and a mild economic slowdown. Unit sales dipped in 1949, and fell further the following year.

Now the major firms felt obliged to act. Just as they had reinvented the cigarette prior to World War I by creating the standards, now they would try to do the same by stressing the kings.

The 1949 sales figures pointed the way. Camel finally regained first place, but Reynolds sold fewer of them that year than it had in 1948. In fact, all the Big Three experienced declines, with Luckies the hardest hit. These brands accounted for only seven out of every ten sales and clearly were on the decline. Philip Morris was rising, but this resulted from the efforts of a new management team rather than a sudden craving for the smoke.

Pall Mall and Tareyton advanced. So did Raleigh, whose popularity was attributed to that cigarette's use of coupons, a popular item during that period, and one designed to keep a strong grip on those who purchased the cigarette.

The most important development that year, however, was the move by industry leaders into the king-size arena. Liggett & Myers led the way. In the summer of 1948 the company tested a larger version of its old pre-World War I best seller, Fatima. That brand had remained on the market during the interwar period, even though L & M devoted most of its attention to Chesterfield. In 1939 slightly more than 300 million were sold, with most going to old-timers in northern urban areas and others who preferred the Turkish blend. Thus, there would be a ready-made market for a king version. Still, Liggett & Myers did not expect too much in the way of increased sales and devoted only a small portion of its 1949 advertising budget to this smoke.

With little advertising or promotion, Fatima sales doubled in 1949, leaving L & M executives both pleased and troubled. They liked the sales figures, of course, but wondered whether they had entered the right kind of a smoke in the king-size market. After all, how many Americans would take to Turkish tobacco after decades of Bright and White Burley?

Lorillard took a different tack. Despite a sales rally for Old Gold, it seemed clear that that cigarette was on the decline. For several years the company had sold longer cigarettes in the export market, its most important entry there being Embassy. This brand had not tested well in the United States on a limited basis in 1947, and so was withdrawn. Lorillard tried again in late 1948, this time with a new package and the commitment of some advertising money. Embassy sold only half a billion units in 1949, not very impressive, but test results were positive. The company felt sure it had the right tobacco mixture, the correct image, and the kind of smoke that could perform credibly against Pall Mall and Tareyton.

Brown & Williamson held back, uncertain as to what was happening. The firm's leading American smoke, Kool, had the menthol field to itself by 1948, and sales were growing. Given its limited ad budget, B & W opted to enter the king market on the cheap side by transforming Wings and Avalon into larger smokes. Larus did the same with Domino, and added another 85 mm, Alligator, to its large stable of low-unit sales cigarettes. None of these four kings demonstrated much appeal in 1949, but then, little had been expected of them.

The big news came from Reynolds, which up to that time had placed all of its bets on Camel. In late March, the company presented its second brand and first king, Cavalier, in test markets in New England, the Midwest, and the Pacific coast. In a press release the company said, "This new long or king-size cigarette was the result of a study for a number of years of the extent of public demand for long cigarettes, for which type of cigarette in recent years a desire has been evidenced by an increasingly large number of smokers."

If the prose was tortured, so was the sales effort. In fact there was almost no such development—no advertising, no special promotion, and not even the usual street giveaways of samples by pretty girls the public had come to expect. What was Reynolds trying to prove? Along Madison Avenue it was thought that the company wanted to see just how far it could go in this market on a pure demand basis, with no selling. After having tested the water it would make its big push, but not with Cavalier. Rather, Reynolds was developing another brand for which Cavalier was a stalking horse.

Despite this, Cavalier performed surprisingly well. By the end of the year it had nationwide distribution and sales of 800 million. Reynolds indicated that some money would be expended advertising it in 1950, but at the same time provided a sharp boost to Camel, showing the industry this would remain its primary brand.

The Reynolds strategy failed. In continuing to rely strongly on Camel and not making an all-out effort for Cavalier or some other 85-mm smoke, the company was signaling its belief that the market for kings was limited, and would soon level off and perhaps decline. This feeling was understandable in 1949. The economy was sluggish and there was some talk of a new recession. The popularity of Raleigh coupons indicated a growing awareness of price differentials. The kings sold at a premium. Furthermore, the price of tobacco was rising that year, and the larger smokes took around 17 per cent more of the weed than the standards.

This seemed to close the argument as far as Reynolds was concerned. The company continued to push Camel in 1950, mounting a major campaign on television. Then came the Korean War, and sales for all smokes rose sharply. Over 418 billion cigarettes were produced in 1951, close to twice the 1941 figure, and Camel was far and away the nation's best-selling brand, accounting for one out of four packs sold in the United States.

Still, the kings continued to win converts, and taken as a group, the Big Three was losing ground. In 1951 the larger smokes captured over 12 per cent of the market, more than double what they had sold three years earlier. Pall Mall was the nation's fifth best seller, having passed Old Gold, and in 1952 it would go to the number-four position ahead of Philip Morris. Camel sales set new records, perhaps the result of the Reynolds ad push. Luckies and Chesterfield declined, this due to smaller advertising budgets, as American and Liggett & Myers showed growing interest in the kings. American was particularly pleased with Pall Mall, which even then had displaced Luckies as the firm's lead item, while Tareyton's popularity was growing steadily. Brown & Williamson was holding firm with Wings and Avalon, but two new entries from Larus—Holiday and Lords—hadn't met with much approval. As for Liggett & Myers, that firm continued to back Fatima, whose sales in 1953 seemed destined to top the 4 billion mark.

Fatima remained a problem. True, it had done better than anticipated, but L & M continued to be troubled about its blend, for as expected, there were a limited number of smokers who liked the Turkish blend. Clearly the company had erred in making this brand its major king-size entry. Changes were possible, however. There was the example set by Camel, whose blend had been altered by Dick Reynolds and then went on to national leadership. Perhaps the same could be done for Fatima.

The industry expected the next step to come either from Reynolds or Lorillard, in the form of a new sales push for Cavalier or a cutback at Old Gold coinciding with a new effort for Embassy. These seemed likely developments in the early summer of 1952.

Then L & M broke the news, the most carefully guarded trade secret since the end of the war. In mid-June the company called a press conference to announce that thenceforth Chesterfield, the nation's number-three best seller and the leader in the New York market, would be available in two sizes, standard and king, and that each would have its own price. On the retail level, this worked out to twenty-one cents for the standard, and only a penny or two more for the kings.

The larger cigarette was an instant success. Liggett & Myers had placed all of its resources behind a major advertising and distribution effort, but within two months it become clear that more work should have been done in the area of production. Retailers complained they couldn't get enough of the smokes to meet the demand, and for a while they were rationed, on an ad hoc basis, to favored customers. Some stores attempted to hike the price, but L & M and the Office of Price Administration cracked down on them, and so the listed price held in most cases. The ad campaign stressed the fact that the new smoke combined the familiarity of the old standard with the novelty of the larger size. If a smoker used Chesterfields in the past, he or she would enjoy them even more in the new size, since there would be more to satisfy the user.

Chesterfield king was on the market for slightly more than half of 1952, but in this period over 8.5 billion of this variant were sold, placing the brand ninth on the national list, behind Kool but ahead of Raleigh. It was third, after Pall Mall and Tareyton, in the 85-mm category, but would have been in second place given a full year for sales and an ability to meet demand. This happened in 1953, when Chesterfield kings sold 14 billion cigarettes and went to seventh place, behind Old Gold but ahead of Tareyton.

This phenomenal showing prompted strategy meetings at all the major firms and along Madison Avenue, attracting much attention at Reynolds and Philip Morris. As they saw it, L & M had succeeded in switching smokers from Chesterfield regulars to the kings. Thus, the firm was cannibalizing its own sales. While it was true that the new kings sold a total of 22.5 billion cigarettes in 1952–53, the sales of Chesterfield regulars dropped by 14.5 billion in the same period, by far the sharpest decline in the industry. In fact, the fall-off was so severe that it appeared inevitable that Chesterfield regular would drop behind Pall Mall the following year. So it did; for the first time since the early 1920s, a newcomer had entered the ranks of the Big Three, and two of the top group—Luckies and Pall Mall—came out of the same company, American Tobacco.

The goal was to expand total corporation sales, thought Reynolds and Philip Morris, and not merely to juggle them around. In fact, L & M was losing ground within the industry. In 1951 the company had 17.9 per cent of cigarette sales, and two years later, 17.4 per cent. As they saw it, the final verdict on the gamble was yet to come.

American Tobacco, Lorillard, and Brown & Williamson had no such doubts; they thought the switch a clear success. American had no need to alter strategy; even prior to the Chesterfield king advent the management had decided the future rested with Pall Mall. Thus, there was no consideration of a Luckies king at that time. Lorillard responded with the creation of Old Gold kings in 1953, which posted 4 billion in sales—mostly at the expense of standard O.G.s, as the Reynolds people were quick to observe. The B & W experience was similar; the new Raleigh kings had 6 billion in sales, while the standard fell to 1.5 billion from 8.3 billion. Philip Morris saw this coming, but in mid-year decided to take the plunge itself, with Philip Morris kings, which sold 9 billion—but the standard's sales declined by almost 10 billion that year.

These major fall-offs in the sales of regular-size cigarettes did not trouble leaders at B & W, Philip Morris, and Lorillard. By early 1954, executives at all three companies were considering plans for phasing out the regulars in favor of the kings. But the rise of the kings meant more than simply an alteration of product. In fact, the success of the Chesterfield 85-mm smoke contained three important messages for the industry, each of which would require some significant response.

The first and most important lesson for immediate strategy was that the major firms had misunderstood the nature of the market for king-size smokes. In the past it had been assumed that those who preferred the larger smokes comprised a separate and distinct group. Indeed, this may have been the case prior to the war. In that period the kings were supposed to appeal to urban sophisticates willing to pay much more per smoke than other people. After 1945, industry leaders made a play for the female half of the population and assumed women would want a different cigarette than the men. This was a large market, but it underwent surprisingly little scrutiny at the time. Twice as many men as women smoked more than a pack a day, and the companies looked upon the females as their last important frontier. The kings were deemed elegant, or at least were being advertised that way.

Yet there were signs that this was not true. Pall Mall's continued rise meant that the middle class, women as well as men, were taking to the smoke, and in fact the differences in brand preferences between the sexes was narrowing, perhaps as a result of the war, continued prosperity, or the increasing number of women holding full or part-time positions. Chesterfield king was a natural development, then—a move to alter a product that had once met consumer demands but would have to change as the market did. Liggett & Myers had adjusted its leading brand to appeal to the offspring of the people who had made the move from Turkish to Burley and Bright cigarettes prior to World War I. Now the other companies would have to fashion their own responses.

The second message had far broader implications. Diversity, and not conformity and uniformity, would be the rule within the cigarette industry and indeed in other areas of the American consumer market. Throughout the 1920s the drift had been in the direction of standardization. For many products, such as automobiles, soap, and food, the number of competing firms and brands had been diminishing because of the growth of mass merchandising techniques, the mania for the efficiency of standardization and the continuing influence of Henry Ford and the trusty Model T. Weak companies were absorbed by the strong in the 1920s; during the next decade, when the market for many products was smaller, they simply folded. A depression America required low-priced goods, and these could be provided through standardization, which in any case was assumed to be the lesson of the mature industrial revolution.

That this was not so became evident to some students of marketing after the war. For one thing, the industrial revolution was not in its last phase; several additional ones seemed in the offing. Too, the market for many goods was not as limited as formerly, but could be extended to previously ignored socioeconomic groups. The poor person who in the 1920s had to settle for a used Model T, and couldn't afford a car in the depression years, now wanted a selection of models. The housewife who relied upon family favorites and old standbys in food, soap, and household remedies now had more discretionary income, was a more sophisticated consumer, and like her husband wanted a choice from among several brands. The sales volume for individual brands would rise, but the enlarged consumer-based economy required manufacturers to offer greater selections and to alter products more rapidly than they had in the past. Thus, while the familiar Camel pack was considered an asset prior to the war, and George Washington Hill's switch in the Lucky Strike color was deemed a bold and even reckless move, the situation had changed dramatically by the early 1950s.

It appeared then that the major alteration would be in the size of cigarettes; at the very most, the kings would dominate the market later in the decade. The success of the larger Chesterfields suggested this would happen by "hitchhiking" upon the names, reputations, and blends of already popular smokes. Thus, the regular-size standards would be replaced by the king-size variety.

This was not to be. The age of standards of all kinds was ending, and one of experimentation beginning. The regulars would not vanish, or even take a minute part of the market, as had been the fate of the Turkish blends of the 1910s. Nor would Pall Mall, Chesterfield kings, and Tareyton ever dominate the market to the extent the Big Three had done in the 1920s and 1930s. Rather, diversity and constant change would be the rule, with plenty of room for the conventional-size smokes, the kings, mentholated brands, cork-tipped, filters, and combinations of two or more—such as the king-size mentholated cork-tipped filters that would appear two decades later.

This much was unimaginable in the early 1950s, but movement in that direction had started and would accelerate. In part this would result from changes in the smoker population and the nature of American society. But even more important were pressures from a familiar adversary that had taken on a new form.

By this time, the anticigarette forces had begun to stress the question of cigarettes and health.

The tobacco companies ignored the more serious charges, but did respond to those relating to minor discomforts. Old Gold's "Not a Cough in a Carload," Camel's "Not a Single Case of Throat Irritation Due to Smoking Camels," and other similar slogans were quite common prior to World War II. The companies claimed that smoking cigarettes actually aided digestion; Reynolds boasted that "More Doctors Smoke Camels than any Other Cigarette." The advertising agencies didn't go so far as to say that cigarettes were of medical benefit, but they came close. Julep was supposed to aid in clearing up head colds, for example, while Kool "guarded against colds." And, of course, implicit in many ads was the idea that smoking somehow made a person more virile.

The Federal Trade Commission brought actions against several companies for these and similar ads and, in many cases, was able to bring campaigns to a halt. Furthermore, claims that one or another brand was milder or smoother than the others were challenged, and fines levied due to false and misleading statements. Always the companies returned with slightly modified campaigns, and these resulted in new suits, with the cycle beginning once more.

The king-size smokes were considered yet another response to the desire for smoother smoking—a way to prevent coughing, throat irritation, and colds. Pall Mall, for example, noted that it was a "longer and finer and milder smoke." This was the reason for the 85-mm length. Pall Malls were "Outstanding, and they are Mild!" What produced this mildness? The greater length, of course, "to travel the smoke further—to make it cooler and sweeter for you." This was so because Pall Mall's "richly-flavored tobaccos" are "the finest quality money can buy," and "fine tobacco is its own best filter."

The key words were mild and longer, or at least this was the thought at the company and along Madison Avenue. In fact, "filter" would prove more significant. For as the medical barrage against the cigarette mounted, methods of removing harmful substances became more important than ever.

If the king-size smokes acted as a natural filter, and this provided a sales boost, why not feature artificial filters, which in fact could remove even more of whatever the doctors decided was harmful?

Filter-tipped smokes were not new to the American scene after World War II. In fact, this variety had been among the first to be manufactured in the United States and, before that, in the form of stiff paper mouthpieces on many Russian and Turkish brands.

But only two of the major firms had produced mouthpiece-tipped cigarettes. After World War I L & M turned out a few hundred thousand Imperiales and Obaks a year for specialized American markets and the overseas trade—and these were abandoned in 1943 in order to save tobacco for Chesterfield. Brown & Williamson had introduced Viceroy filters in 1936, but they played a small role in that company's plans.

Benson & Hedges of New York, a small but rising firm in 1945, was the third manufacturer of mouthpiece smokes. A specialty tobacconist of the old school, with offices and shop on New York's Fifth Avenue, it had done fairly well by selling fine cigars, pipe tobacco, and Turkish-blend cigarettes to the city's upper class. Benson & Hedges was decidedly English in tone. For a while during the 1930s the firm had been controlled by several Philip Morris executives, and before that had been an affiliate of the London firm of the same name. The company obviously played upon snob appeal, and after the war there were plenty of clients for the company's products.

As a concession to changing tastes (and also in order to survive during the Great Depression) B & H had introduced two new cigarettes with American tobacco blends and European mouthpieces. Parliament and Virginia Rounds, as they were called, came in cardboard boxes and sold at a premium price, usually twice that for the standard brands. They were not advertised, since the smokes were only for B & H clients. Those who preferred a Burley-Bright mixture purchased Parliament, while Virginia Rounds was an English-style smoke with a Maryland and Virginia blend. However, the tobaccos were less important than the mouthpieces. These were constructed of cardboard, and contained the usual small wad of cotton as a filter. They set apart the Parliament and Virginia Rounds smoker from the crowd. For those who could afford the price, the premium smokes seemed a small luxury.

Sales for both brands were never more than a hundred thousand or so units per year prior to the war. Americans who visited London and enjoyed du Maurier filters there would switch to Parliament when they returned home, but there weren't many such travelers during the depression.

Shortages in 1942–45 made them more popular, and the continuation of the wartime prosperity enlarged their clienteles. Still, in 1944, they only sold less than one tenth of 1 per cent of the national total, and by 1946, less than half of that. The Americans were switching back to their old brands, and it appeared Parliament and Virginia Rounds would return to their prewar niches. However, this did not happen. By 1948 sales increased dramatically, and without advertising of any kind.

Joseph Cullman, Jr., the Benson & Hedges president, tried to uncover the reason for this advance, which though modest by industry standards had an important impact upon the firm's business. Some thought that the wartime experience had altered cigarette tastes somewhat, or that Americans who had been in Britain during the conflict had developed a taste for mouthpiece smokes, but these explanations were rejected. Rather, it seemed that more than a few New York doctors were recommending Parliaments to their patients and were doing so for health reasons. On the basis of an increasing number of scientific papers, unavailable to, and unknown by, the general public, they had concluded that smoking was harmful to the health. They urged their patients to stop smoking, but most were unable to do so. For these, the doctors recommended a filtered smoke, which they assumed passed less tar and nicotine to the lungs. Virginia Rounds contained a blend that did not appeal to people raised on a diet of Camels, Luckies, or Chesterfields. Thus, Parliament became the cigarette of choice for doctors, or at least for those who were moved to react to the information regarding health.

Parliament was not advertised in the conventional media, but word of the smoke passed from one person to another. The Benson & Hedges Fifth Avenue shop was deluged with orders, not only from smokers, but retailers as well. But it remained a small company, with sales of $3.9 million in 1947. The following year, however, the figure reached $4.9 million, and Cullman began advertising in selected newspapers and magazines. For 1949, Benson & Hedges posted $7.2 million, and its two brands sold 600,000 cigarettes—out of an industry total of 353 billion.

Did filtered cigarettes have an important future in the United States? American and Liggett & Myers thought not, preferring instead to concentrate upon the developing potential for kings. Reynolds stayed out of the contest, as though hoping there would be no change at all and that Camel would lead the way to a return to the standards. Brown & Williamson was in an unusual position. Each of the company's three major brands appealed to a special market—Kool to mentholated smokers, Raleigh to the coupon collectors, and Viceroy to those who wanted filters. At the time it seemed Kool could accomplish everything Viceroy might and, in addition, already was a national, popular brand. For the moment, B & W stood pat on filters.

Lorillard hesitated, for the company was in the mood for experimentation. Its Old Gold clearly was a fading brand, and although the Lorillard king, Embassy, was making a good showing, there was some question as to whether it could make the grade against Pall Mall and Chesterfield king. So Lorillard decided to act and, in the spring of 1952, introduced a new cigarette, Kent, which was named after its president. Kent had an attractive package, a national advertising campaign, and a different kind of filter.

Kent's sales for the next eight months were half a billion. For all of 1952, Viceroy sold 2.7 billion and Parliament, 1.6 million. The rest of the industry was interested, but not overly impressed. Brown & Williamson was a specialty company, while Benson & Hedges clearly had only one string to its bow. But Lorillard was one of the larger firms, and so its effort bore watching. Still, all the talk that year was of hitchhiking and kings. Only a major shock could alter the situation.

That came in 1953.

X

A Matter of Health

In 1921 Dr. Moses Barron of the University of Minnesota Medical School noted a remarkable increase in the frequency of lung cancer being treated at his hospital. A review of autopsy records there showed only four cases of the disease from 1899 to 1919. In contrast, eight victims were treated in a one-year period ending on June 20, 1921. Barron wasn't certain what was causing this sharp increase, and of course such a small sampling couldn't be extrapolated from the nation as a whole.

In 1930 researchers in Cologne, Germany, made a statistical correlation between cancer and smoking and found that a far greater percentage of cancer patients were heavy smokers than was found in the general population.

Eight years later Dr. Raymond Pearl of the Johns Hopkins University presented statistics on the length of life and smoking. He concluded that smokers did not live as long as others in the population.

In 1944 a spokesman for the American Cancer Society said, "Although no definite evidence exists concerning the relation between the use of tobacco and the incidence of lung cancer, it would seem unwise to fill the lungs repeatedly with a suspension of fine particles of tobacco products of which smoke consists. It is difficult to see how such particles can be prevented from becoming lodged in the lungs and when so located how they can avoid producing a certain amount of irritation." Dr. E. Cuyler Hammond of the Society went further; he reported "a strong statistical correlation" between heavy cigarette smoking and lung cancer.

The following year Drs. Ernest Wynder and Evarts Graham of the Washington University School of Medicine investigated the smoking habits of 605 men with bronchogenic cancer of the lung and found that almost all of them had smoked more than a half a pack of cigarettes per day for twenty years. Only eight of the group were nonsmokers.

Richard Doll and Bradford Hill, both British doctors, compared lung cancer patients to a sample of other patients of the same age, sex, and general background. In 1952 they reported that the cancer patients tended to be heavy cigarette smokers.

Literally hundreds of scientific papers dealing with the effects of smoking upon health, especially with the incidence of cancer, had been published during the first half of the century. All of them could be found in scientific and similar journals. The Wynder and Graham study was entitled: "Tobacco Smoking as a Possible Etiologic Factor in Bronchogenic Carcinoma: A Study of Six Hundred and Eighty-four Proved Cases," while the Doll-Hill report was: "A Study of the Etiology of Carcinoma of the Lung." One study was published in the *Journal of the American Medical Association* and the other in the *British Medical Journal* and so were seen by most doctors in both countries, as well as many more elsewhere in the world. These studies showed a strong statistical correlation between cigarette smoking and the incidence of lung cancer. In other words, smokers tended to suffer more cancers on a per capita basis than did nonsmokers. Moreover, it appeared that the heavier the use of tobacco, the greater the incidence of the disease.

This did not mean that the doctors and researchers had proven clinically that smoking caused cancers, but rather had shown that the two seemed to go together. At that time researchers could induce skin cancers in laboratory animals by painting them with mixtures of tars and nicotine. They could not do the same for lung cancer, however, and the researchers said as much.

There was an important difference between correlation and proof, they would say, and this could be found in the matter of causation. Proof implied that the researchers could demonstrate that the application of A resulted in the condition of B, and do so under controlled laboratory conditions. Correlation simply indicated that A and B were found together. The discovery of a correlation could be the first step toward finding a proof, but again, the matter could rest there. For example, the death rate from lung disorders of various kinds is higher in Arizona than most other places in the nation. Does this correlation indicate there is something in the Arizona diet, climate, or even political structure that causes respiratory disease? The answer, of course, is no. Rather, individuals with lung problems seek the Arizona climate, and some of them die there. In this case, correlation does not lead to causation, but quite the reverse.

The researchers had learned that cigarette smoking tended to be one of the attributes of lung cancer victims, but they could not prove that the latter resulted from the former. To argue that smoking led to cancer was as sensible and scientific as claiming that precancerous conditions helped develop a craving for nicotine in certain individuals, or that some people who are cancer-prone also are of the type that like to inhale tobacco smoke.

This is not to say there was no causal relationship between cigarette smoking and lung cancer. Rather, on the basis of the evidence available in 1952, no such relationship had been proven.

But the issue did not revolve around a dissection of the use of logic or the nature of the scientific method. Even those who defined the word "proof" in its narrowest sense had to be impressed by the correlations. In 1900, for example, when relatively few men and almost no women smoked cigarettes, cancer deaths for each one hundred thousand of the population was sixty-four. Half a century later, at the height of the cigarette age, this number was up to one hundred forty deaths from cancers.

Even this could be explained without recourse to a cancer-cigarette link. Malignancies appeared far more often in older people than in the younger age brackets. The life expectancy of Americans rose by almost twenty years in this period, and so the deaths from cancers might have been expected to rise as well. But most of this advance had resulted from improvements in the treatment of childhood ailments of various kinds. The differences in life expectancy for a thirty-year-old male in 1950 was not that much better than it had been in 1900, and the same was true for women.

Finally, lung cancer was predominantly a disease of males, though of course some women were in the group. In 1950 there were indications that more women were turning up with lung cancer. The great increase in cigarette smoking by women had taken place in the 1920s and 1930s. Two and three decades later there was a similar increase in the incidence of lung cancer among women. In fact, the upward curve for cigarette use for any given time and group in the past half century was remarkably similar to that for lung cancer twenty or so years later.

It remained just a correlation. Causal evidence had not been presented. But it was enough for many doctors, who switched to pipes and cigars, went over to the kings, or gave up smoking completely.

The general public knew little of this in the 1950–52 period. The vast majority of Americans never saw the articles in the journals, and if they did, couldn't have understood them or, for that matter, known what the titles meant. Of course, there was talk of a cancer-tobacco link, but in early 1952 this seemed an extension of the old fears that smoking cut down on the breath or caused smoker's cough or raw throats. Everyone knew of individuals who smoked two or three packs a day and then came down with lung disorders that shortened their lives. On the other hand, there were other heavy smokers who lived to ripe old ages and who attributed their longevity to the use of tobacco. Habitual smokers who knew of the available medical evidence rationalized it away, perhaps because they were unwilling or unable to stop smoking, or even cut down on their consumption. Fear might turn the trick against cigarettes, but there wasn't much of it in the early 1950s. The reason was not a lack of information regarding the correlations between cancer and smoking, but the inability of the researchers to deliver their findings and ideas to the general public.

This changed in late 1952.

The *Christian Herald* was one of a small number of limited circulation journals that published anti-smoking articles on a regular basis. Most were written by Roy Norr, the editor and owner of *Smoking and Health News,* an almost-unknown paper sold in health food stores and similar outlets. Norr tended to dramatize his points, and his exposé-style writing usually was more sensational than illuminating. "Smokers are Getting *Scared*" was the title of a long Norr article appearing in the October 1952 issue of the *Christian Herald.* In it the author charged the organized medical profession with doing nothing while "800,000 adolescents [are] recruited each year for addiction." He referred to an American Cancer Society project on lung cancer as "a death watch" and charged the "medical bureaucracy" with helping "the tobacco industry obscure the truth." So it went. Norr wrote of conspiracies and cover-ups, and, in general, this article seemed simply another exercise in preaching to the converted.

It was more than that. DeWitt and Lila Wallace, editors and publishers of *Reader's Digest,* were keenly interested in the antismoking movement, and had some experience in leading consumer crusades. Their magazine had the largest circulation in the nation and carried no advertising; the Wallaces boasted that this made them more independent than other magazines, which had to rely upon ads, cigarette and liquor ads in particular, for their well-being. Millions of middle-class Americans looked to the Wallaces to filter out the chaff and present them with the best reading available, in shortened, easy-to-take form. The couple knew their audience well and concentrated upon upbeat nonfiction, popular novels, and short humorous pieces, often with a religious tone. The magazine was scorned by intellectuals but loved and trusted by its readers.

The *Digest* had two reputations, one for excellent editing and rewriting. The other, hotly denied by the Wallaces, was for planting important stories in obscure magazines in order to reprint them later on, usually the next month, in a featured spot in the *Digest.*

Whether or not this was the case with the Norr article is un-known, but it did appear, almost completely rewritten and with a different title, in the December issue. Gone was the purple prose and intimations of conspiracy, all cleaned away by the magazine's expert editors, who also came up with the new title, hard-hitting and catchy in the magazine's tradition: "Cancer by the Carton."

The *Digest* version was only two pages long and contained the gist of the Norr article in such a way as to alert readers to the dangers of smoking, make them aware of medical work in the field, and present a reasonable call for action. "Cancer workers want something done, and done now on the basis of present clin-ical knowledge, to alert the smoking public."

Neither article went so far as to claim that cigarette smoking caused cancer of the throat or lungs. Rather, each observed that research indicated strong links between the habit and the dis-ease. In his *Christian Herald* article Norr called upon the gov-ernment to "break the stranglehold of the tobacco huckster on the people's air," and to "rip off the mask from cigarette claims," by federal action if necessary. This was omitted from the *Reader's Digest* version. But to the layman who subscribed to and trusted the *Digest,* the message was clear and forthright: Stop smoking or risk a horrible death. In fact, the contents of the article really didn't matter. What remained in the mind was the title and the implication that smokers were getting cancers along with their cartons.

The article received a good deal of attention in the other parts of the mass media. The story was picked up by radio and televi-sion news programs and was the subject of comment in the news magazines. In the late 1940s articles on smoking and possible connections with cancer had appeared in popular science jour-nals. "Cancer by the Carton" changed the situation dramatically. The story was taken to the public by a wide variety of maga-zines, so that it could not be avoided by any literate smoker. The titles of articles appearing in the two years following the *Reader's Digest* condensation told the story. "What Smoking Does to You," "Cigarette Smoking and Lung Cancer," "Lung Cancer Increase," "Cigarettes and Cancer," and such strong statements as "Beyond Any Doubt" and "ACS Nails Smoking as Cancer Cause."

In fact ACS—the American Cancer Society—had done no such thing at the time, but it hardly mattered. The public was somewhat confused by claims and counterclaims, but as one writer put it, many Americans assumed that "Where there's smoke there's fire—and cancer." Even those who took the trouble to investigate the evidence, and therefore knew the vital link had not been uncovered, concluded it was only a matter of time before convincing proof was published.

Why wait? Magazines carried stories on ways to break the cigarette habit. "Withdrawal clinics" opened and did a booming business. There was talk of the formation of "Smokers Anonymous," which would function like Alcoholics Anonymous to assist "habitual smokers." Once considered a sign of sophistication, in some circles cigarette smoking was coming to be seen as an indication of moral weakness. There was a sudden upswing in the use of pipes—pipe smoke was not inhaled—and cigars. Roy Norr celebrated, calling for federal legislation against cigarette advertising, prosecution of those firms making false claims, and the mounting of a new crusade. By 1953 the spirit of Lucy Page Gaston was everywhere. As Norr put it in another of his *Christian Herald-Reader's Digest* articles, "Now *Everybody's* Scared."

That year, for the first time in twenty-one years, cigarette sales declined, going to 423 billion from 1952's record 435 billion. This was not a fluke, an aberration that would pass with the arrival of the next day's news. Medical reports began piling up, and all of them seemed to corroborate the claims of a cancer-cigarette connection. In early 1954 several new investigations disclosed significant relationships between heart diseases and heavy smoking, and some of these could be verified by laboratory experiments on animals.

American Cancer Society studies completed in 1953 indicated some hope for smokers, however. It appeared that former smokers had a longer life expectancy than smokers and less susceptibility to lung cancer and other ailments. In fact, the longer one abstained from smoking, the closer one came, statistically, to the profile of the nonsmoker. The message stated: Stop smoking and you might escape this horrible fate. The reports were a blend of science and religion, combining as they did an appeal for repentance with the paraphernalia of the laboratory. For years the major companies had used medical men in their advertisements, where they testified on the mildness and health-fulness of cigarettes. Now doctors were telling smokers they should abstain, and they spoke with the zeal of the Anti-Cigarette Leaguers of 1900.

Cigarette consumption declined sharply, to 401 billion, in 1954. The industry realized it was facing a crisis and would have to react swiftly and effectively. There were emergency meetings with advertising companies to develop strategy. All the leading firms except Liggett & Myers agreed on the need for a direct re-sponse to the American Cancer Society—L & M thought it unwise to enter the arena with the doctors. At the same time, all the ciga-rette companies realized they would have to develop new prod-ucts and revamp ad campaigns.

On January 4, 1954, the major firms (except L & M) an-nounced the formation of the Tobacco Industry Research Com-mittee, an independent group funded by, but not answerable to, the industry. The birth of the TIRC was proclaimed in full-page advertisements in 448 newspapers. In them the companies said they were confident cigarette smoking had no harmful effects, and that they were "pledging aid and assistance to the research effort into all phases of tobacco use and health." The committee was to be headed by "a scientist of unimpeachable integrity and national repute." A few days later Dr. Clarence Cook Little, a geneticist and cancer specialist who at one time had been man-aging director of the American Society for the Control of Cancer —the predecessor of the American Cancer Society—accepted the post of scientific director. Little was a man of unquestionable in-tegrity, and so the TIRC claim appeared serious and even gener-ous.

It was a sensible move, for the companies knew that the cigarette-cancer link had not been proven and were certain Lit-tle would have to back them up on this point. Furthermore, to-bacco processing had reached the point where the industry's own scientists could remove any substance that medical researchers identified as causing cancer, or any other disease.

The TIRC made several grants for research during its first

year, and in general Little supported industry allegations that the causal connection between smoking and diseases had not been proven. But statements from the committee had minor impact, in the face of the onslaught from the antismoking groups. Still, those members of the public interested in such matters were discovering much about tobacco and smoking in the process.

They learned, for example, that American cigarettes burned at over 1,600 degrees Fahrenheit, and that the temperature was not affected by the size of the cigarette, the length of the puff, or blend variations. The extra few millimeters in a king-size cigarette had only a minor effect on the temperature of the smoke as it entered the lungs. So much for industry claims for "coolness." For that matter, mentholated tobacco burned at a higher temperature than did regular leaf, and so those brands that featured that form of tobacco were actually "hotter" than the others.

Did heat cause cancers? If so, there wasn't much the companies could do about it, though a cooling mechanism of one kind or another was possible, and in fact American Tobacco would come out with just such a smoke—Waterford—a dozen years later.

What about nicotine? By the mid-1950s the careful reader would have learned that while nicotine was addictive, and in large enough doses poisonous, it did not cause cancer. In addition, only about 20 per cent of the nicotine in a cigarette actually got into the mouth, the rest being burned or filtered out along the way.

Did "tars" cause cancer? This could not be determined, but for certain there were no tars as the term was commonly understood in cigarettes. Rather, the word was used to indicate a variety of substances found in tobacco—some 685 of them. Each could be identified and, if necessary, removed from the cigarette. In fact, the tobacco companies could have produced a smoke almost entirely free from tars or nicotine—or both, for that matter. Only from 5 to 10 per cent of the smoke contained particles (the rest was air) and of that, most was water vapor. But this was what gave the cigarette much of its taste. So the industry could create a low or no nicotine-tar cigarette, but having done so, could it be sold? The answer seemed to be no.

For a while in 1954–55 there was talk that the cigarette paper might be the culprit, the carcinogenic element. Paper comprised around 4 per cent of the cigarette by weight and could easily be replaced by sheet tobacco. There was no substance to this idea, however, and little was heard of it thereafter.

What was the reader of articles on smoking in popular journals to make of all this? What he or she really wanted to know was whether or not cigarette smoking caused cancer, and no answer was forthcoming. In a detailed study published in February 1955, *Consumer Reports,* no friend of the industry, wrote that "in summing up the evidence, it seems established that smoking is harmful in vascular disorders of the extremities and the eyes; and in active peptic ulcer. Inhaling smoke is also definitely irritating to the nose, throat, and larynx. The evidence is inconclusive with respect to the effects of smoking on athletic ability, and on heart disorders." As far as lung cancer was concerned, "the reasonable view" was that the disease was caused by a variety of factors—air pollution being one—and partly "to excessive cigarette smoking."

This hardly answered the question. Two years later, in March 1957, the editors concluded that "the cancer linkage is still not clear," adding that "for anyone to argue that everyone should stop smoking because of its hazards would be highly unrealistic." Perhaps the positive aspects of the habit should be taken into consideration. In a most carefully worded and hedged sentence, *Consumer Reports* noted that "the stimulating or comforting effects of tobacco may be so valuable to some persons that they are willing to risk *whatever* physical harm *may be associated* with the habit [emphasis added]."

What were these harmful effects? Was cancer one of them? The magazine could do no better than come in with a Scotch verdict—not proven. This, five years after the beginning of the modern antismoking crusade. The question vital to millions of Americans and a major industry still had no conclusive answer. But the public did respond, with a question of its own. "Why take chances?"

That a large segment of the public had taken the health crusade seriously was evident and beyond dispute. This could be seen in the popularity of books and articles dealing with ways to break the habit, the spread of withdrawal clinics, and most im-

portant, the appearance of several new cigarette holders containing filters. The industry had always been known for its careful
attention to public tastes and shifts in sentiment. Now it strug-
gled to refine old techniques and develop new ones in this area.

The marketing and advertising executives poured over the
1954 sales figures, attempting to divine their meaning. Had the
health scare alone caused the sharp decline? Some executives
noted that the economic recession may have had something to do
with the lower sales. Others pointed out that cigarette taxes had
been raised in several states in 1953. A third group referred to
the meager "baby crop" of the 1930s, that came to smoking age
in the 1950s, and predicted poor results until the demographic
outlook was better.

However, these arguments were easily disposed of. The close
to 5 per cent drop could not be explained by the slow decline in
births in the mid-1930s. Sales held strong in those states and
cities where the taxes had been increased. Most important, the
decline was entirely out of proportion to the relatively minor
economic fall-off of 1954, and in any case, smoking had risen during previous recessions. Finally, there were the performances of
those cigarettes that became more popular in 1954—Pall Mall,
Raleigh kings, Old Gold kings, Cavalier, and other 85-mm
smokes, along with the filter brands led by Viceroy. All of these
sold for higher prices than the standards. Despite this, the standards had sharp losses, led by Chesterfield and Old Gold, both of
which were down by more than 20 per cent, due in part to
switches to their king-size partners. But Camel, which had no
king equivalent, sold 16 per cent fewer smokes in 1954 than in
1953, though it retained a strong lock on first place within the industry.

Clearly the future rested with the kings and the filters, and
given the continuing strength of the antismoking crusade, more
with the latter than the former. All the major firms agreed.
Reynolds came out with Winston, a filter brand that sold 7.5 billion cigarettes in its first year, placing it slightly behind L & M
filters, which came to the market in late 1953 and was the second
most popular filter brand after Brown & Williamson's Viceroy.
Tareyton filters performed poorly for American Tobacco, and
that company seemed to be placing most of its future on the

kings—Pall Mall and Tareyton regulars. Philip Morris kings weren't doing well, but that company solved its problem by purchasing Benson & Hedges early in the year and mounting a strong effort for Parliament.

The situation at Lorillard was more complex. The smallest of the major firms in terms of sales, assets, and production facilities, its brands had been declining in popularity since shortly after the close of World War II. And in 1954 Kent was the only filter brand to experience a sales decline, which was most puzzling. The cigarette had arrived in 1952, complete with full-scale ad campaign, attractive wrapper, and the usual promotions. It had a unique filter, "developed by researchers in atomic energy plants," which the company called "micronite," to indicate its fine filtration abilities and to give the smoke a touch of space-age flavor. Why was it failing?

The answer seemed to be that the filter was doing too good a job. Smokers complained that there was no "kick" in Kent—because the filter removed so much of the nicotine and tars. At a time when most cigarettes had well over 3 mg of nicotine, Kent delivered .5 mg, while its tar content was 2 mg—when the standard smokes had over 20 mg, and the supposedly mild Pall Mall came in at close to 25 mg. Furthermore, this efficiency had been accomplished through the use of a dense filter, which made it difficult to draw the smoke into the mouth.

The new filter brands of 1953–54 had utilized cellulose mouthpieces not very different from the simple cotton of Parliament. L & M had a "Pure White Miracle Tip of Alpha-Cellulose," which the company claimed was "just what the doctor ordered," for example. Tareyton filters used cellulose too and, in addition, a small amount of activated charcoal, "a filtering substance world famous as a purifying agent." None of these was as effective as the Kent filter, of course, and the leaders at Lorillard reasoned that might be why those brands were more successful. Without meaning to, the company had stumbled upon an important discovery—that filters were just another sales gimmick, not unlike those utilized in the industry for the past half century.

During the 1920s and 1930s the industry's advertising agencies had claimed that smoking cigarettes led to romance, admiration, and even longevity. Later on, Pall Mall and the other king-size cigarettes had become status symbols, both to the user and those who watched him or her. After a while the smoker became habituated to his brand, through the narcotic effect of nicotine, so that even if he wanted to stop smoking, to do so would be difficult if not impossible. But this was not what attracted individuals to cigarettes initially. That had been accomplished by advertising and public acceptance.

Now smokers were frightened, half-convinced that cigarette smoking would cut years from their lives. At the same time, most people really wanted to continue on with their habit. So the companies would respond with another image-creating campaign. If Luckies transformed the user into a version of Sam Spade, and Pall Mall endowed him with the aura of a Douglas Fairbanks, Jr., why couldn't a filter brand satisfy his craving to be a safe smoker? The companies would imply that filters removed harmful substances from the smoke, and so rendered the cigarette safe. Whether this was true or not was beside the point. What mattered was that the smoking public would accept the idea. This was behind the success of L & M and other new filter brands—which delivered image, not reality. Kent was failing because Lorillard truly believed it had to create an efficient filter, thus giving the smoker a new kind of product, one which it found most smokers really didn't want.

Late in 1954, without announcements or advertisements, Lorillard provided Kent with a looser filter, one that drew easier, permitting additional tars and nicotine to enter into the mouth and lungs. In addition the mixture was reformulated, giving the cigarette a greater amount of both substances. Thus the company could state, in all candor, that Kent had the most effective filter in the industry, while at the same time delivering to its smokers what they really wanted: a conventional taste combined with the aura of safety and health. In fact, Kent did have less tar and nicotine than most smokes, but the percentages of both were higher in 1955 than they had been the previous year. This was known within the industry and along Madison Avenue, but not to the general public.

By then it seemed the companies were settling down in a new pattern. Filters would be the coming category, with new brands entering the market every few months. Kings would remain steady; their growth would continue, but not much faster than the industry as a whole. As for the standards, they would be sold to an increasingly older segment of the population and eventually be phased out completely or at least play a very small part in the industry. What Camel had done to Sweet Caporals in the 1910s, Pall Mall and Viceroy might do to Camel and Luckies in the 1960s and 1970s.

The 1955 statistics appeared to bear out this statement. Sales of the regular-size smokes were down by almost 11 per cent, while those for the kings declined by 1.5 per cent. Meanwhile the filtered smoke doubled in sales, taking 20 per cent of the market. Overall, sales reached 412 billion cigarettes, 11 billion more than the previous year but far below the record established in 1952. Still, the industry's leaders could congratulate themselves. The impact of the health scare seemed to be lessening, in large part as a result of the growth of filter smoking. The government indicated as much. Commenting upon the prospects for the coming tobacco crop, the Department of Agriculture stated that while the initial reaction against cigarettes in 1954 had been most negative, the major effect "of the publicity concerning cigarettes and health appears to have occurred during 1954." The Department forecast a continued growth of smoking in the foreseeable future.

That the industry believed its troubles were ending could be seen in the way it adjusted to the new atmosphere and the manner by which it marketed old and new products. The rush to filters continued, in what was the most radical revamping operation since the turn to the standards forty years earlier. The best performance for 1955 was turned in by Winston, which went from sales of 7.5 billion and thirteenth place in 1954, the year of its introduction, to fifth place with sales of 23 billion in 1955. That any cigarette could rise so rapidly in less than two years indicated the increasingly volatile nature of the business in the filter age. This was accomplished through a blitz campaign on television and in newspapers, featuring the slogan, "Winston Tastes Good, Like a Cigarette Should." Almost immediately grammarians attacked the company for its improper use of the language—"As" rather than "Like" would be proper. The company continued to employ the original slogan, and this opened a curious national debate on the matter, which involved the degradation of the language, the role of advertising, and the ignorance displayed on Madison Avenue. In the process, Winston gained a great amount of free publicity, which apparently did it no harm.

If Madison Avenue indeed was staffed by barbarians, they were more devious and clever than were their critics. The key word in the Winston slogan was "Taste," not "Like." This filter cigarette was not being marketed on the basis of health, but on the old standby, satisfaction. Feeling sure of itself, the industry was beginning to downplay the health issue. Marlboro, introduced by Philip Morris in 1955, featured a hard flip-top box as well as the conventional soft pack. Both could fit into vending machines, and customers found each appealing. Marlboro sold 6.6 billion cigarettes in 1955, placing it ahead of such old standbys as Tareyton filters and both versions of Old Gold. The slogan hit all bases: "Filter, Flavor, Pack or Box," preceded by "You Get a Lot to Like in a Marlboro," and the chant was heard on television and the words seen in print ads. Thus the filter, an extra long one in this case, was given equal billing with flavor. Late in the year, however, Marlboro ads promised to "Deliver the Goods on Flavor," indicating a switch in tactics. The same was true for Viceroy, which in 1954 stressed its "20,000 filter traps" and now talked about aroma and taste. The standards used the same theme. Camel claimed "It's a psychological fact: Pleasure helps your disposition." "For *more* pure pleasure, have a Camel" and "No other cigarette is so *rich-tasting*, yet so *mild*." As for Lucky Strikes, American Tobacco stated that they "taste better, cleaner, fresher, smoother," while Pall Mall stressed "the pleasure of smooth smoking."

These trends continued into 1956, when sales went up again to 424 billion, and by which time the antismoking groups were clearly on the defensive. Repeated attempts to induce lung cancer in laboratory animals had failed, and the tobacco industry did all it could to publicize this. Even the American Cancer Society had to backtrack on some of its earlier claims. It would be "gratifying" if it could "cut through the smoky turbulence and produce a neat final answer" to the question as to whether or not cigarette smoking causes cancer. Unfortunately, wrote the ACS,

"It cannot." The tobacco industry tried to let the matter rest at this point. It was impossible to prove a negative, said company executives, and since the critics had failed to show the link, there was none.

The crusade had transformed the industry, however, altering the prospects of the leading firms. Reynolds, which had entered the king area so reluctantly and thus performed badly in the late 1940s and early 1950s, recouped ground with filters. Winston continued strong in 1956, with 34 billion units, up by more than 50 per cent. Salem, a new king-filter-mentholated brand, also performed satisfactorily, though Cavalier was on the way down. In all, Reynolds had a third of the filter market, while the ever-declining Camel still held on to first place within the industry.

American had been the big winner with kings, and so had hesitated prior to going over to the filters. Tareyton filters had only a small following, while a new entry in 1956, Hit Parade (the slogan: "Your Taste Can't Tell the Filter's There" indicated clearly the thrust of advertising in this period) was proving a dud. American had only 5 per cent of the filter market.

Brown & Williamson's Viceroy and Raleigh filters by now were that firm's leading sellers, enabling it to retain almost a quarter of the market. But both brands were old and, at a time when novelty was prized, didn't appear to have much of a future. Marlboro, the rising star at Philip Morris, enabled that firm to hold on to 14 per cent of the filter trade. The company was devoting an increasingly large amount of time and money to this brand and, in the process, pushing Philip Morris standards and kings into the background. The same situation existed at Liggett & Myers, where L & M filters were replacing Chesterfield regulars and kings as the firm's flagship brand. That cigarette's strong showing enabled L & M to obtain 18 per cent of the filter following.

Lorillard was in trouble in 1956. Old Gold was sold in three versions—regular, king, and filter—and none were doing well. Embassy had almost vanished from the scene and was about to be discontinued. The company considered new products, but given its lack of cash, prospects seemed poor.

Kent, the firm's leading entry in the filter field, had sold only 3.4 billion cigarettes in 1956, fewer even than the moribund Old

Gold filters. It had been Lorillard's major disappointment, but it was not discarded. Rather Lewis Gruber, who became president in 1956 and had been identified with that cigarette from the first, started a new research program, to give it one last push. Gruber and others knew that without a major king filter, Lorillard was doomed.

The antismoking groups continued with their work in this period. Understanding that Americans would not give up on smokes easily, they turned to methods by which cigarette users could minimize harmful effects. Cutting down on consumption was one way, of course, and smokers could take fewer puffs from each cigarette. Several new filter holders appeared promising, and there was talk of a nontobacco cigarette in the offing. Most important, however, was the publicizing of tar and nicotine contents in cigarettes. Clearly the lower the amounts of each, the better they would be.

In July of 1957 *Reader's Digest* published an article by Lois Mattox Miller and James Monahan entitled "The Facts Behind Filter-Tip Cigarettes." It began by noting that at a convention of the National Association of Tobacco Distributors the previous March, a study group on smoking and health found that "the sum total of scientific evidence established beyond reasonable doubt" that cigarette smoking was a cause of cancer.

Nothing of the sort was discovered, however. The group had made a survey of correlations and found them quite strong, even convincing, but not "evidence" as scientists usually use the term. This was not the point, however. Rather, the authors wrote that the tobacco men at the convention were unruffled. The head of the NATD said "This will blow over like other blasts." A Kansas City wholesaler took a practical view of the matter. "People enjoy smoking and aren't going to quit. But they *will* go to filters."

Miller and Monahan conceded the correctness of the thought and, working on that assumption, presented evidence on the tar and nicotine contents of leading brands. There were few surprises among the plain-tipped smokes. Cavalier had most of both substances, with Old Gold kings in second place. Camel was low in tar but high in nicotine, while Luckies was at the bottom of the list in nicotine and Old Gold, in tars.

There was startling news in the statistics for filter brands. Old Gold king filters, for example, had more tar and nicotine than Old Gold standards, without the filter. L & M, Hit Parade, Winston, and Marlboro all showed up as stronger smokes than many unfiltered brands. But the truly important news was to be found at the bottoms of both lists, the places and smokes readers were bound to note and act upon. Among the better-known filter brands, only Viceroy showed up as being low in both tars and nicotine. At the very bottom of the two lists, however, was Kent regulars, the fading Lorillard brand.

After praising Kent, Miller and Monahan claimed to have learned "*the* 'trade secret'" that would interest smokers most! "*It is entirely possible to manufacture filter tips much more efficient than any now on the market.*" Although it didn't say as much, the article implied that such a filter might be the best response to the health issue, a compromise that would satisfy both sides in the controversy.

Meanwhile there was Kent regulars, the best in the field.

The following month Miller and Monahan published another article in the *Digest*, this one entitled: "Wanted—and Available —Filter Tips that Really Filter." Most of this piece was devoted to Kent. The authors wrote that Gruber and his associates, working round the clock, had managed to develop a new version of the micronite filter. Scientists from Tennessee Eastman assisted in the project. "While the Eastman laboratories in Tennessee are the center of much hush-hush filter-tip research, Lorillard claims that this development is essentially its own." This new filter contained "tiny natural fibers (so small to the naked eye, the stuff looks like fine powder) added to the cellulose-acetate tow after it reaches the Lorillard plant in Greensboro, N.C." The article went on to note that the new Kent king "yields 14 percent less tar than Tareyton; 23 percent less than Marlboro; 36 percent less than L & M; 40 percent less than Old Gold." As far as *Reader's Digest* was concerned, "The new Kent may not be the best filter-tip possible . . . But it is a big step in the right direction."

There was little in the way of brand loyalty in the filter field; there simply were too many new brands, and smokers usually switched from one to another searching for the "right taste." Of course, the vast majority of filter-tip cigarette smokers used that variety for health reasons, or at least in the belief they were less harmful than the non-filtered brands. Now they were being told by the most popular and trusted magazine in America that Kent was the best brand currently available, and in such a way as to stop just short of an official endorsement.

As luck would have it, Gruber had lowered the Kent regular-size price a few months earlier, so as to compete with the standards and get a slight edge on the other filter brands. This had been a desperation move, and hadn't yielded much in new sales. Now all of this changed. These two articles created a rush to Kent. For the rest of the year the company was unable to keep up with demand, and in some areas retailers sold Kent by the pack, and not the carton, to make certain of a fair allocation. Sales went from 3.4 to over 15 billion in one year. In 1957 Lorillard's output of cigarettes rose by close to 50 per cent. The next best performing major firm, Philip Morris, showed an advance of only 4.5 per cent, while American Tobacco and Liggett & Myers experienced declines from the previous year. Nor was this a one-year fluke. Kent sales for 1958 reached 36 billion, making it the fifth largest brand in the nation, second among filters behind Winston, and the hottest performer in the industry.

It also saved Lorillard from ruin and demonstrated to all within the industry that the health issue would not disappear. Rather, it would take several paths. The hard-liners would demand a total end to cigarette manufacturing. Centrists would concentrate upon health warnings on packs and the curbing of advertising, especially in those areas where the ads might reach young people. The moderate reformers might settle for effective filters. During the next few years the tobacco companies would try to please the moderates, weaken the positions of the centrists, and isolate the hard-liners.

In 1957 this seemed the best and most workable strategy.

XI

The Political Issue

George Washington Hill was the subject of a story making the Madison Avenue rounds in the late 1950s. "Hill would have known what to do about this health business," said one executive. "He would have made cancer fashionable."

This grim form of humor was in vogue at the time, and of course the point is obvious. Actually, Hill would have been out of place in the cigarette industry of that period. He had operated during what in retrospect seems a time of product stability and industry security. The challenge that came from the economy brands in the early 1930s was a simple matter when set beside that from the "health establishment" after World War II. Hill had known that the worst possible resolution of the conflicts of his day would have been an industry-wide switch to the cheaper smokes. A quarter of a century later there was talk of the utter destruction of the industry, of a prohibition as drastic as that for alcohol in the 1920s.

The 1930s had been a period of brand loyalties, and the companies looked upon advertising expenses as long-term investments in an immutable product. Just as Brooklyn Dodger fans weren't supposed to cheer a different club, so smokers of Lucky Strike, once confirmed with that brand, were expected to remain with it for life. Even the slogans were long-lasting—two decades of smokers were supposed to have been willing to walk a mile for a Camel. Writing of the business in his 1952 year-end report in *Printer's Ink*, tobacco analyst Harry Wootten said that "Few if any industries in America offer such a glowing testimonial to the power of advertising." Wootten especially noted "the sheer selling force of the 'agate line'" in cigarette ads. One hardly could open a newspaper or magazine without being hit with testimonials for several major brands.

The situation was drastically different in the late 1950s. Not only did the brands proliferate, but so did the sizes, shapes, forms, packages, and advertising campaigns. Hill had pondered the dropping of the Lucky Strike green pack for years before acting, and it took a similar period for American Tobacco to switch to Pall Mall as its top smoke. In the late 1950s packs were redesigned in a matter of weeks, and new brands dropped immediately if their initial impact seemed unfavorable. In 1959, for the first time, the industry sold more filter tips than regulars, while sales of king-size unfiltered smokes were closing in on those for the old standards.

That also was the last year Camel appeared in first place. Pall Mall took the lead in 1960, but five years later would relinquish it to Winston, the top filter brand. To further complicate matters, the fastest rising smoke of the period was Salem, the Reynolds mentholated king-size filter, which sold only 4 billion in 1956 and 35 billion by 1960.

Mentholated king filters seemed the wave of the immediate future, at least. When Brown & Williamson realized the new Reynolds smoke was catching on, it switched Kool to that form. Then Lorillard introduced Newport, and L & M came up with Oasis. As the sole king menthol filter in 1956, Salem had 1 per cent of the total cigarette market. This group took 5 per cent of sales the following year. All the old rules seemed of little use. Lorillard added Spring to its roster in 1959, even though it would compete with its stablemate, Newport, and in 1960 Brown & Williamson added Belair, despite the fact that Kool was going strong. The Philip Morris version, Alpine, was introduced in 1959, when American Tobacco weighed in with Riviera. By then the king menthol filters had 10 per cent of the market, and by 1962 it would rise to 15 per cent.

The changes in the two decades since the beginning of World War II had been striking, even revolutionary. Of the ten best-selling cigarettes of 1941, one (Pall Mall) was king-size and three (Sensation, Marvel, and Avalon) were economy brands. The same list, twenty years later, contained two (Camel and Lucky Strike) standards, one (Chesterfield) that sold in both king and regular sizes, one (Pall Mall) king, one (Salem) king methol filter, and five (Winston, Kent, L & M, Marlboro, and Viceroy) king filter—and the Viceroy came with two different kinds of filters.

TOP TEN CIGARETTE BRANDS AND SALES, 1941 AND 1961

1941		1961	
BRAND	SALES (BILLIONS)	BRAND	SALES (BILLIONS)
Lucky Strike	49.5	Pall Mall	71.2
Camel	48.5	Camel	66.5
Chesterfield	37.5	Winston	58.8
Philip Morris	17.5	Lucky Strike	41.6
Raleigh	11.0	Salem	41.5
Old Gold	6.0	Kent	38.4
Pall Mall	4.8	Chesterfield	25.9
Sensation/Beechnut	5.5	L & M	25.5
Marvel	4.0	Marlboro	24.1
Avalon	4.0	Viceroy	19.9

SOURCE: *Printer's Ink*, February 6, 1942, and December 1961

The top ten sold 188.3 billion of the 206.4 billion total that year, or over 91 per cent of sales. In contrast, 1961's best sellers had slightly more than 83 per cent of the market—413.4 billion units out of 495.4 billion industrywide. Kool was eleventh on both lists, but its one form—regular-size—in 1941 had slightly more than 1 per cent of the market, while Kool regular and filter combined accounted for over 3 per cent in 1961.

Traditionalists might have taken some comfort from the persistence of brands like Kool, and the fact that four—Camel, Luckies, Chesterfield, and Pall Mall—appeared on both lists. But the changes were more striking than the similarities. To compare cigarettes once again with automobiles, the nation's top three sellers in 1941 were Chevrolet, Ford, and Plymouth, in that order, and twenty years later, the same three, in the same order of popularity, were on the scene. This was not the case with cigarettes, and such stability would never again be enjoyed by the corporate descendants of George Washington Hill.

That the age of standard smokes had passed by 1961 was not as significant and unsettling as the decline of brand loyalty in the same period. The young person who in 1951 might have started out with Camel, because that was his father's smoke, could have switched to Pall Mall by 1955, and then gone on to Kent two or three years later, only to wind up with Salem by 1961. Along the way he probably sampled a wide variety of smokes, without feeling much in the way of loyalty or commitment to any of them, and in fact he might have tried to stop smoking altogether on several occasions, or tested cigars or pipes.

In some ways the decline of the old-brand loyalty was as worrisome as the health issue, for while the doctors could be countered with new arguments and the industry could count upon habit as an ally, the new vogue for switching struck at the heart of the industry: its advertising campaigns.

Was it possible to devise a marketing program that would lure smokers and keep them hooked? In other words, was it possible, in the early 1960s, to develop the kind of slogans that helped boost Camel to the top and popularized Winston in more recent times? Many Madison Avenue executives said it couldn't be done, for two essential reasons. First, loyalties of all kinds were on the decline in many areas of American life. In politics there was the rise of independent voting, in autos one could point to the successes of the imports. Marriage vows appeared to mean less than they did in earlier times—witness the rising divorce rate. Even in sports loyalties meant little: the Dodgers had moved to the West Coast. So there was little wonder that increased brand switching took place in cigarettes.

In addition, there was the problem of advertising media. Most of the Madison Avenue executives of that period had been raised in Harry Wootten's "agate line" tradition. They had learned how to sell products through the use of magazine, newspaper, and billboard. By that time most were proficient in radio too, but the truly great, successful campaigns had always begun with the print media, to be transferred to radio later on.

There would be one more major print campaign directed at brand loyalty. It featured smiling, attractive, young people, cigarettes in hand—and black eyes. The caption: "Us Tareyton Smokers Would Rather Fight Than Switch." This was not the case, to be sure, and the agency knew it, which perhaps was why it attempted to stress brand loyalty. Nor did the campaign perform particularly well on television, and of course it would have made no sense to put in on radio. Increasingly, the campaigns would be geared to television, and then be transferred to print, or the two media would be used in unison. No matter what was attempted, however, there seemed no effective way of solidifying a consumer base.

Thus, while the industry as a whole had to face the problems involved with the health issue, the individual companies were obliged to develop new marketing strategies at a time when brand loyalties were fading and the tempo with which new products were coming to view was increasing. Just as advertising had been paramount in Hill's period, so product research and development led the way thirty years later. This too would help reshape the industry, harming some large firms while enabling others to rise rapidly.

In 1961 the relative rankings of the major companies hadn't altered much from what they had been in 1941. At that time, American and Reynolds were neck and neck for industry leadership, followed by L & M, Brown & Williamson, Philip Morris, and Lorillard. Reynolds was number one in 1961, with American in second place. Then came L & M, Lorillard, B & W, with Philip Morris in last place among the major producers. This order would change sharply with new product development and presentation. In these areas Philip Morris proved spectacularly successful, as did Brown & Williamson, the former with Marlboro—in many manifestations—the latter with a variety of smokes, led by Viceroy and Kool. Meanwhile, American foundered, unable to come up with new brands that appealed to a broad section of the smoking public or to revive old ones. Reynolds managed to retain its share in this span, but Liggett & Myers suffered the same problems as American. Neither of these two old firms was able to adjust either by uncovering a new technology of smoking or developing a flagship brand which for one reason or several could exert a hold on its users.

CIGARETTE COMPANIES BY MARKET SHARES,
1961 AND 1971

1961		1971	
COMPANY	SHARE	COMPANY	SHARE
Reynolds	32.7%	Reynolds	32.3%
American	25.6%	Philip Morris	18.0%
Liggett & Myers	10.7%	American	17.5%
Lorillard	10.4%	Brown & Williamson	16.7%
Brown & Williamson	9.8%	Lorillard	9.0%
Philip Morris	9.4%	Liggett & Myers	6.4%
Others	1.4%	Others	0.1%

SOURCE: *Printer's Ink,* December 1961, and *Business Week,* November 29, 1971

In the early 1960s, the industry had been successful in repulsing the initial anticigarette assault. Attempts to limit advertising, or to ban cigarette ads completely, had been turned back by a coalition of industry lobbyists, politicians from tobacco-growing states, and civil libertarians troubled by free-speech issues. A feeble effort at ending the subsidies given to the growers had been brushed aside. Reports out of the Tobacco Industry Research Committee challenged claims that smoking caused cancer. Industry spokesmen observed that more than 58 million Americans smoked cigarettes, while only 39,000 cases of lung cancer had been reported and recorded in 1960. Since some of the victims were not smokers, it would appear that a smoker wasn't running much of a risk by continuing with his habit. And to add to this, several studies conducted independently of the Institute rejected the correlation, while others observed the continued failure to induce lung cancer in laboratory animals. A few of those who had condemned smoking in the mid-1950s fell back to a new position, arguing that many environmental factors, especially air pollution, caused cancer, and that cigarette smoking

added to the cancer-inducing environment and should be eliminated on that basis.

This is not to say the anticigarette movement was declining.
Rather, the initial shock had passed. Doubtless some individuals
stopped smoking entirely and others cut down or switched to cigars and pipes, but more went over to kings, filters, and
menthols, or combinations of two or three of these. The statistics
told the story. In 1953, when cigarette sales declined due to the
Reader's Digest articles and similar broadsides, sales were 2,702
per capita; by 1961 this had increased to 2,830.

Around this time Maurine Neuberger emerged as a leading
anticigarette figure in Washington. Until 1960 she had been
known as the reform-minded wife of Senator Richard Neuberger,
a liberal former New York *Times* reporter and author who had
gone from the Oregon legislature to the Senate in 1955. Richard
Neuberger had been a heavy cigarette smoker. In March 1960, at
the age of forty-eight, he died of lung cancer. His wife won the
election to fill his seat and arrived in the Senate that November.
Almost immediately she became involved in the issue of banning
cigarette advertising.

It wasn't a promising issue, not for the opponents of smoking or those who defended the habit. The reason was clear
enough: if cigarette smoking did cause cancer, then the practice
should be ended, and no American should be allowed to purchase or use cigarettes. Tobacco might have been classified as a
drug; it did contain nicotine and other substances that were labeled as such. Should it be proven a harmful drug, it could have
been banned, much as cyclamates would be in the early 1970s.

What if the case against tobacco could not be proven in the
laboratory? Then cigarettes would continue to be sold, and the
modern antismoking crusade would have ended. What would be
needed, then, was scientific, causal proof that smoking resulted
in lung cancer. But none existed in 1960, so a different tack had
to be taken. Failing in the crusade for a total ban, the anticigarette forces turned to the matter of advertising, which was
regulated by the Federal Trade Commission and the Federal
Communications Commission, with a possible connection with
the Interstate Commerce Commission.

The Legal and Monetary Affairs Subcommittee of the House

Government Operations Committee had held hearings on cigarette advertising in 1957 and had issued a report which stated
that "the cigarette manufacturers have deceived the American
public through their advertising of cigarettes." It went on to
argue that claims for filters had been exaggerated, and in fact
the filter brands contained low-grade tobaccos with high concen-
trations of tars and nicotine. Nothing came of it. The subcommittee was dissolved shortly thereafter, with the anticigarette forces
claiming this indicated the power of the tobacco lobby.

John Kennedy had been elected President in 1960 by a narrow
margin and with the aid of the southern states—tobacco-growing
states included. There were strong Democratic contingents in
both houses of Congress, and key committees were headed by
southern legislators, whom Kennedy would have to woo in 1961.
Thus, the industry had reason for confidence.

The American Cancer Society, which from the first had been
the spearhead of the movement, rallied its forces for a show-
down in the spring of 1961. Together with the American Public
Health Association, the American Heart Association, and the National Tuberculosis Association, it sent a letter to the White
House calling for the establishment of a presidential commission
to study "the widespread implications of the tobacco problem."
Kennedy brushed the matter aside, but Maurine Neuberger
brought it to the Senate floor by asking for passage of a resolution in favor of the commission. Simultaneously the various associations urged the public to flood Washington with letters and
petitions supporting the Neuberger motion. In May, a reporter
asked the President about his stand on the tobacco issue, and
Kennedy tried to side-step it as gracefully as possible but promised he would look into the matter.

In the end Kennedy decided to accept the Neuberger position.
Two months later the White House announced the formation of
the Surgeon General's Advisory Committee on Smoking and
Health. The Surgeon General himself, Luther Terry, would chair
the Committee, while its members were drawn from leading
figures at the nation's top medical schools and universities.

The Committee spent a year in investigations and several
months in preparing its 387-page report, entitled *Smoking and
Health,* which was released on January 11, 1964. Its message was

clear and to the point. "Cigarette smoking is *causally* [emphasis added] related to lung cancer in men; the magnitude of the effect of cigarette smoking far outweighs all other factors. The data for women, though less extensive, point in the same direction." The report went on to say that the average cigarette smoker is nine or ten times more likely to be struck by lung cancer than is the nonsmoker and that the more a person smoked, the more likely he was to get cancer. Specific carcinogenic agents were identified as being in cigarette smoke, among them cadmium, polycyclic hydrocarbons, DDT, and arsenic. The Committee concluded, unanimously, that "Cigarette smoking is a health hazard of sufficient importance in the United States to warrant appropriate remedial action."

The tobacco companies rushed to print with rebuttals, featuring charges that the Committee had not produced evidence to substantiate its findings. In fact, the Committee had reworked old reports that showed correlations, but not causation. Still, the report had a major impact upon sales. As had been the case eight years before with "Cancer by the Carton," *Smoking and Health* frightened many Americans into cutting down on consumption or quitting altogether. Several months later the industry conceded that cigarette sales had declined by almost 20 per cent in January and February. Then, as time coupled with heavy advertising took its effects, there was a rebound. The old pattern seemed to have been re-established by the end of the year, and there were indications that a new record might be posted in 1965.

But the industry was badly shaken. Some executives believed the scare would pass, as it had in 1953, but most knew otherwise. *Smoking and Health* was a government project and not an article in a magazine. Further action would be taken, and by the government. What would that be? Already there were signs of action. The Surgeon General ordered an end to the free distribution of cigarettes in all hospitals under the control of the Public Health Service, and the Federal Trade Commission indicated it soon would take steps against cigarette advertising. Dr. Terry spoke out in favor of this. "We intend to support the Federal Trade Commission in its proposed action," he said, "because we are convinced that the American people have been deceived and misled by cigarette advertising—and their health has been harmed as a consequence."

This would be the issue around which the anticigarette movement would coalesce, the battlefield for both industry and critics.

The Surgeon General's report had said that smoking was causally related to cancer in men, and perhaps in women as well. The accepted method of demonstrating causal effects was to induce the disease in laboratory animals, if necessary through the use of massive doses of the substance suspected of being harmful. This would be the way cyclamates, certain food dyes, and saccharin would be attacked in the next decade. For years laboratory animals had been raised in what amounted to smoke-filled environments, and still no cases of lung cancer had been induced. The Advisory Committee must have known it lacked documentation to prove causal links and, for that matter, so did the industry. Yet both sides in the dispute elected to fight matters out on the rather narrow grounds of advertising. The press took little notice of this, and the public didn't stop to think about it.

Why was this so? Perhaps all involved decided to take the lesser risk and so chose advertising as the issue. If the government could have proven a causal link did exist, cigarette production would have to cease, and this would have resulted in economic and social dislocations, unemployment, a large dent in the export picture, and the creation of an irate smoking population. Bootlegging would have been introduced, with all of its obvious problems. But should the government fail to prove its contention, all would be as it was, though the anticigarette crusade doubtless would have continued, but in a lower key than before.

It was prudent to deflect the issue. Curbs on advertising would be harmful to Madison Avenue, but it would recover. Tobacco growers might suffer a loss of income, but this too might be borne (and the idea of dropping farm price supports was never given serious consideration). The industry itself would be intact. It was a compromise approach to a difficult problem, which all sides seemed to accept, though there is no sign or evidence that prior agreements had been entered into by government, industry, or reformers.

It was a replay of the Lucy Gaston experience. She had begun by trying to save the country from tobacco, and failing this, the youth, and when that seemed out of reach, young females. At that, Miss Gaston had more success than those who imitated her in the 1960s. She had managed to convince many state legislatures and city councils that an outright ban not only would work, but was necessary, given the evil effects of cigarettes. The American Cancer Society and the Surgeon General would not go that far, even though their evidence showing links between smoking and diseases was more convincing and less emotional than any that existed prior to World War I. The perceived failure of alcohol prohibition, the strength of the cigarette habit in 1964, the power of the tobacco lobby, and the national mood of the period militated against any such replay of the Gaston crusade.

So did the nature of media. Although the antismoking movement cut across all political and ideological lines, generally speaking it had the atmosphere of a crusade and as such found allies among those involved in other movements. One of these was a large, nebulous, and unorganized population that was wary of the impact television was having upon Americans, especially the young people. As they saw it, the freedom of speech issue did not apply here, for television was under the purview of the Federal Communications Commission, and the stations and networks were supposed to function "in the public interest," since in theory the public owned the airwaves.

What was this public interest? At the time, many pressure groups argued against violence on television, and attempts were being made to limit mayhem, especially on programs aimed at young audiences. Some of these same groups attacked commercials that might encourage what they considered harmful habits. This was not a new approach; from the first, the stations had been forbidden from showing hard-liquor ads, though beer commercials could be shown. Now the reformers insisted that cigarette commercials join the short list of banned items, and so the television crusaders united with the anticigarette movement.

It was a powerful and broad coalition with what amounted to limited objectives. Both groups wanted to ban advertisements from television and radio. There was some hope that all forms of cigarette advertising could be ended, but this ran afoul of fears of newspaper and magazine censorship. The anticigarette forces wanted to find some more direct way of warning smokers against the habit. That was as far as they were prepared to go. Given the proper tactics and forum, this coalition had every reason to expect success.

Leaders of the cigarette industry understood the situation and, as might have been expected, hoped to mitigate any penalties decided upon. They knew they could count upon powerful support in Congress, so that any anticigarette bill introduced there would be watered down considerably before it passed. For their part, the antismoking groups recognized the power of politics and so attempted to obtain a ruling from the Federal Trade Commission on advertising, in this way bypassing the legislative process entirely.

In the end the matter was considered both by the Commission and the Congress, and in that order. The FTC hearings on cigarette advertising began in early 1964. Industry and anticigarette witnesses were called to testify, as well as experts on the impact of television upon young people. The industry's tactics were clear: witnesses would both defend tobacco against charges that it caused disease, while at the same time arguing that any curbs on advertising should be voted upon by Congress, since the FTC did not have jurisdiction in the matter. In responding to this, several Commission members warned that they had the right and obligation to issue bans against the use of any harmful product, and that there was evidence that cigarettes fell into that category. Picking up on this, F. J. L. Blasingame, a spokesman for the American Medical Association, wondered why the only action against smoking was in the realm of advertising. "The health hazards of excessive smoking have been well publicized for more than ten years and are common knowledge," he said. Curbs on advertising and labeling cigarettes as being carcinogenic were not the answers, for smokers would ignore the warnings—that had been the experience in those countries where they had been employed—and would smoke even when not hit by television ads. Rather, Blasingame called for more research and then, if proof of harmful effects was produced, he implied a total ban should be considered.

No one followed up on Blasingame's suggestion, and nothing more was heard of a total elimination of cigarettes from the marketplace. The FTC hearings lasted only three days, and Chairman Paul Dixon indicated that a full report would be forthcoming, complete with recommendations.

The industry did not wait for the release of the report and, instead, acted on three fronts simultaneously. First, it continued to argue that the Commission lacked jurisdiction and made it clear that any attempt to force changes in advertising procedures and content would be challenged on that basis.

At the same time, the industry tried to anticipate such changes, by announcing the formulation of a code of fair advertising, to be administered by Robert Meyner, former New Jersey governor. Shortly thereafter, Meyner called a press conference, where he pledged to put an end to claims that smoking was good for the health, to halt ads in comic books and on children's television programs, and in other ways curb excesses in the field. Later on, ad campaigns in college newspapers were halted, as were campus promotional programs, such as the distribution of free cigarettes.

Finally, the industry pressed for hearings before "the proper congressional committee" on the matter, this too in order to force the Federal Trade Commission to back down.

But Dixon and the Commission majority would not be deterred. While the controversy over rights and powers intensified, the FTC ruled that manufacturers would have to "disclose, clearly and prominently, in all advertising and on every pack, box, carton, and other container in which cigarettes are sold," a warning that "cigarette smoking is dangerous to health and may cause death from cancer and other diseases." The Commission wanted a strong, bold statement, and it hinted that further regulations were being considered, among which were some relating to television. Meanwhile it set a deadline of January 1, 1965, for the inclusion of the health warning.

The FTC ruling was not as harsh as the anticigarette forces wanted; however, the industry felt it could get better treatment from Congress and prepared to do battle there. Even before the decision came down, the companies had retained Earle Clements, former Kentucky senator, to co-ordinate the defense. He would be assisted in his work by Hill and Knowlton, a New York public relations firm that had been taken on by the Tobacco Institute. It was a wise selection. Clements had been a protégé of Majority Leader Lyndon Johnson in the 1950s and had served as acting leader while Johnson was recuperating from his heart attack. Many Democratic senators owed him favors, and in addition Clements was a man of great personal charm. Now Johnson was President, and Clements the chief lobbyist for the tobacco industry.

Clements knew that the hearings would take place before the FTC and even before they opened had a good idea of what would happen. In fact, he was somewhat pleased by the development, for he feared that if the FTC did not handle the case, the antismoking people might go to the Federal Communications Commission, which had the power to ban cigarette commercials from radio and television. So rather than concern himself with this matter, he spent much of 1964 cultivating his old friends on Capitol Hill and developing tactics and strategies.

Hearings were scheduled before the House Interstate and Foreign Commerce Committee and the Senate Commerce Committee. Clements knew he could count upon strong allies in both for support. The House panel was chaired by Oren Harris of Arkansas, a firm believer in price supports and other programs to aid agriculture. Horace Kornegay of North Carolina was a strong procigarette voice and, in fact, would leave Congress in 1968 to become vice-president of the Tobacco Institute. Seven other members of the thirty-three-member committee came from tobacco-growing regions and through exchanges of favors could convince others to support their position. In the House, the industry would use economic arguments—cripple the tobacco industry, and hundreds of thousands of jobs would be lost. Congressmen understood such things; they would reject radical proposals.

Maurine Neuberger was the major anticigarette voice on the Senate Commerce Committee, but she lacked seniority and allies. Republican Thruston Morton of Kentucky and Democrat Ross Bass of Tennessee had both. Vance Hartke of Indiana owed Clements a favor. Democrat Daniel Brewster came from the tobacco state of Maryland. Others were irritated by Maurine Neuberger's crusading zeal—she was not a typical get-along-by-going-along legislator. Thus, Clements felt he could rely upon at least half the senators for support.

The House hearings proceeded as anticipated. Some medical evidence was introduced, but for the most part the congressmen seemed intent on developing the economic argument. Destroy the cigarette—and that was the intent of the antismoking people, so they said—and an entire region of the nation would be crippled. "The tobacco plant stands as the defendant in this trial," said Kornegay. "This plant and millions of Americans stand in serious jeopardy today. The health factor is tremendously important," but the precise relationships between smoking and health hadn't been determined. "There is a definite need for more research to find out what, if any, health hazards exist." And so it went, through late June and early July of 1964.

In the end the House Committee recommended a measure to require health warnings on cigarette packs. At the same time it agreed to bar the FTC from acting on its own. In August, Chairman Harris asked Paul Dixon to delay implementation of the FTC ruling, and Dixon agreed to do so.

The hearings before the Senate Commerce Committee, which took place the following March, were quite similar. Dr. Thomas Carlile of the American Cancer Society testified that "lung cancer can be produced in human beings by prolonged inhalation of at least several different substances such as dust containing radioactive material, chromates, or nickel. Thus it is clear that lung cancer is not purely an hereditary, hormonal, or infectious disease." He went on to say that "Prolonged exposure to certain chemical substances, called carcinogens, can produce cancer of various tissues in experimental animals, and in man. Such substances are present in cigarette smoke. In fact, cancer has been produced repeatedly by the application of tar condensed from cigarette smoke to the skin of experimental animals." Other witnesses drew attention to the fact that while some substances might be called carcinogenic, none or only small traces of them could be found in cigarette smoke. Also, the cancers Dr. Carlile referred to had been produced by painting the skin of rats with highly concentrated tars. The lesson, said one industry spokesman, is to avoid having anyone paint your back with tars. He and other witnesses went on to note the inability to produce lung cancer in laboratory animals. Also introduced into evidence was an article with a statement by the president of the American Medical Association, James Z. Appel. "There must be a relationship between cigarettes and lung cancer, but I—for that matter, anyone else—don't know what it is." "The only evidence we have is primarily statistical . . . perhaps a little more than that, but that's about all." And as though responding to Dr. Carlile's comments, Dr. Thomas Burford of St. Louis said, "Many of us feel that cancer will eventually be proven to be due to a virus or a viruslike substance and that it will very probably require a very special set of circumstances within the host for the cancer to develop. So long as the cause of cancer is unknown it would seem only reasonable that to raise an alarm about cigarette smoking is unwarranted."

As before, there was testimony on both sides, some of it convincing, most only partially so, and even more of the polemical nature. Dr. Alvis Greer of Greer Clinic in Houston may have struck a responsive chord when he quoted Dr. Joseph Berkson of the Mayo Clinic, who said: "Without false modesty and, quite frankly, I do not know the cause of cancer. Moreover, I am going to say, without the slightest fear of contradiction, that no one else does either."

The congressional hearings were not medical forums, however, but a method of arriving at a legislative resolution of a problem that had moral, economic, social, medical, and, most important, political overtones. Whether or not cigarette smoking caused cancer was not the issue; had it been, one would have argued the case before a more qualified set of committees or perhaps before a nonpolitical group or groups. What really mattered was what would be done to resolve the contest between the industry and its lobbyists on one side and the anticigarette forces and its allies on the other. Votes and political pressures counted in this struggle, and not laboratory evidence and statistical charts.

In this contest the tobacco companies had more experience, sophistication, and clout than did the anticigarette lobby. Subtle and direct pressures were brought to bear against senators and congressmen. Through several associates, President Johnson let it be known that he favored a moderate measure. Meyner and others pointed to the results of self-regulation, for the more blatant advertising campaigns indeed had come to an end.

The Cigarette Labeling and Advertising Act passed both houses of Congress in mid-June. Under its provisions a health warning would appear on cigarette packs. The Federal Trade Commission was informed that henceforth the industry would come under congressional purview.

The anticigarette forces were irate. When *Smoking and Health* had been released in January 1964, they had hoped some way would be found to control the habit or even eliminate it over a period of time. The FTC stance later that year indicated that while a ban would be out of the question, stringent controls on advertising would be created and enforced by an agency that could not be swayed easily by political pressures. It had been a step back for the crusade, but this was a beginning, and a promising one at that. Now the FTC had been chastised, and Congress passed a weak measure requiring a health warning on packs, and nothing else. Senator Neuberger attempted to amend the bill so as to make it stronger, but her amendments were rejected. The antismoking coalition petitioned President Johnson to veto the measure and ask for a stronger one. He said nothing and signed it into law on July 27.

Beginning on January 1, 1966, all cigarette packages would have to carry a label stating: "Caution—cigarette smoking may be hazardous to your health." That was all. Given the problems that it faced in 1964, and the fears of what might be done as a result of the Surgeon General's report, this must be considered a major victory for the industry. The tobacco lobby had a large majority in Congress and a friend in the White House. Chairman Dixon's assertions to the contrary, the FTC had all but been eliminated from the scene, at least insofar as controlling this industry was concerned.

This did not mean the contest was over, however, or that the corporation leaders felt confident of victory. In fact, the opposite feeling prevailed in the board rooms. Much had been accomplished, but the antismoking forces did have a narrow victory, and they meant to mount another assault at the next session of Congress. In addition, they would use the courts and try to work through the Federal Communications Commission. Already there was talk of litigation, and one fringe group wanted to have tobacco reclassified as a drug, obtainable only upon prescription and subject to regulation under the terms of the Pure Food and Drug Act. The industry would not be crushed by such blows, but it could be nibbled into a state of malaise, if not terminal illness.

Cigarette sales for 1965 were 562 billion. On a per capita basis this came to 2,896. It was a new record.

XII

The Industry Responds

There was little jubilation at tobacco company headquarters after the limited victory in Washington. The industry
believed that there could be no final resolution of the conflict.
Even prior to the congressional vote, the antitobacco coalition let
it be known that a new campaign was in the works. This one
would include the usual mix of remedies and penalties—requests
for limitations on advertisements, further health warnings, and
an end to subsidies—as well as one new one: there would be
demands that the tobacco companies themselves support antismoking messages, on television and in print media, to undo the
damage they had caused.

The companies and the Tobacco Institute were pretty certain
they could block all of these efforts, but having been dealt both a
scare and a message in the early 1960s, they didn't intend to take
risks. Their responses took two forms, the first conventional, the

second more drastic and an anticipation of the worst possible resolution of the conflict.

The companies understood that while new victories might be scored in Washington, defeats were becoming more common in the rest of the country. The health issue simply would not vanish or even fade. At the same time, smokers had demonstrated an inability to give up cigarettes or at least an unwillingness to do so. The drive to combine health and smoking—pleasure and safety—continued. There would be further growth in the filter, king, and menthol markets, but the old standards of the "pre-cancer days" would continue their steady decline. Thus, the new-product mania of the early 1960s would go on for at least the rest of the decade.

Robert B. Walker, who became president of American Tobacco in 1963, was the most flamboyant advocate of brand proliferation. He took over at a time when American was declining because of its late entry into the filter and menthol markets and its undue reliance on a single brand, Pall Mall. A marketing man for most of his professional life, Walker was expected to turn the company around by taking a fresh approach in this area. American had great expectations for its new chief, who seemed an updated version of George Hill, and who loved to lecture his fellows with what to outsiders seemed trite and garish speeches but which were much appreciated within the industry. "The law of the marketplace like Darwin's Law of Evolution is change or perish," he told the National Industrial Conference Board. "With the persistence of the scientist, we must probe for new concepts, new insights into consumer behavior, new marketing techniques. And with the courage of the explorer, we must be willing to turn from the old that is tarnishing to the new that sparkles with promise. . . ." And so it went.

Walker employed a buckshot approach to the cigarette market. No one within the industry expected a return to the old days, when a single brand, or two or three, dominated the field. A generation earlier a major smoke might capture and hold one out of every five consumers. Walker and his counterparts at the other large firms would have rejoiced if one of their brands proved profitable in its second year, showed gains for the next three, and remained in the field a decade after its introduction.

There would be major celebrations at company headquarters if any such product captured 5 per cent of the market. Thus, the companies would create and market many new brands, in the hope that one or more would catch on, while the others would be discarded as soon as their lack of appeal was detected.

Walker showed the other firms how to do this. In January 1964, he released Carlton, a king filter that had its low tar and nicotine contents printed on the package in clear view of would-be purchasers. Furthermore, American advertised the Carlton figures that surprised and pleased some anticigarette crusaders, who had advocated such publicity in the past. But Carlton didn't perform as well as Walker had hoped. He wanted his smoke to cut deeply into Kent sales, which it failed to do.

Roi-Tan was released in March, as a hybrid cigarette-cigar, an attempt to open up a new market for American. The antismoking people had all but exonerated cigars, and as a result sales of that form of tobacco reached a historic high in 1964. American long had been a leader in this field, with Roi-Tan one of its major brands. Now it was a small cigar—or standard cigarette, depending upon how it was viewed—with a filter and packaged twenty in a soft container. Was it to be inhaled like a cigarette or puffed as a cigar? The ads didn't say. But neither cigar nor cigarette smokers took to this new product, and soon it was withdrawn from the market.

Walker made a play for pipe smokers in April 1964, when he released Half and Half, which was made from the old mixture of that name and had its fragrant aroma and sweet taste. The ads called upon smokers to "Enjoy America's best-tasting pipe tobacco in a filter cigarette!" The antismoking forces hadn't attacked the pipe, and like cigars, sales of pipes and tobacco were rising. As with Roi-Tan, the purchaser wasn't told whether or not he should inhale. Half and Half never performed very well.

American released Montclair in May. This was what amounted to a mentholated version of Carlton, which also had an "air-vent" filter that was supposed to further cool the smoke. Walker had hoped Montclair would take some of the play away from Salem and Kool, but this brand too failed to gain more than a modest foothold in the field.

Now Walker turned to a variant of what had been known as

hitchhiking a few years earlier, when L & M had come up with Chesterfield kings. In August he released Luckies filters, which captured a decent share of the market, though at the expense of the regulars. Other mutations followed, so that within two years smokers could purchase Luckies in any of seven different forms —regulars, regular or king filters, regular menthols, 100 mm (what Walker called "luxury length" to distinguish it from kings), and king or 100-mm mentholated filters. The same was tried for Pall Mall, which in January 1965 was released in the new 100-mm form, with a mentholated version out in October. The previous month, Walker announced a "radical new filter" for a fresh brand, Waterford. As the name indicates, this cigarette's filter was impregnated with droplets of water in an encapsulated form, which were released when pressed gently. Waterford was supposed to combine the benefits of the water pipe with the convenience of the cigarette and, of course, provide coolness of smoke to those who did not relish the taste of menthol. "From the oldest idea in smoking . . . comes the newest taste in cigarettes," read the ads. But Waterford didn't attract customers and was withdrawn after a national test of slightly more than a year.

Failing to make a significant dent with his new brands, and not doing particularly well with the family approach, Walker turned to an old favorite. Sweet Caporal, that best seller of the pre-Camel era, was revamped and released nationally in October. "Sweet News for You From 1870!" read the ad. "Gee whiskers! Sweet Caporal Cigarettes are back. Back with old-time flavor. Back with a filter. Today, treat yourself to this great-tasting 95-year-old cigarette. You'll be sweet on Sweet Caps." Of course, the cigarette blend was changed—modernized was the word. Instead of the old Virginia mix, American put forth one based upon Bright tobacco, heavily flavored with sugar. Old-timers didn't recognize the blend; new smokers merely assumed the name had to mean the smoke was sweet. Some tried the brand for a while but then returned to old favorites. By 1966, Sweet Caps were all but gone from the scene once more.

"Brand-a-Month Walker," as he was being called by the trade, was not dissuaded. In 1967 he came out with Bull Durham cigarettes, attempting to capitalize upon the name of the old plug brand, and also put Tareyton out as a 100-mm brand. The following month Walker introduced Silva Thins in both regular and menthol versions. This 100-mm smoke was designed for women and featured an elegant pack, "upper-class" ads, and a more slender cigarette (which also meant less tobacco). Silva Thins had moderate success and was the only one of the new Walker brands that did even fairly well. Colony, which was tested in several regions that year, lasted less than six months, and the same was true for other smokes that came out of the American stable in this period.

Walker's only success came with 100-mm brands, but despite this all his forays were imitated by one or more of his rivals. Reynolds released Tempo in 1964, the same year L & M came out with Devon and Philip Morris arrived in a "multi-filter" form. L & M's Masterpiece appeared in 1965, along with P.M.'s Galaxy. The following year the latter firm introduced Marlboro Green—a mentholated form of that smoke—while L & M had a slew of new smokes, none of which made it nationally, and Lorillard introduced True.

In 1967 there was a veritable explosion of new offerings based primarily on Walker's success with Pall Mall 100s. Reynolds came out with Winston and Winston Menthol in that length, and Salem went to 100 mm as well. So did Brown & Williamson's Kool, and that company also had a new 100 mm called Capri. At Philip Morris, Marlboro and Benson & Hedges went to 100 mm. Lorillard put Kent into that length, while creating True Menthol toward the end of the year. And of course, there were L & M 100s, in both the menthol and regular tastes. In fact, the entire industry seemed taken with the drive to greater length. L & M capped the fight by putting out Chesterfield 101s—which were advertised as being a "tiny millimeter" longer (and presumably better) than the rest.

This family approach to brands that had begun with Chesterfield had been carried to its logical conclusion by Walker in the 1960s. It was one of the two most important merchandising developments of the decade, the other being refinements in television ads. Winston, which was the nation's leading smoke in 1969, came in four models—king filters in soft pack, 100 mm, menthol 100s, and 85 mm in boxes. Pall Mall, in second place, had three different forms, while Marlboro, the nation's number-three smoke, could be purchased in five different ways—king boxes, king softs, 100-mm boxes, 100s soft, and Marlboro Greens. That year there were four different forms of Luckies and Philip Morris and three for Benson & Hedges, and Parliament. Not a single one of the top ten that year came in only one form. Liggett & Myers, the smallest of the major firms with only 7 per cent of the market, had only three brands—L & M, Chesterfield, and Lark. But the first two came in at five each. Chesterfield, which had started the movement, now could be had in regular, king, and 101-mm sizes, with filters, and mentholated. In addition, Liggett & Myers was experimenting with coupons in some parts of the country, so that the Californian who purchased the smokes received a coupon, while the Tennesseean did not.

Brand proliferation and this family approach indicated both weakness and fear. The former reflected the inability to create a cigarette that could capture a sizable segment of the total market, and the latter was derived from a desire to capitalize upon whatever proven assets and brand loyalties remained from an earlier period. Together, they were signs of either industry maturity or decay, depending on whether the analyst was optimistic or pessimistic regarding the future of smoking in America. As might have been expected, the industry tended to take the former position, while the anticigarette forces adopted the latter. The companies could point to the 573 billion smokes produced in 1969 as an indication that the habit was not on the way out. This was a record, and coming off a bad 1968, a sign that further growth was in store. On the other hand, per capita consumption was 2,836, continuing the steady erosion of this figure which began in 1966.

Without the anticigarette movement, both figures would have been much higher, while the industry would have been anticipating a boom era for the 1970s. The baby crop of the late 1940s was moving into the age where it would be taking to smokes. There was a war on in Vietnam and disturbances at home, and, in the past, wars and internal tensions had helped boost cigarette sales. This time they did not. Some sociologists claimed young people were taking to marijuana and hard drugs in place of tobacco, but others noted that drug users often tended to be heavy cigarette smokers as well. Walker and industry leaders spoke

bravely of their hopes for the industry before Wall Street analysts and service club meetings, but in private they must have
known they were in serious trouble.

The antismoking crusade had not faded. The early legislative
setbacks did not dissuade the reformers from their work. Rather,
they regrouped and planned a new assault upon cigarette ads,
this one in the courts, before legislative committees, and at the
Federal Trade Commission and the Federal Communications
Commission.

Given the statistics, the failures in product development, and
the persistent crusade, the corporation leaders embarked upon
the second and more drastic of their responses. Gradually, with
careful planning and often brilliant execution, the companies
began to ease themselves out of complete dependence upon tobacco in general and cigarettes in particular. Just as Buck Duke
had transformed the tobacco industry of the 1880s into the cigarette industry of the early twentieth century, so his legatees at
American, Reynolds, Philip Morris, Lorillard, and Liggett &
Myers turned to other products that offered more promise in
sales and profits. Only Brown & Williamson refused to diversify,
perhaps because its parent firm, British-American Tobacco,
wanted to avoid troubles with the government, which might
have frowned at the prospect of a foreign company taking over
another American concern.

Diversification seemed both sensible and possible, given the
business atmosphere of the early and middle 1960s. In fact, the
industry might have gone on an acquisitions binge even without
the impetus of the anticigarette movement. This was the great
era of conglomerate construction, when such major empires as
LTV, Litton, Textron, and International Telephone & Telegraph
emerged from much smaller companies as a result of acquisitions
of nonrelated businesses. The theory was simple enough. The
most important part of any company, so it was believed, was its
management. Assets could be bought and sold; management
remained, to be changed through evolution, not revolution. The
management of a machinery company wasn't that much different
from the leadership of a supermarket chain, and so a moribund
concern in the former industry might attempt to purchase ownership of a promising operation in the latter. The important

question, at all times, was: "What experience and talents do managements possess?" and not "How can we expand our present business?" Thus, Gulf & Western, a supplier of auto parts, used its stock to acquire a sugar refiner, a zinc producer, several machinery companies, and an entertainment complex. G & W even entered the tobacco field, through acquisition of Consolidated Cigar, one of the oldest, largest, and most prestigious firms in the industry, and in this way became a direct competitor for American Tobacco, which remained first in cigars though lagging in cigarettes.

If G & W could diversify into the tobacco field, why couldn't one or more of the cigarette companies do the same into auto parts, metals, and entertainment? Not only was it possible, but the idea was sensible given the problems faced by cigarette manufacturers in the 1960s.

As was the case with other developments in the postwar period, Philip Morris led the way. In 1957 it acquired Milprint, and the following year, Polymer Industries. Milprint was a manufacturer of packaging, and some of its products could be used for cigarettes. As for Polymer, this was a chemical company, which had no direct relationship with tobacco. In 1960 Philip Morris obtained control of American Safety Razor and, three years later, Burma-Vita and Clark Gum. In the mid-1960s, the company purchased several small hospital-supply operations. The biggest and most important acquisition came in 1968, when Philip Morris obtained majority control of Miller Brewing Company. Later on, the rest of the stock was acquired for a total cost of close to a quarter of a billion dollars. Then Philip Morris diversified into land development and even took a flyer into Australian wines. In 1978 it acquired Seven-Up.

With the exception of Polymer and part of the Milprint operation—P.M.'s first forays into diversification—all the other companies were in the field of consumer goods, and each required marketing skills of a high order. This was what the cigarette business had stressed from the outset. It was the link that ran from Buck Duke and Richard Reynolds through George Washington Hill to the Cullmans and on to Robert Walker. Philip Morris took an inventory of its assets and found that one of the more important of these was the ability to create products for consumers and then market them effectively. In the past these talents had been used to create and then sell cigarettes. Now they would be employed to merchandise such varied products as gum, razors, shaving cream, wine, soda, and beer.

Reynolds cast its net more widely. In 1963 it purchased Pacific Hawaiian Products (the manufacturer of Hawaiian Punch and other drinks), and two years later, Penick & Ford (Brer Rabbit and Vermont Maid syrups, My-T-Fine desserts, and a variety of other food products). Then Reynolds went into Chinese foods (Chun King), Latin foods (Patio Foods), and other consumer goods. But it also diversified into petroleum and packaging and, in 1970, spent close to $200 million to obtain McLean Industries, the major factor in the field of containerized freight. For a while it seemed that Reynolds would become a transportation and food conglomerate. After assuming control of McLean the firm changed its name to Reynolds Industries and set out in an abortive move to take over at U. S. Lines, the largest American oceanic shipper, a good match for McLean. But this attempt resulted in much litigation and in the end was called off. Like Philip Morris, Reynolds remained a tobacco company, utilizing its merchandising expertese in food and related areas.

American Tobacco was of two minds regarding mergers. Walker seemed intent upon making the firm the leader in cigarettes and would not concede defeat, either to Reynolds and Philip Morris or the antismoking groups. While the other tobacco companies sought out merger candidates, Walker concentrated upon new brands and configurations. Still, he did bow to internal pressures by entering into conversations with Consolidated Foods, which was almost half as large as American and the producer of a wide variety of consumer goods, including Sara Lee cakes and pastries. Nothing came of the negotiations, but Walker did take a stock interest in Gallaher, Ltd., a major British cigarette company. As it had since the end of the war, American went on its own way, contrary to that taken by the rest of the industry. And as had been the case with filters and mentholated brands, it "converted" later in the game, abandoning a failing philosophy on the brink of corporate disaster.

American's big move came in 1966, when it purchased Sunshine Biscuits and James Beam Distilling Company, the former one of the nation's largest bakers, the latter a major producer of bourbon whiskies. Two years later Sunshine purchased Bell Brand Foods, while another American subsidiary took over Duffy-Mott. Swingline, a manufacturer of office equipment, was acquired in 1970, along with Acme Visible Records, Master Lock, and Andrew Jergen, the last a medium-size cosmetics company. By then, close to half of American's sales and profits were derived from nontobacco products and services. To signal this new independence from cigarettes, the company changed its name to American Brands, Inc.

Liggett & Myers followed American into the liquor field, by purchasing control of Paddington (the importer of J&B Scotch, Bombay gin, and other leading brands) and Star Industries, an important liquor distributor, in 1966. Earlier they had taken control of Allen Products, the canner of Alpo dog food and a leader in that industry. Other acquisitions followed. In 1976, Liggett & Myers changed its name to Liggett Group, to signal its new incarnation.

Lorillard took a similar path to a more drastic conclusion. First the company purchased Usen Canning, the second largest firm in the cat food business, then Golden Nuggets Sweets, a candy manufacturer. However, these mergers did Lorillard little good; the company stagnated, unable to expand its cigarette business, while pet foods and candy offered little potential for growth. Lorillard could not hope to become a major conglomerate like American or Reynolds; nor did there seem much prospect of true growth, as was the case at Philip Morris. Resigned to an ignoble fate, the company permitted itself to be acquired by a fast-moving conglomerate, Loews Corporation, in 1969.

The anticigarette movement might have destroyed the tobacco companies of the 1960s, just as the prohibitionists of 1919 smashed the distilleries and breweries of that period. But the reformers hardly could do as much to Reynolds Industries, American Brands, Liggett Group, and Loews, while Philip Morris increasingly was more interested in beer than cigarettes. Corporate leaders spoke enthusiastically about new opportunities for management and staffs, interesting possibilities in merchandising, and the growth cycles for pet foods, alcohol, and other consumer products.

The contrast between them and George Hill couldn't have been sharper. Hill had lived for Luckies and couldn't have conceived of his company featuring any other cigarette, much less product. The men at American Brands saw profits in smokes but would have discontinued production had such a move served corporate requirements.

The combination of these two responses resulted in a mood of failure and drift in cigarette circles. Part of the reason for this went beyond the relatively narrow limits of the cigarette debate and involved the national mood during the middle and late 1960s. The country seemed to be dividing into rival camps on such issues as race, the Vietnam War, and what was euphemistically called "life styles." This division was replete with symbols, most of which were oversimplified and bordered on caricature but nevertheless were powerful and pervasive. On one side was the young, dungareed, bearded, opponent of the Vietnam War and racism, who called for revolution, disdained middle-class values, refused to seek conventional success, ate natural foods, and used drugs, usually soft, at times hard, which were consumed at rock concerts or sit-ins. His opponent was middle class and middle-aged, supported the war, feared integration would destroy property values, ate and dressed conventionally, drank liquor, and smoked cigarettes. Again, these were caricatures, but the mood was such that they were accepted as reality.

Each acted as though the other was out to destroy society, and reacted accordingly. The middle class wanted to ban demonstrations by the revolutionaries, who in turn presented a list of demands: end the war, end racism, end control of the people by corporate interests. And end pollution as well, of the air, the seas, the earth, and the lungs. This meant a fight against cigarettes, or more than that, a crusade, for the late 1960s was the period for such movements and symbols.

In other words, the antismoking coalition enlisted new cadres during these years. Of course, this was not the focal point for their interests—not while the war, racism, and sexism were prime issues. But the antiestablishmentarians did provide drive, emotion, and even recruits who worked hard for the cause. At the same time, those individuals who were in control of major institutions and power centers often appeared uncertain and were willing to bow, compromise, or even capitulate. It happened in the universities, in governments, and at the regulatory agencies and in the courts. Some of those in power hardened their stance. Others cried *"mea culpa"* and joined the critics. This, too, served the interests of the antismoking people.

John Banzhaf III, who became the symbol for and leader of this next stage of the fight against cigarettes, did not fit the stereotype for revolutionaries. He was a young lawyer interested in copyrights, computer programming, and the good life. Banzhaf was marginally involved in some of the political protest movements of the period, but not to the extent that the activities would divert him from a career.

In 1966 he became concerned with the way cigarettes were advertised on television, as much through questioning of federal policy as anything else. At the time the FCC was considering the rights of television and radio stations to present editorials, and the rights of interested groups to respond. Banzhaf saw no reason why this should not apply to advertisements as well, especially when the goods being sold were of questionable value. He wrote to WCBS-TV in New York, asking for free air time to respond to its cigarette commercials. The request was rejected. Not only would this be opposed by sponsors, but such ads would be costly to the station. Furthermore, such a concession would open a nest of problems. Did this mean that antisugar groups would reply to commercials for breakfast cereals? And what of those individuals who opposed beer, cosmetics, autos, and other products? As was to have been expected, the station hoped Banzhaf would forget the matter, and that no one else would take up the fight.

Banzhaf did not let the matter rest. He wrote other letters, both to the station and the Federal Communications Commission. The station continued to ignore him, but Banzhaf did better with the Commission, which in mid-1967 ruled that the fairness doctrine indeed did apply to commercials. On the other hand it rejected the claim for equal time. "The practical result of any roughly one-to-one correlation would probably be either the elimination or substantial curtailment of broadcast cigarette advertising," said the FCC. The station would have to provide some time for other points of view, and do so without charge, but this need not be equal to that purchased by the tobacco companies. Finally, "this requirement will not preclude or curtail presentation by stations of cigarette advertising which they chose to carry."

Banzhaf considered this a limited victory, and he immediately filed additional briefs before the Commission. Shortly thereafter he quit his job at a New York law firm for full-time work in the anticigarette movement. He organized ASH—Action on Smoking and Health—whose major goal was the complete elimination of televised cigarette ads. With the aid of Senator Neuberger and other veterans of the struggle, as well as that of some newcomers (including Robert Kennedy), he seemed capable of winning the fight.

The tobacco companies appeared to recognize this. Banzhaf and his group stressed public ownership of the airwaves and the fact that children could be influenced by the ads to start smoking and maintain the habit. Clearly the 1967 decision would be the first of several, which would finally result in an end of televised ads. Believing this, the companies adjusted their strategy and tactics accordingly. They would fight ASH to the end, not only by maintaining their old positions, but through analysis of television revenues—without cigarette ad revenue, the media would be crippled. Would a cigarette advertising ban create a precedent? It was then that the companies raised the specter of dozens of special interest consumer group lawsuits for equal time. In an extreme statement, one agency noted that automobiles killed far more people than died each year of lung cancer. How would the FCC respond to demands that anticar fanatics be granted access to the airwaves?

Much of this was hyperbole, a futile attempt on the part of the cigarette companies and advertising agencies to raise unreasonable fears and gain allies. And they knew it at the time. They wouldn't go down without a struggle, and perhaps some kind of compromise would be reached. For example, the tobacco companies might volunteer to stop using television if the government would promise to end some forms of "harassment."

Many company executives thought this kind of deal would prove beneficial for all concerned. Not only might moderate antismoking forces accept it, but an end to televised commercials might actually benefit the companies. In fact, by the late 1960s television had proved a media of dubious net value. This had not been the case during the 1950s, when few new national brands were being introduced, and television time and production costs were quite low. There were many new brands at the time Banzhaf filed his briefs, however, and ad time and charges were high. Furthermore, there was no convincing evidence that television did a better job of selling particular brands than did print media. No one company would withdraw by itself however, but all might benefit if the government obliged all of them to leave the air simultaneously. Too, the industry feared the impact of antismoking ads. And if there were no cigarette ads, the equal time provision would not apply.

The antismoking commercials (if they could be called that) which began in 1968 were imaginative and effective. Some of them, featuring actors Tony Randall and Tony Curtis, urged the public to throw away their cigarettes and wear a button that read, "I quit." Others showed sagging middle-aged men and women smokers who, upon stopping the habit, became athletic and jumped in the air to click their heels. The motto there: I kicked the habit. One was a takeoff on the Marlboro man, a tough-looking Westerner who smoked "a man's brand." It featured one such individual in a Western saloon, unable to draw his gun on a clean-cut nonsmoker because he was overcome by a coughing fit. The slogan: "Cigarettes—they're killers." Several urged the answer of "yes" to the question, "Do you mind very much if I smoke?"

The most effective ad featured William Talman, who had played Hamilton Berger in the popular Perry Mason television series, and so was a familiar figure. Looking drawn and obviously close to death, Talman spoke of his wife and children and the good life he had enjoyed and was about to lose. Referring both to his use of cigarettes and the television role, Talman told the audience, "I have lung cancer. Take some advice about smoking and losing from someone who's been doing both for years. If you haven't smoked, don't start. If you do smoke—quit. Don't be a loser." The fact that Talman was dead by the time the commercial reached the air made the appeal all the more moving and effective.

The cigarette companies had no way to respond to such an appeal. And it did work—some sources claimed that as many as ten million Americans quit smoking from 1967 to 1970. Yet with all of this, total sales were on the upswing. Perhaps the public had become inured to ads on both sides. The vast majority of smokers kept their packs.

These, then, were the crosscurrents within the industry and among reformers in 1968. Banzhaf filed appeals in the district courts, and some of them argued that stations which accepted cigarette ads should lose their licenses, since they operated against the public interest. The National Association of Broadcasters entered the cases and spoke out for economic freedom and against unwarranted interference in the promotion of what was a legal product. As for the tobacco companies, they continued to spend large sums of money for network television and tried to create the atmosphere for compromise. This became more desirable as it grew evident that the antismoking commercials were having an impact, and that the diversification moves were bearing fruit in the form of sales and profits.

In February 1969, the FCC announced its intention to ask for a ban on cigarette advertising on radio and television, on the grounds that smoking was a "hazard to public health." The broadcasters responded by announcing they would fight the ban on First Amendment grounds. As for the Tobacco Institute, it called the statement "arbitrary in the extreme." Just as the cigarette industry had bypassed the FTC in 1965 through an appeal to Congress, so it would do the same in regard to the FCC four years later.

Earle Clements began making trips to the Capitol once more and seemed in full control when the House Committee on Interstate and Foreign Commerce opened hearings in April. Once again he did his job well. The Public Health Cigarette Smoking Bill, reported out of committee in May, would have extended the life of the 1965 measure for six years and called for a strengthening of the health warning; instead of "Caution: Cigarette Smoking May Be Hazardous to Your Health," the message would be, "Warning: The Surgeon General Has Determined That Cigarette Smoking Is Dangerous To Your Health And May Cause Lung Cancer And Other Diseases."

The tobacco and cigarette lobbies weren't pleased with the wording, but they lacked the power to block antagonists on this issue. On the other hand, no hard-and-fast ban had been recommended. Both sides in the fight knew the situation would be different in the Senate Commerce Committee, however, for Senator Philip Hart of Michigan vowed he would fight to the end for the elimination of televised commercials. Appraising the situation carefully, counting votes and knowing the industry stance, Clements approached Hart with an offer. The industry would cease all television and radio commercials voluntarily, in return for immunity from legal actions in the case. On the surface it appeared fair enough. All the companies wanted were assurances that they would not be prosecuted for ending their ad campaigns. Thus, they would be protected from the networks on the one side and the government on the other.

Hart rejected the offer. Instead the committee, under his leadership, reported a draft measure calling for an end to televised cigarette ads by January 1, 1971, at the latest. On the other hand, the proposed new health message for cigarette packs would be less severe than that recommended by the House Committee—"Warning: Excessive Cigarette Smoking Is Dangerous to Your Health."

As far as the public was concerned, Hart and his Senate colleagues were being harsher on the industry than was the House Committee. But the cigarette manufacturers actually preferred the Senate version. Walker of American Tobacco went so far as to offer to end all televised ads by January 1970, if the Congress would find some way to help him break his contractual obligations to the networks. By late 1969, then, the fight over televised ads was between the media and the reformers. The tobacco companies were on the sidelines in this struggle, awaiting the verdict with a measure of assurance that no matter what happened, they would do well.

This attitude meant the Senate version would become the basis for the new legislation, and so it was. Cigarette ads would be banned from radio and television, but the date for the ending of such messages would be midnight, January 1, 1971—so that the companies could place their ads on broadcasts of the New Year's Day football games. Also, the message on the side of cigarettes and in print ads also would be altered, with the final version being, "Warning: The Surgeon General Has Determined That Cigarette Smoking Is Dangerous to Your Health." President Nixon signed this measure into law on April 1, 1970. The newspapers and news magazines heralded the legislation as a major turning point in the history of the cigarette habit. Perhaps now it would loosen its grip upon the American public.

The evidence that this was so is spotty. As previously indicated, cigarette production for 1969 actually rose, going to 573 billion units from the previous year's 570 billion. But the advance was due largely to increased exports and additions to inventory made necessary by brand proliferation. Actual consumption did decline, from 1968's 528 billion to 520 billion. In its year-end industry survey, *Marketing/Communications* noted that "For years people have talked about breaking the smoking habit. Now for the first time it's apparent many are doing it." *Business Week* echoed the thought: "There is no getting around it. The cigarette business has long been what economists call 'mature,' and now it has become a declining business."

Was this really the case? Combining their needs for additional revenue with the pose of crusading for health, many states and municipalities had raised cigarette taxes in 1969, so that, on a national basis, this charge advanced by more than 50 per cent. A recession began in 1969, and this may have aggravated the situation somewhat. This is not to say that higher prices and lower incomes resulted in the decline in smoking, but neither could it be claimed with conviction that the anticigarette message had finally taken hold.

The tobacco company executives believed more time would be needed before any serious assessment could be made. Meanwhile they prepared for the last year of televised commercials, the switchback to the old media, and the introduction of new brands. Reynolds placed emphasis upon campaigns for Doral, which was test-marketed in 1969, and Vantage, a 1970 brand, both of which featured filters and low-tar and -nicotine contents. American had no new brands for 1970, but Walker hadn't run out his string. Toward the end of the year he announced that Maryland 100s, featuring air-cured menthol tobacco, would be marketed nationally the following January—the first of the post-

television cigarettes. Brown & Williamson offered Flair and Hallmark, both in 100-mm regulars and mentholated, but neither of
them made much of an impact. In late November the company
announced the development of Laredo, which featured tobacco,
paper, and a roll-your-own machine, the use of which would cut
the cost of smoking considerably. Philip Morris came up with
New Leaf, Liggett & Myers with Eve (a smoke aimed at the female market), and Lorillard with Kent mentholateds.

None of the new brands was deemed a threat to the industry
leaders, and there were no breakthroughs in product design—
though Hallmark had "windows" in the paper to allow more air
in the mix, and presumably less smoke in the lungs. Yet while
cigarette production declined somewhat as a result of the working off of inventories and a dip in foreign sales, actual consumption rose slightly in 1970, going to 524 billion units.

The industry was mature. Its attackers had won several major
victories. Antismoking propaganda had reached a new high in
both volume and sophistication in 1970. Smoking no longer was
deemed the mark of status and worldliness. There was talk of
banning the practice in public places, and already some restaurants were telling customers they should refrain from smoking in
dining rooms. With all of this, growth resumed, in absolute
terms, if not on a per capita basis.

The antismoking contingent looked forward to the television
ban, thinking it would alter the situation significantly. Without
advertising the habit would wither and, after a generation, actually vanish. To them the television ban was the equivalent of the
national prohibition of alcohol after World War I, only this time
the ban would be effective. Heartened by the 1970 statistics and
surveys, the cigarette companies were willing to await the verdict of the marketplace. Although they appeared to have lost the
congressional battles of 1969–70, they did not consider the defeat
a serious blow. In fact, they had every reason to be content with
the situation as it stood on New Year's Day, 1971. Now there
would be no more cigarette ads on television. On the other hand,
the anticigarette forces would have to pay for those ads they
chose to show. The companies would boost their advertising expenditures in newspapers and magazines, and in 1971 it seemed

unlikely these would be obliged to carry free antismoking messages.

Viewed in this light, the industry defeat was really a victory of sorts. The companies would survive and so would the cigarette. Furthermore, the fortunes of the companies and the product no longer were as closely interrelated as they had been a decade earlier. In all, the companies were in better shape in 1970 than they had been in 1960, this the result of wise diversification. The firms would have stuck to their lasts were it not for the antismoking agitation. As it was, due to their acquisitions, they had become revitalized. Neuberger, Banzhaf, and others of their groups may have threatened the cigarette, but their efforts actually had aided American, Reynolds, and Philip Morris, all of which were well prepared to enter the post-television age by 1971. While it might be argued that the individuals who stopped smoking were the major beneficiaries of the crusade, there was pleasant fallout for the stockholders of those companies whose existence seemed threatened throughout the early 1960s.

XIII

The Habit

The advent of the television ban on January 2, 1971, was a fine symbol for the anticigarette forces, which rejoiced in their victory. Their next step would be an effort at eliminating smoking in all but designated areas in public facilities. This already was the case in hospitals, many schools, and theaters. Now the reformers tried to do the same for restaurants, airplanes, elevators, and other public places. The nonsmoker should not be obliged to inhale air fouled by cigarettes. The smoker was free to kill himself, so they said, but he must not be permitted to inflict the residue of his noxious habit on innocent people.

Energy and the national mood was in favor of some such measures. Bans like these probably could not be enacted on a national level, and no attempt was made to do so. But throughout the nation, and especially in large northern cities, smoking in public places was circumscribed. A subtle and important change had taken place by the mid-1970s. Prior to that time "No Smoking" signs were placed in those areas where the habit was not allowed. Now "Smoking Permitted" notifications appeared, indicating an assumption that elsewhere in the area the habit would not be tolerated. Airlines reported a steady growth in that part of the passenger population asking for seats in the no-smoking section. It became fashionable for nonsmokers to demand that users of cigarettes leave their presence, or at least snuff out their butts. Guests on television talk shows volunteered information on how they "kicked the habit," and would urge others to do so. In the early 1950s Edward R. Murrow smoked or held a cigarette between his fingers while on camera; a quarter of a century later Johnny Carson took pains to drag on his cigarette only when commercials were being run and often seemed embarrassed when the camera switched to him suddenly, in the midst of a puff. Fashionable restaurants established smoking and no-smoking zones. In reporting on these in newspapers and magazines, writers made it appear that "the beautiful people" of both sexes —tall, elegant, and poised—favored clean lungs and chilled chablis, while the coarser more frustrated smokers drank scotch and bourbon. In 1978 wines and no smoking were "in" while cigarettes and hard liquor were "out." The smoker was on his way to becoming a pariah, at least in the "right" circles.

The great debate over the link between cigarette smoking and lung cancer all but ended. Most Americans took it for granted that one existed, for they had been told by respected medical men and journalists for years of the connection. The tobacco companies, which at one time had mounted a major effort aimed at countering such claims, simply allowed them to stand. Yet the linkage still hadn't been demonstrated clinically—that is to say, by way of inducing lung cancer in laboratory animals by subjecting them to a smoke-filled environment. In 1971 Drs. E. Cuyler Hammond and Oscar Auerbach, working under an American Cancer Society grant, claimed to have caused lung cancers to develop in twelve beagles by raising them in a smoky environment. Later on it was learned that only two minor tumors had been created in the test animals and, more important, that two dogs in the control group had developed similar tumors. The American Cancer Society placed a lid on the story and refused to permit the evidence to be examined by independent researchers and scientific journalists. This episode and others similar to it had little impact upon public conceptions of the cigarette-cancer link.

Government documents issued in the 1970s took the connection for granted. In the Surgeon General's report on *The Health Consequences of Smoking* issued in 1971, for example, it was claimed that "Epidemiological evidence derived from a number of prospective and retrospective studies, coupled with experimental and pathological evidence, confirms the conclusion that cigarette smoking is the main cause of lung cancer in man." But even then, the experimental evidence was nonexistent, although the statistical material on the subject was most impressive, and certainly had convinced many scientists they should stop using cigarettes.

There was an even more important demonstration of the health hazards of smoking, at least insofar as the television viewer was concerned. Detective Sam Spade seemed always to be lighting up a Lucky Strike. Humphrey Bogart, who portrayed him that way in *The Maltese Falcon,* etched on the public mind the image of the tough guy hero who chain smoked. Bogart is dead—of lung cancer—and one of his television counterparts, Telly Savalas, has given us Theo Kojak, the tough cop who is trying to kick the smoking habit by sucking on lollipops.

With all of these negative factors at work, one might have expected cigarette production and consumption to have declined. But this did not happen. The elimination of cigarette ads meant the end of the free commercials against the habit, and the elimination of the former was more than compensated for by the decline of antismoking messages. Smoking was on the increase in 1972 and afterward, and this could be demonstrated by almost any statistical measurement. Total production in 1970, for example, was 562 billion, or 2,754 on a per capita basis. More than 593 billion were turned out in 1972, which on a per capita basis came to 2,850. Two years later production reached 652 billion units, and that was more than 3,100 for every American man, woman, and child.

The industry's vigor and the persistence of the habit resulted from several factors, some of which were obvious to even the most casual onlookers.

The habit persisted for several reasons.

First, cigarette smoking is both physiologically and psychologically addictive, facts that could be testified to by hundreds of thousands of regular smokers who tried to quit and failed to do so. Many joined groups which, for a fee, promised to have one off the weed in a matter of weeks or months. One of the largest of these organizations, SmokEnders, Inc., was organized in 1968, and during the next nine years it claimed to have processed well over 200,000 people through its nine-week course. SmokEnders and similar programs claimed a good success ratio, but even more impressive is the number of people willing to undergo such sessions at a high price. Clearly, large numbers of Americans want to stop smoking and are unable to do so on their own or, for that matter, even in a structured group. These individuals, and those who smoke and have no intention of ending their habit, comprise a large group of consumers for which cigarettes are almost as important as food and drink, or perhaps more.

Population statistics worked in favor of greater sales. The "baby boom" of the postwar period was coming of age—smoking age—in the late 1960s and early 1970s. These individuals tended to smoke more cigarettes per day than their parents, even though the antismoking crusade had convinced many others never to start the habit. For a while there was some thought that the growing popularity of marijuana would cut into cigarette sales. In fact, the opposite was true. Indications were that marijuana smokers tended to be heavy users of tobacco as well. They preferred some varieties and brands more than others. Mentholated smokes were especially popular, with Kool a particular favorite. This preference was partially responsible for the sales boom enjoyed by that brand, which became the nation's third best seller by the late 1970s.

The antismoking groups and their publicity contained a class, geographic, and even political bias. Most of the leaders came from either the East or West Coast and were well to do. Actors and actresses, social activists, and even some politicians tended to overshadow the words and images of the medical men who led the American Cancer Society and related organizations. As previously mentioned, for some of them the fight was a continuation of the struggle against evils in American life, which included the Vietnam War, racism, and sexism, as well as exploitation of the poor by the rich corporations. But poor people and those comparatively less educated were not included in the anti-smoking coalition. Commercials against smoking were made by individuals like Tony Curtis and Jack Lemmon, but working-class media stars, like Charles Bronson and Clint Eastwood, continued to project the images of hard-fighting and heavy-smoking strong men, the kinds supposed to be admired by working-class people. Interestingly enough, there was one such hero who could have been used for that purpose. John Wayne stopped smoking after learning he had lung cancer. Wayne made no secret of his belief that smoking almost cost him his life, and perhaps he would have spoken out loudly, and often, against the habit if asked to do so in a commercial. But he was at odds politically with most in the movement and so was never approached.

Thus cigarette smoking, a sign of poverty or at least lower-class status in the late nineteenth century, once again took on some of these attributes in the late 1970s. This is not to say that poor people were the only ones who smoked. Rather, the anti-smokers seemed concentrated in the middle and upper parts of the social pyramid. One saw it on commuter trains. The non-smoking sections would be filled with attaché-case carrying exec-utives, while blue-collar workers were more evident in cars re-served for smokers. Airline reservation clerks noticed that planes out of the Midwest, South, and Rocky Mountain states had an overflow in the smoking section, while the reverse was true for flights from either coast. Some surveys indicated as much. Lower-class middle Americans smoked more than upper-class New Yorkers or Californians. It was not chic to be a smoker in a Manhattan prep school, but large numbers of students in lower-class area high schools took smoking breaks. These young people hadn't been reached effectively by the antismoking crusade. Their parents would not be found at SmokEnders and similar programs, since they lacked the time and money, even if they had wanted to quit. Rather, they would continue to smoke, and many of them actually increased their intakes considerably in the 1970s.

The industry proved more successful than its opponents in adjusting to the post-television advertising age. As anticipated, the antismoking groups were unable to obtain free space in newspapers and magazines. For a while, some journals refused to run the more blatant kinds of cigarette ads, and others would not accept them without the inclusion of clear health hazard notices. The companies protested these actions as violations of their First Amendment rights, but this attempt to conform to the spirit of the TV ban soon ended. Meanwhile, the companies spent huge amounts for large-scale advertising blitzes, more than doubling their output for magazines and increasing those for newspaper ads nearly tenfold.

The tobacco companies even attempted to re-enter television "through the back door." Philip Morris introduced Virginia Slims, its "female cigarette," and then sponsored a women's tennis tournament by that name. The sports contest was televised, with no ads for the cigarette, but the name itself sufficed. Other brands did the same, and there was nothing the networks, the FCC, or the antismoking groups could do to halt the practice. They could prevent more blatant forays, however. In 1972 some of the companies considered putting out pipe mixes in packages that resembled those of cigarettes, and then giving them the names of existing cigarette brands. These could be advertised on television, they argued. It wasn't clear whether or not pipe tobacco came under the ban, but in any event the idea was quickly dropped. The companies did create some new thin cigars, which really were cigarettes—Winchester, out of Reynolds, was the leader—and their ads did appear on television for a while.

Still with all of this, cigarette advertising costs declined since print media cost so much less than television. Total charges for promotion fell by almost 20 per cent in the two years following the ban. For decades critics had claimed that hard-sell advertising campaigns had lured millions into smoking. The experience under the ban did not disprove this contention, but it did show that brand loyalty was not necessarily a function of advertising costs. More to the point, it demonstrated that established, popular brands could do well without television and, in fact, become more profitable. This lesson, similar to the one learned in the 1930s regarding the weak relationship between advertising expenses and brand popularity, did not result in a change in strategy. The companies still spent large amounts to push new brands onto the market, and maintained them for old brands clearly on the way down. Habit, tradition, inertia—and uncertainty—had as much to do with advertising decisions as did anything else. The companies demonstrated no evidence of wanting to alter the pattern. Why should they? Sales were up, and so were profits, after the most concerted and certainly most successful antismoking crusade in history. That was all that mattered.

As they were prior to the ban, the research and development divisions and teams remained central afterward. However, this strategy changed. In the uncertain 1960s the firms had concentrated upon the creation of families of brands, hitchhiking, and the scattergun approach exemplified by Walker at American. Having survived the onslaught while at the same time learning from the experience, the leading firms felt free to explore new opportunities in cigarettes. This is not to say that proliferation ended—by 1978 there were more than 190 different brands and configurations of them on the market, more than ten times as many as had existed at the end of World War II. Rather, imitation had become the rule; if one major firm developed what appeared to be a winner, the others would take similar brands to market without pretesting. And there seemed a rationale for each new introduction. Gimmicks such as those used for Waterford and Laredo were out. So were attempts to transform pipe and cigar names into cigarettes. However, now the leading companies set out in three directions simultaneously, knowing precisely where they were going and what they hoped to accomplish. They would concentrate upon the female half of the market, the expanding demand for longer smokes, and the need for cigarettes with lower tar and nicotine contents. As had been the case in the past, attempts would be made to combine two and in some cases all three of the varieties, to create the ultimate smoke for the late 1970s—the long, slender, low-nicotine and -tar cigarette aimed at women.

But was there such a thing as a woman's cigarette? During the 1920s and 1930s women as well as men smoked Camel, Lucky Strike, and Chesterfield. There was some evidence that women preferred a milder tobacco, but not enough to encourage the manufacturers to alter their blends. Smokers of both sexes took to the filter and mentholated brands in the 1950s and 1960s. Advertising campaigns and brand image had little to do with preferences. Pall Mall, originally conceived of as a brand with a special attraction for women, was enjoyed equally by both sexes. Similarly, evidence indicated that Marlboro, the smoke with the most masculine image in the 1960s, had a strong following among women smokers.

Did it make sense to create a cigarette that would make a blunt, direct appeal to women? Two things made this seem so in the 1960s. First of all, fewer women than men smoked cigarettes. Perhaps nonsmoking females could be attracted to smoking by a brand created especially for them. Second was the movement for women's equality with men. The cigarette manufacturers and their advertising agencies weren't certain how to deal with this phenomenon. On the one hand, the women in the movement claimed they wanted equality with men, which would support the idea that the same cigarette should be marketed for both sexes. On the other hand, these same women clearly wanted to be differentiated from men—to have symbols of their liberation —and this might mean success for a woman's cigarette, even if men and antiliberation women rejected it.

In an attempt to regain the trailblazer reputation it had enjoyed in the pre-World War II period, Reynolds decided to test the market. In 1969 the company introduced Embra, the first brand designed exclusively for women. The ad made it clear. "Embra. For My Woman." At the same time, the word "my" seemed to fudge the issue. Whether it was due to this, or because the time wasn't right for the concept, or because the cigarette itself was not very different from others on the market, Embra was a failure and vanished from the scene after a short trial.

Virginia Slims, which was introduced by Philip Morris shortly after Embra, performed far better. Its advertising campaign was imaginative and the slogan "You've come a long way, baby" was the catchiest since those for Marlboro and Winston. The Virginia Slims television campaign was especially effective, featuring a humorous treatment of the women's liberation movement. Furthermore, they were the kinds of ads that could be transferred with relative ease to the print media, so they did not suffer when the ban went into effect. Neither Eve from Liggett & Myers nor Brown & Williamson's Flair did as well. By 1976, Virginia Slims

was the fifteenth best seller in the nation, as well as one of the
fastest growing brands in the field. But they were the exception,
and in any case, by the mid-1970s it appeared evident that the
vast majority of women smokers preferred the other two innovations of the decade.

There was a plethora of new brands in the summer of
1974, most of which were unimaginative and soon were discontinued. For years Lorillard had attempted to find a counterpart to Marlboro—a full-flavored smoke with a western motif. It
had marketed Maverick, Redford, and Luke, all of which failed.
Now it introduced Zach, which in tests featured a pack that
looked like blue denim. Zach lasted less than a year. Brown &
Williamson had even less luck with Tramps, an attempt to cash
in on a revived interest in Charlie Chaplin. Although Chaplin's
face and form weren't used in commercials, the company paid
the retired actor two cents per pack in royalties so as to be able
to suggest the connection. American Tobacco had Safari and
Super M Menthol; L & M tried the market with St. Moritz, and
Philip Morris produced Philip Morris International. This last
smoke, a longer version of the old standard, did find a following,
but the others were gone by early 1975.

Only Reynolds had success that model year. For some time
the company had tried to find a new kind of cigarette that would
appeal to urban smokers. Camel, its old flagship brand, had done
well in the cities but the new sales leader, Winston, was considered a "middle American smoke," or at least this was the judg-
ment of the firm's marketing experts. Heartened by the initial
success of Winchester, aware of the growing popularity of the
100-mm brands, and adept at the creation of new products, Reynolds came out with More, a 120-mm cigarette that looked like a
long, thin cigar.

More was not the first brown cigarette. Several specialty
tobacconists, the most famous of whom was Nat Sherman in
New York, had marketed various colored cigarettes for years. In
the 1930s the Philip Morris brown pack was deemed to have the
look of class, though the cigarette was white. Winchester's
brown wrapper helped it win a portion of its market. On the
other hand Adam, a brown 1973 brand out of Liggett & Myers
(it also featured a pack that looked like leather) had failed.

The 120-mm length was a novelty, but only in the mass market. Some smokes of that length had been sold by the specialty shops, and in 1972 a European cigarette, named Mahawat, featured the long look. More, then, was a combination of the Mahawat length and the Winchester color.

And there was reason to believe More would succeed in capturing a limited segment of the male market. For decades, heroes in period-piece motion pictures—especially those set on Mississippi riverboats—would puff on long, thin cigars. The image already was there; Reynolds hoped to fill it with the new cigarette. Also, More was to be a "full-flavored" smoke, meaning it would have relatively high contents of both tars and nicotine. Yet the public identified length with filtering qualities, and so the 120-mm size would imply health safety.

More was a surprising success, quickly carving a niche for itself without cannibalizing sales from other Reynolds brands, an accomplishment considered a near miracle in the mid-1970s. That this transpired was as much the result of good fortune as careful planning. The Reynolds executives had thought More would appeal to urban white males who in their fantasies pictured themselves as a Clint Eastwood or Charles Bronson, dealing out the cards on the *River Queen* while puffing on a cheroot. More managed to appeal to such individuals, but also was remarkably strong among female smokers. In fact, more than half the sales were to women. Furthermore, the new cigarette became the status smoke for black urban males, who prior to this had favored Kool. According to one potential smoker, questioned in New York's Harlem, More was a sure winner. "Man, I can just see myself blasé-in' it up to the bar and orderin' my Chivas Regal. I lights up my More and I've made my point."

More's success resulted in imitation. Philip Morris, which by then had made a practice of following Reynolds into new fields, came out with Saratoga, a 120-mm smoke with a white wrapper, which soon became the second best seller in this market. Then the other companies presented their imitations. As had become its custom, American developed several new brands, among them Long Johns and Tall, and as was equally the case for that company, both were relative failures. Lorillard entered the field with Max, and Brown & Williamson came out with Suede and Phoenix, none of which did very well.

As might have been anticipated, most manufacturers tried to transform one or more of their 100-mm brands into 120s so as to cut into the More market. Reynolds appreciated what was happening and countered with an expensive ad campaign as well as the creation of a mentholated version of More, which did almost as well as the original and made still deeper inroads into the market.

With all of these, the 120-mm smokes, as a whole, had less than 3 per cent of the market in 1978, and they were not considered likely to do much better than that in the future. The large smokes fetched a premium price, were bulky to carry, and could not fit into vending machines. More important perhaps was the fact that all of the 120s had high-tar and -nicotine contents at a time when smokers were becoming increasingly sensitive to such statistics.

The 120-mm cigarette was not as significant an innovation as it seemed to be—because the only major change *was* the appearance. Smokers would wave them as they might a baton. They did attract attention and evoke glamorous memories. In essence, however, they were the old smokes Americans had used for decades, with a longer length and in the case of More, a different color. They were not as adaptable as the conventional smokes (one hardly would light a More in order to "grab a few puffs") and they seemed to fit in only at polite gatherings or after work; men and women somehow looked ostentatious when smoking a Saratoga while mowing the lawn. Clearly the 120s were novelties —important ones, no doubt, but novelties just the same. They never would become standards, and no brand seemed capable of cracking the top-twenty list.

Carlton, on the other hand, was a portent of the future. One of the few products of the Robert Walker administration at American Tobacco that found buyers, it featured its low-tar and -nicotine content on the package, for all to see, in 1964. Carlton was the nation's twenty-sixth best seller in 1969, with 1.2 billion units sold, and was headed upward. It also sparked interest within the other companies, Reynolds in particular.

Reynolds had developed a method for "expanding" the leaf so

as to use less of it for each cigarette. This resulted in savings but also meant that each puff would contain less tar and nicotine and more air and water vapor. When wedded to porous cigarette paper and improved filters (and remembering that filter material cost less than the tobacco it replaced) one had a mild smoke that the anticigarette people might consider safer than those already on the market. Some of the ads developed by the American Cancer Society and similar organizations urged smokers to cut down if they couldn't stop smoking altogether, and to use milder cigarettes. Although this was not deemed a plug for the Carlton-type product, it certainly helped its sales.

Building on this, Reynolds introduced three low-tar and -nicotine cigarettes—Now, Doral, and Vantage. These were lumped together with Carlton and some other brands—True and Lark, among them—as "high filtration," or "hi-fi" brands, and within the industry this meant a tar content of 15 mg or less. For a while the hi-fis were distinguished from the "medium-fis" which had from 15 to 20 mg, while the "low-fis" had more than 20 mg of tar. The low-fis also were called "full flavor" smokes, and were advertised as such. More, for example, had 22 mg, which placed it squarely in the full-flavor category.

By 1970 it had become clear that the smoking population would divide into two camps, one insisting upon the old kind of flavor, the other accepting milder flavor in order to have low-tar and -nicotine contents. All the major companies had entries in both categories, but even then it was evident that the big push was behind the hi-fis. Not only were they a more effective cigarette insofar as meeting the health issue was concerned, but they were cheaper to produce as well. Also, the industry discovered that many smokers would keep their daily doses of tar and nicotine at a fairly constant level. The user of Marlboro (which had 18 mg of tar and 1.1 of nicotine) might switch to a hi-fi with half as much of each. Then he would increase his consumption from one to two packs per day. The net result was higher profits for the company, while the smoker could feel, unjustifiably, that he had done the right thing by his lungs and heart.

Of course, the ads for the hi-fis claimed these new smokes "delivered" taste as well as health, but most experienced smokers could tell the difference between them and the low-fis. Carlton and Vantage were as different from Winston and Marlboro as those cigarettes had been from Camel and Luckies, which in turn marked a drastic changeover from Sweet Caps and Murad. By the mid-1970s the hi-fis had been recognized as the coming trend in cigarettes, the best, perhaps the only, answer to the cancer issue. All other varieties would decline, stagnate, or settle for a modest share of a segment of the total market. The manufacturers began converting their established brands to hi-fis and in other ways preparing for the next step in the development of the cigarette.

This is not to say the major firms abandoned their old standbys. Change in this industry came slowly, and after spending millions of dollars and years in establishing a semblance of brand loyalties, the companies could be counted on to protect their investments. The newspaper ads created for Winston in the mid-1970s featured handsome, rugged-looking men, with the slogan, "If I'm Going to Smoke, I'm Going to Do It Right," and the additional statement: "Some people smoke a brand for its image. I don't. You can't taste image. I smoke for taste." Winston remained Reynolds' low-fi leader, while Vantage sales began to soar. Tar and nicotine contents, not taste, were featured in ads for that cigarette. A similar situation existed at Philip Morris, as the company stressed taste in Marlboro and Benson & Hedges ads and tar and nicotine when speaking out for hi-fi brands. Philip Morris introduced Merit in late 1975. This cigarette, the first to have a tar content below 10, was an instant success; the following year it became the nation's nineteenth best seller, ahead of the American Brands' hi-fi leader, Carlton. Wouldn't this new brand threaten Marlboro? Chairman Joseph Cullman didn't seem concerned. "We would just as soon sell Merit as sell Marlboro."

The introduction of Merit, and its surprising success, set off a production and advertising contest among the brands, as all the hi-fis began lowering their tar and nicotine contents. If 9 mg was good, so the thought went, 8 would be better. By 1976 Carlton was down to 1 mg of tar and 0.1 of nicotine per smoke, a challenge Reynolds responded to by creating Now, which featured the identical statistics. This meant that there was more of both substances in one Winston cigarette than in an entire pack of Carlton or Now. In fact, these brands were so mild that veteran inhalers rejected them after initial trials, and they became the cigarette of choice for many individuals who were seeking to stop smoking entirely.

By 1978 the cigarette makers had demonstrated an ability to adjust the tar and nicotine contents of their products at will. "We can produce some [cigarettes] that don't have any tar at all," said one experimenter in the field. "The trouble is, they don't have any taste at all. The lower the tar and nicotine, the lower the taste." In order to overcome this blandness, the companies had to resort to stronger and increased use of additives. Philip Morris recognized this problem and went so far as to advertise Merit as having taste added on as "enriched flavor." The company called this "a scientific breakthrough," which it was not. But Merit managed to create a tobacco taste where none existed and combine it with low tar and nicotine, and this translated into high sales and profits.

Reynolds responded to the challenge in mid-1977 by introducing Real, which had 9 mg of tar and 0.8 of nicotine. The name was a slap at Merit; Real would not use artificial flavorings and yet could match the tar and nicotine contents of Merit. The company provided the new cigarette with a $40 million advertising budget.

At stake was domination of the industry. Cullman had boasted that Philip Morris would assume first place by the early 1980s. He could accomplish this by taking a commanding lead among young smokers with hi-fi brands. If this indeed was the future of the industry, then Philip Morris and Reynolds would be the dominant forces, with the others far behind. By 1977 it was clear that the older people had remained loyal to Camel, Luckies, and Chesterfield, while the young men and women who had taken to Marlboro and Winston in the 1960s were approaching middle age by the late 1970s. Merit and Real were supposed to slug it out for the young person's patronage in the era of the hi-fis. Which would succeed? Alex Richy, the brand manager for Real in this campaign, thought he had an excellent chance for victory, which in this business was made up of "one-third advertising, one-third packaging, and one-third product."

THE TEN BEST-SELLING CIGARETTES, 1977

RANK	BRAND	COMPANY	SALES (BILLIONS)	MARKET SHARE
1.	Marlboro	Philip Morris	98.4	16.4
2.	Winston	Reynolds	88.1	14.7
3.	Kool	B & W	60.0	10.0
4.	Salem	Reynolds	53.9	9.0
5.	Pall Mall	American	39.9	6.6
6.	Kent	Lorillard	30.6	5.1
7.	Benson & Hedges	Philip Morris	24.6	4.1
8.	Camel	Reynolds	24.4	4.1
9.	Vantage	Reynolds	17.2	2.9
10.	Merit	Philip Morris	14.9	2.4

SOURCE: *Business Week*, October 31, 1977

Real was a dismal failure by any standard, capturing less than 1 per cent of industry sales within the first half year of its introduction. The public appeared uninterested in its claims to be a natural smoke, and no amount of advertising could alter the situation. "If a brand doesn't make it after six months, I don't care how much money you spend, it just doesn't make it," said Herbert Horvitz, president of Royal Wholesale Cigar Co. Some supermarkets dropped the brand, and most vending machine companies did not give it space or publicity. Reynolds officials said it was too soon to make a decision regarding the future, but early in 1978 the company introduced Camel Lights, which had a somewhat better reception, and in addition gave new impetus to the drive toward hitchhiking.

The hi-fis had more than 18 per cent of the market by 1977 and sales were growing so rapidly that it was evident this category would be the leader by 1981 at the very latest. Over 145 billion of these cigarettes were sold that year, against 105 billion in 1976. They commanded half the advertising budgets, around $365 million. One out of every three brands or configurations were in this group. They included some early entries such as Vantage, Kent, and Carlton, and many old brand names revamped for this market, including Marlboro, Winston, L & M, Tareyton, and Pall Mall. The "third wave," which included Merit and Real, was the fastest growing, and the general feeling within the industry is that from this group will emerge the sales leaders for the 1980s. Of course, such projections are common in this business, and it also is common for them to be wrong.

In the process of converting the industry to hi-fis the average amount of tar and nicotine in the American cigarette dropped sharply. In 1955 the figures had been 43 and 2.8 mg respectively. By 1978 they were 18 and 1.2 and headed downward.

THE TEN BEST-SELLING HI-FI BRANDS, 1977*

RANK	BRAND	COMPANY	SALES (BILLIONS)
1.	Vantage	Reynolds	17.15
2.	Merit	Philip Morris	14.91
3.	Salem Lights	Reynolds	13.85
4.	Winston Lights	Reynolds	11.92
5.	Kent Lights	Lorillard	11.62
6.	True	Lorillard	11.00
7.	Marlboro Lights	Philip Morris	10.53
8.	Parliament	Philip Morris	8.60
9.	Carlton	American Brands	8.07
10.	Kool (Lights)	B & W	7.59

SOURCE: *Barron's,* November 28, 1977

* The statistics are for the light varieties for each brand, and figures have been added together where several configurations for each brand exists (for example, Parliament comes in a hi-fi and a lo-fi brand, and only hi-fi figures are included here. Vantage comes in four different forms in the hi-fi group).

CIGARETTE OUTPUT BY COMPANY, 1977

COMPANY	TOTAL OUTPUT (BILLIONS)	PER CENT OF DOMESTIC MARKET	HI-FI OUTPUT (BILLIONS)	PER CENT OF MARKET
R. J. Reynolds	222.01	32.5	52.47	8.6
Philip Morris	188.16	26.3	42.02	6.9
Brown & Williamson	102.39	15.7	15.63	2.6
American Brands	83.58	13.1	9.57	1.6
Lorillard	57.65	8.8	23.20	3.8
Liggett Group	26.80	3.6	2.60	0.4
Others	.45	—	—	—

SOURCE: *Barron's,* November 28, 1977

There was talk in Congress regarding legislation to limit the amounts of tar and nicotine to a low level. Curtis Judge, president of Lorillard, thought that even without such a law smokers' preferences would all but eliminate the high-tar and -nicotine brands from the market. "You're not going to have any cigarettes of consequence over 15 mg. [of tar] in eighteen months or two years time," said Judge in late 1977. To back his views, he announced that Lorillard would commit more than $25 million in 1978 to advertise Kent Golden Light, its entry in the field.

The development and growing popularity of the hi-fis pleased the antismoking contingent, both in Congress and within the public interest groups. They rightly considered this their major success and noted with approval the steady decline in tar and nicotine contents. Still, a generation of effort and publicity regarding the health aspects of cigarettes hadn't cut appreciably into the ranks of smokers—there were some 60 million of them in 1978. On the other hand, clearly the movement had had a major impact upon the industry and American smokers, one that will be felt for many years to come.

The future of the cigarette is in the hands—and between the lips—of teen-agers. "If you can convince them that smoking is bad for their health when they are eighteen or so," said one critic, "you have a good chance of keeping them clean for life."

A Gallup survey taken in late 1977 indicated that around a quarter of the nation's teen-agers smoked cigarettes but that the vast majority were light smokers (a half a pack a day or less) and that only 3 per cent of the sample smoked more than a pack a day. As many women as men smoked cigarettes, confirming suspicions that more women used cigarettes in 1977 than a decade earlier, and that the percentage of male users had declined.

More important for the future of the habit, almost 90 per cent of the sample answered "yes" when asked if they thought cigarette smoking was bad for their health. Why did they smoke? Almost half of those polled did so "to act grown up," and four in ten smoked as a result of "peer pressure." One in five were emulating parents, relatives, or close friends.

A quarter of those teen-agers polled by Gallup said they had quit smoking for health reasons, and perhaps this reflected the effectiveness of the anticigarette crusade. (But a Daniel Yankelovich poll of this period indicates that 43 per cent of teen-agers agreed completely or partially with the statement "It's safe to smoke low-tar cigarettes." Perhaps the cigarette ads were even more convincing.) Four in ten quit smoking because they found they didn't like the taste or smell of cigarettes. Clearly the results of the poll were difficult to analyze.

Still, the rate of sales increases had declined in the 1970s. The advance was less than 1 per cent in 1976 and a like amount the following year—this when the fifteen- to thirty-four-year-old age group increased by 5 per cent. The hi-fis were doing very well, but all of their sales had been cannibalized from other types of smokes. Slightly more than 600 billion cigarettes were sold in 1977, for a per capita consumption of 2,730 a year, 4 per cent below the 1972 figure.

In addition, the industry had become more sophisticated in its reaction to the crusaders. Perhaps the public had become inured to talk regarding health hazards, for these no longer had the impact they had twenty years ago. This may explain why the tobacco industry executives said little when, in early January of 1978, Joseph Califano, Secretary of Health, Education and Welfare, announced a new government program to fight the cigarette. Not only would millions of dollars be spent to publicize health problems, but Califano wanted a higher tax per pack and the complete elimination of smoking sections on passenger planes. Califano announced the program on the "Today" show. During an interview he was asked whether he was certain smoking caused cancer. The Secretary shied from the verb, and instead talked of "links." Later on he said, "Last year, smoking was *a major factor* [emphasis added] in 220,000 deaths from heart disease, 78,000 lung cancer deaths, and 22,000 deaths from other cancers." The words were selected carefully but were not precise; did Califano mean to say that smoking had some relationship to *all* of these deaths, those for nonsmokers as well as for smokers? Of course he didn't; nor was this the case. But it further illustrated the difficulties of precision in this area.

Tobacco industry leaders responded that this was one more example of Washington trying to interfere with the private lives of citizens, a case of the bureaucracy dictating the way Americans lived. This approach struck a responsive chord in the post-Watergate period. In an article that appeared in the New York *Times* the following day Ross Milhiser, Philip Morris president, noted that not all scientists agreed with critics of smoking and, in fact, some believed the practice was beneficial. For example, Ulf von Euler, Nobel Prize in Medicine laureate, thought additional research in the subject was needed. "Nobody would believe that so many people would use tobacco or products containing substances similar to nicotine unless it had positive effects." Harvard anthropologist Carl Seltzer denied some health claims; "It has not been reasonably established that cigarette smoking causes coronary heart disease." Dr. Philip Burch of the University of Leeds said, "Studies that purport to show a causal connection between cigarette smoking and various cancers—particularly lung cancer—fail when examined critically to establish the causal claim."

Califano was treated far more harshly by the anticigarette forces, which claimed he had not gone far enough. The Secretary had spoken of an initial grant of $6 million for the work. Dr. Sidney Wolfe of the Health Research Group (affiliated with Ralph Nader's Public Citizen, Inc.) responded that if the government could spend a quarter of a billion dollars to fight swine flu "it should spend at least as much on smoking." John Banzhaf of ASH thought it "a very weak program, since most of its elements are merely suggestions."

Some newspaper and television reporters noted that two years earlier Califano had been a three-pack-a-day smoker and inferred that he displayed the kind of zeal one ordinarily expected from a convert or repentant sinner. His program received little attention in the press—the *Times* printed the story on page 15, on a slow day for news when the front-page headlines dealt with a decline in the jobless rate. Little more was heard regarding the program thereafter, but the press in general wasn't very kind to the Secretary. Earlier, in a series of articles on his department, Washington *Star* reporter Cristine Russell discovered that many top HEW personnel smoked and did so, visibly, on the job. In fact, there were cigarette smokers in the Department's National Cancer Institute. Reporter Russell is a nonsmoker, but her editor for the series proclaimed that he had smoked for twenty-two years and had "no intention to quit."

Nor did the Califano blast mean a Carter administration campaign against the cigarette was about to commence. When asked to comment on the suggestion that tobacco subsidies be ended, Press Secretary Jody Powell replied, "It is not the view of this Administration that we should impose upon the tens of thousands of families whose futures would be ruined if we terminate the farm program with regard to tobacco." On the same day of the Califano speech, President Carter announced his intention to organize a separate Department of Education, an idea the Secretary strongly opposed. Without intending to do so, by his timing Carter had further undercut Califano. To make matters worse, news of the Carter statement appeared on the front pages of many newspapers and was given more prominence than was the Secretary's announcement.

Dr. Peter Bourne, Carter's Special Assistant for Health Issues, already was on record against a public ban for smokers. In an address before the Ad-Hoc Committee on Tobacco and Smoking Research of the American Cancer Society, Bourne warned against excessive repression of individual rights. "There is a small minority of people who have a hypersensitivity to smoke; we cannot write the laws to protect this small group, overlooking a much larger group who are entitled to the same basic rights." Bourne thought there was nothing wrong with no-smoking sections, but he came out against the proposition that airlines and restaurants should ban the practice entirely. "Private proprietors could simply be required to notify the public of their policy regarding smoking, no smoking, and public sections."

If there would be no crusade against the cigarette in 1978, there were signs that the earlier drives hadn't lost all their impetus. Some airlines agreed to enlarge their non-smoking sections to as much as 65 per cent of the planes' seats, for example; and prior to the Califano statement, they went so far as to ban pipes and cigars. But they rejected suggestions that cigarettes be included as well.

There is no clear indication that cigarette smoking will decline very significantly in the future. Thirty million Americans already have given up cigarettes, and doubtless there will be more. In all likelihood present trends will continue—slow growth in sales combined with lower per capita consumption. The hi-fis doubtless will gain more converts; some within the industry believe that by 1982 they will account for more than 90 per cent of sales.

Indications are that the number of cases of lung cancer will continue to rise, as they have for several decades. Also, lung cancer in women is increasing, and anticigarette forces are convinced this is due to the added numbers of female smokers. Still, the vast majority of smokers haven't abandoned their habit, and most have no intention, or will power, to do so.

It might be different if they were offered clear evidence that cigarettes actually *cause* cancer. For example, if researchers could demonstrate that laboratory animals who inhale the equivalent of two or more packs a day become cancerous at a greater rate than does a test group, and if this evidence was presented on television and in the press, the situation might change. As it is, many people are confused by what they read. Clearly the statistical evidence and high correlations alone won't do the job.

Perhaps this is so because cigarettes have become as much a part of the national diet as hamburgers or cola drinks. It had been so for the first three quarters of this century, since the glory days of Buck Duke. An ad put out for Chesterfield in 1977 told the story well, and in only three words.

"They *Still* Satisfy."

Bibliographical Essay

Harry Wootten, whose year-end surveys of the industry were published in *Printer's Ink* from 1941 to 1961, knew more about the history of the cigarette than did any other person during his lifetime. His annual reports, together with the many Wootten articles that appeared elsewhere during these two decades, comprise one of the most valuable sources. John C. Maxwell, Jr., continued in the Wootten tradition, and his annual reports also were published in *Printer's Ink* and its successor, *Marketing/Communications*. Maxwell also wrote for *Barron's* and other financial and business publications during the 1960s and 1970s. Finally *The Maxwell Report* is an invaluable compendium of information and ideas regarding cigarettes. Without a doubt Maxwell is the leading student in this area today; had he written his own book, I wouldn't have attempted mine.

Business Week also reports on the status of the industry at least once a year, usually in lead articles. *Fortune* has covered most of the major firms in essays which, sad to say, have declined in value and quality in recent years. In the process of conducting research, I have gone through several hundred articles in various magazines; with the exception of automobiles, no consumer product has attracted as much journalistic attention as has the cigarette. A list of these articles would be of use only to a few readers, and so has not been included here. I refer those individuals to the *Reader's Guide to Periodical Literature* and the *Industrial Arts Index,* which is where I went to gather my readings. Also, see the indexes for *Advertising Age* and *Media Decisions,* along with less-known magazines in the advertising field. In addition, diligent students would do well to explore the Department of Agriculture reports on the tobacco industry, published annually.

Many articles and reports on the health implications of smoking may be found in various medical and psychological journals, in particular *Lancet, Psychopharmacologia,* and *Journal of Personality and Social Psychology,* the *Journal of Experimental Research in Personality,* and the *Journal of Experimental Psychology.* Articles critical of smoking often appeared in *Reader's Digest* and the *New Yorker* as well. R. C. Smith's "The Magazines' Smoking Habit" in the *Columbia Journalism Review* (January/February 1978) is a critique of the way the subject has been handled in magazines.

The Tobacco Institute has published several pamphlets dealing with tobacco culture and cigarette history, but none is particularly informative, and all clearly are based on easily available books and monographs. The same is the case for many of the brochures published by the American Cancer Society. Each of the individual companies in the industry has a reference library and a public relations bureau. One can obtain a good deal of information regarding the current activities of the firms from these sources, but none are particularly interested in what happened more than a few years ago. None of the companies has been covered by a decent history; there is a picture-book essay dealing with American Tobacco called *Sold American!,* but it hardly qualifies as a serious work. Joseph Robert's *The Story of Tobacco in America* is a useful survey and contains an excellent bibliography. Nannie Mae Tilley's *The Bright Tobacco Industry, 1860–*

1929 is a magnificent work, clearly the best book on the industry and the product. Richard Tennant's *The American Cigarette Industry: A Study in Economic Analysis and Public Policy* and William Nicholls' *Price Policies in the Cigarette Industry: A Study of "Concerted Action" and Its Social Control, 1911–1950* are more interesting than their titles indicate. Both are based upon documents released during the antitrust case of the 1940s, and so are quite similar to one another. More complete bibliographic information on these and other books may be found in the following compilation.

Finally, one of the more important sources used in gathering information and ideas for this book were men and women in advertising agencies, as well as several who have retired to other occupations. Through them I learned much regarding the creation and marketing of cigarettes, as well as anecdotes concerning leaders in the field. I quickly discovered that none of them would speak openly unless I promised to respect their confidentiality, and so I will. But those researchers hoping to work in the field of cigarette and tobacco history would do well to contact leading agencies to speak with concerned account executives. It may be difficult to get past the front door, and impossible to have long interviews with prominent people, but it is worth the effort.

Bibliography

Adams, Walter. *The Structure of American Industry.* New York: Macmillan, 1950.

Agran, Larry. *The Cancer Connection.* New York: Houghton Mifflin, 1977.

Akehurst, B. C. *Tobacco.* New York: Humanities Press, 1968.

Allen, William, Angermann, Gerhard, and Fackler, William. *Learning to Live Without Cigarettes.* New York: Doubleday, 1968.

American Tobacco Co. *Sold American!* New York: American Tobacco, 1954.

Anon. *The Great Industries of the United States.* Hartford: J. B. Burr & Hyde, 1872.

Apperson, G. L. *The Social History of Smoking.* New York: G. P. Putman's, 1916.

Arnold, B. W., Jr. *History of the Tobacco Industry in Virginia from 1860 to 1894.* Baltimore: Johns Hopkins University Press, 1897.

Asbury, Herbert. *Carry Nation.* New York: Knopf, 1929.

Baer, Willis. *The Economic Development of the Cigar Industry in the United States.* No Publisher: Lancaster, Pa., 1933.

Baker, Sam Sinclair. *The Permissible Lie.* New York: World, 1968.

Bernays, Edward L. *Biography of an Idea: Memoirs of Public Relations Counsel Edward L. Bernays.* New York: Simon & Schuster, 1965.

Billings, E. R. *Tobacco, Its Culture, Manufacture, and Use.* Hartford: American Publishing Co., 1875.

Bolles, Albert. *Industrial History of the United States.* Norwich: Henry Hill, 1881.

Boyd, W. K. *The Story of Durham.* Durham: Duke University Press, 1927.

Brooks, Jerome. *The Mighty Leaf.* New York: Little, Brown, 1952.

Corina, Maurice. *Trust in Tobacco.* New York: St. Martin's Press, 1975.

Corti, Count. *A History of Smoking.* London: G. Harrys, 1931.

Cox, Reavis. *Competition in the American Tobacco Industry, 1911–1932.* New York: Columbia University Press, 1933.

Davis, Franklin. *Come as a Conqueror: The United States Army's Occupation of Germany, 1945–1949*. New York: Macmillan, 1967.

Davis, Jerome. *Capitalism and Its Culture*. New York: Farrar & Rinehart, 1935.

Durden, Robert. *The Dukes of Durham*. Durham: Duke University Press, 1975.

"Eminent Literary Men." *One Hundred Years' Progress of the United States*. Hartford: L. Stebbins, 1870.

Evans, Eli. *The Provincials: A Personal History of the Jews in the South*. New York: Atheneum, 1973.

Fairholt, F. W. *Tobacco: Its History and Associations*. London: Chapman & Hall, 1859.

Fisher, Robert. *The Odyssey of Tobacco*. Litchfield, Conn.: Prospect Press, 1939.

Flannagan, Roy. *The Story of Lucky Strike*. New York: American Tobacco Co., 1938.

Ford, Henry. *The Case Against the Little White Slaver*. Detroit: Henry Ford, 1916.

Fritschler, A. Lee. *Smoking and Politics*. New York: Appleton-Century-Crofts, 1969.

Gehman, Jesse. *Smoke Over America*. Patterson, N.J.: Becoma Publishing Co., 1943.

Gottsegen, Jack. *Tobacco: A Study of Its Consumption in the United States*. New York: Pittman, 1940.

Gunther, John. *Taken at the Flood: The Story of Albert D. Lasker*. New York: Harper & Bros., 1960.

Heimann, Robert. *Tobacco and Americans*. New York: McGraw-Hill, 1960.

Hunt, William. *Learning Mechanisms in Smoking*. Chicago: Aldine, 1970.

Jacobstein, Meyer. *The Tobacco Industry in the United States*. New York: Columbia University Press, 1907.

Jenkins, John. *James B. Duke*. New York: George Doran, 1927.

Kolodny, Joseph. *4000 Years of Service*. New York: Farrar, Strauss & Young, 1953.

Lehman Brothers. *About Tobacco*. New York: Lehman Bros., 1955.

Lewine, Harris. *Good-Bye to All That*. New York: McGraw-Hill, 1970.

Lingeman, Richard. *Don't You Know There's a War On?* New York: Putman's, 1970.

Lorillard (P.) & Co. *Lorillard and Tobacco*. New York: P. Lorillard & Co., 1961.

Mackenzie, Compton. *Sublime Tobacco*. London: Chatto & Windus, 1957.

Mausner, Bernard, and Platt, Ellen. *Smoking: A Behavioral Analysis.* New York: Pergamon, 1971.

Miller, J. G., *The Black Patch War.* Chapel Hill: University of North Carolina Press, 1936.

Nicholls, William. *Price Policies in the Cigarette Industry.* Nashville: Vanderbilt University Press, 1951.

Peterson, Lorin. *The Day of the Mugwump.* New York: Random House, 1961.

Robert, Joseph. *The Tobacco Kingdom.* Durham: Duke University Press, 1938.

——. *The Story of Tobacco in America.* New York: Macmillan, 1949.

Rundell, Walter. *Black Market Money.* Louisiana State University: Louisiana State University Press, 1964.

Sandulescu, Jacques. *Hunger's Rogues: On the Black Market in Europe, 1948.* New York: Harcourt Brace Jovanovich, 1974.

Smith, Ralph. *The Health Hucksters.* New York: Crowell, 1960.

Sobel, Robert. *The Entrepreneurs.* New York: Weybright & Talley, 1975.

Tennant, Richard. *The American Cigarette Industry.* New York: Archon, 1971.

Tilley, Nannie Mae. *The Bright Tobacco Industry, 1860–1929.* Raleigh: University of North Carolina Press, 1948.

Towns, Charles. *Habits that Handicap.* New York: Century, 1916.

United States. Industrial Commission. *Report of the Industrial Commission on Trusts and Industrial Combinations.* Washington: USGPO, 1901.

——. Congress. House of Representatives. Committee on Government Operations. (85th Cong., 1st Sess.) *False and Misleading Advertising (Filter-Tip Cigarettes).* Washington: USGPO, 1957.

——. Congress. Senate. Committee on Commerce. (89th Cong., 1st Sess.) *Cigarette Labeling and Advertising.* Washington: USGPO, 1965.

United States v. American Tobacco Co. 164 F. 700, 704 (1908); reversed and remanded, 221 U.S. 106 (1911); 191 F. 371 (1911).

Wagner, Susan. *Cigarette Country.* New York: Praeger, 1971.

Watkins, Sylvestre. *The Pleasures of Smoking.* New York: Henry Schuman, 1948.

Werner, Carl. *Tobaccoland.* New York: Tobacco Leaf Publishing, 1922.

Whiteside, Thomas. *Selling Death.* New York: Liveright, 1971.

Winkler, John. *Tobacco Tycoon.* New York: Random House, 1941.

Wood, James. *The Story of Advertising.* New York: Ronald, 1948.

Index

Adam (brand), 227
Additives, tobacco, 24–25, 30, 48, 73–74, 93, 130, 137, 139, 232
Advertising, 14, 23, 29, 30, 38–41, 45, 70, 92–106, 107, 109–13ff., 243; antismoking TV commercials, 213–15, 223–24; and brand loyalty, 140, 183, 185–86, 232; and health issue and legislation, 159ff., 170, 174–75, 176–77, 178, 181, 187–99, 202, 211–18, 219, 224–26, 230–31, 233; Lucky Strikes (Hill) and, 92–106; and post-World War II sales, 151, 153, 154, 155; Reynolds and, 76–77, 78; television ban and, 206–18, 219, 221, 224; and World War I sales, 83–85, 92ff.; and World War II 83–85, 92ff.; and World War II sales, 128, 131–32, 134, 135, 140
Air-Flow (brand), 139
Airplanes, smoking ban and, 219, 220, 223, 236, 238
Alcohol use and prohibition, 51, 52, 53, 54, 86, 87–88, 182, 192, 209, 217
Allen & Ginter, 20, 32, 38, 41, 45, 46
Allied Tobacco League, 88
Alpine (brand), 184
American Beauty (brand), 59, 108
American Cancer Society (ACS), 3, 106, 164, 167, 169–70, 177–78, 189, 192, 196, 220–21, 222, 230, 242; Ad Hoc Committee on Tobacco and Smoking Research, 238
American Cigarette and Cigar, 122
American Medical Association, 193, 197; *Journal,* 164
American News (brand), 38
American Snuff (company), 48
American Tobacco Company, 45–63, 74, 75, 76, 78–82, 87, 90–106 *passim,* 108–25 *passim,* 201–6, 215, 227, 234, 242; as American Brands, Inc., 209–10; and brand loyalty, 183, 184, 186–87, 233; and brand proliferation, 201–5, 216–17, 225, 228; and health issue, 162, 171, 173–74, 177, 181, 183, 184, 206,
218, 229–31, 232, 234; and mergers (diversification), 206, 207, 208–9; and post-World War II sales, 150–62 *passim;* and World War II sales, 130–46 *passim*
American Tobacco Trust, 45–60, 62, 71, 74–75, 79, 108, 118, 125
Andrews, James, 110
Antismoking movement (anticigarette crusade), 16–17, 49–56, 58–63; coalition (late 1960s), 210–18; 1890s, 49–56, 58–63; and health issue (legislation and bans), 61–62, 89, 187–99, 200–18 *passim,* 219, 222, 223–25, 230–39 *passim;* post-World War II, 148; and public facilities ban, 219–20; and TV commercials, 213–15, 223–24; World War I, 86–89, 91
Appel, Dr. James Z., 197
ASH (Action on Smoking and Health), 212, 237
Auerbach, Dr. Oscar, 220
Avalon (brand), 117, 118, 121, 152–53, 154, 184
Axton-Fisher (company) 108, 115, 118, 123–24, 137–38, 139

Baker, Ray Stannard, 57
Banzhaf, John, III, 211–14, 218, 237
Barron, Dr. Moses, 163
Barter Market (World War II), 143–45
Bass, Ross, 195
Bedrossian Brothers, 18, 37
Belair (brand), 184
Belding, Don, 105
Belgian Soldiers' Tobacco Fund, 85
Belt, Benjamin, 110
Benson & Hedges, 160–62, 174, 204, 205, 231, 233
Berkson, Dr. Joseph, 197
Bernays, Edward, 95–97
"Big Three plus One," 107–25 *passim,* 138, 139–40, 151, 154
Black market (World War II), 136, 138, 143
Blacks: and More brand, 228; and slavery, 27, 30 (*see also* Slavery)
Blackwell, William T., 28–29

Robert Sobel is the author of more than twenty books on a wide range of subjects, including *For Want of a Nail: If Burgoyne Had Won at Saratoga,* which was nominated for a Pulitzer Prize in 1973. In addition to writing books, Mr. Sobel has been a columnist for *Newsday,* a scriptwriter for both television and radio, and a historical researcher for Warner Brothers. He is currently professor of history at Hofstra University.